Information Technology Law in the United States of America

Information Technology Law in the United States of America

McKay Cunningham
Timothy Murphy

This book was originally published as a monograph in the International Encyclopaedia of Laws/Privacy and Technology Law.

Founding Editor: Roger Blanpain
General Editor: Frank Hendrickx
Volume Editor: Jos Dumortier, Pieter Gryffroy, Ruben Roex & Yung Shin Van Der Sype

Wolters Kluwer

Published by:
Kluwer Law International B.V.
PO Box 316
2400 AH Alphen aan den Rijn
The Netherlands
E-mail: lrs-sales@wolterskluwer.com
Website: www.wolterskluwer.com/en/solutions/kluwerlawinternational

Sold and distributed by:
Wolters Kluwer Legal & Regulatory U.S.
7201 McKinney Circle
Frederick, MD 21704
United States of America
E-mail: customer.service@wolterskluwer.com

ISBN 978-94-035-4975-0

e-Book: ISBN 978-94-035-4645-2
web-PDF: ISBN 978-94-035-4655-1

The Authors

Professor McKay Cunningham was born in Honolulu, Hawaii in 1974. He earned his undergraduate degree and his juris doctor degree at Baylor University in Waco, Texas. He was a tenured law professor teaching courses in U.S. constitutional law, property law, data privacy and security law, and torts. His scholarly research and publications focus on cybersecurity, data privacy, and constitutional law. Before joining academia, Professor Cunningham clerked for Judge Joel F. Dubina on the Eleventh Circuit Federal Court of Appeals. He then practiced law for nine years, including four years as a Staff Attorney on the Texas Supreme Court. Professor Cunningham has represented tech industry organizations in litigation and has been certified by IAPP as a data privacy professional. Professor Cunningham lives in Boise, Idaho, is married to Susanne Cunningham, and has four children, Ray, Calvin, Cleo, and Lula.

Timothy Murphy is an Assistant Professor of Law at the University of Idaho College of Law, Idaho and teaches Contracts and various intellectual property and cyberlaw courses. Tim researches and writes in the area of intellectual property law and in particular, trade secrets issues. Prior to this current appointment, Tim was a clinical professor for three years, teaching in entrepreneurship clinics in Idaho and at the University of Michigan Law School. Before entering academia full-time, Tim was Senior Patent and Trademark Counsel at Micron Technology, Inc. His responsibilities at Micron included managing a portion of Micron's patent and non-patent IP portfolios and the legal terms on Micron's websites. Tim also spent many years in-house doing intellectual property licensing in support of M&A, joint venture, and joint development programs, in addition to supporting day-to-day business operations. Prior to joining the Micron legal team, Tim practiced as a patent attorney/agent for several years in the U.S. Northwest doing patent and trademark prosecution, IP litigation, and general commercial litigation work.

The Authors

Table of Contents

Table of Contents

List of Abbreviations

AAA	American Arbitration Association
ACPA	Anticybersquatting Consumer Protection Act
ADR	Alternative Dispute Resolution
AESC	American Engineering Standards Committee
ANSI	American National Standards Institute
API	Application Programming Interface
AT&T	American Telephone and Telegraph Company
ATM	Automated Teller Machine
BIS	Bureau of Industry and Security
CAN-SPAM Act	Controlling the Assault of Non-Solicited Pornography And Marketing Act (CAN-SPAM Act)
CATV	Community Antenna Television
CCL	Commerce Control List
CFAA	Computer Fraud and Abuse Act
CFPB	Consumer Financial Protection Bureau
CFR	Code of Federal Regulations
COPPA	Children's Online Privacy and Protection Act
CSA	Controlled Substances Act
DMCA	Digital Millennium Copyright Act
DOD	Department of Defense
DOJ	Department of Justice
DSL	Digital Subscriber Lines
EAR	Export Administration Regulations
ECPA	Electronic Communications Privacy Act
EDI	Electronic Data Interchange
EFTA	Electronic Fund Transfers Act
EULA	End-User License Agreement
EU	European Union
FAA	Federal Arbitration Act

List of Abbreviations

FAR	Federal Acquisition Regulation
FCC	Federal Communications Commission
FDIC	Federal Deposit Insurance Corporation
FERC	Federal Energy Regulatory Commission
FITARA	Federal Information Technology Acquisition Reform Act
FOIA	Freedom of Information Act
FRCP	Federal Rules of Civil Procedure
FTC	Federal Trade Commission
GIF	Graphics Interchange Format
GSA	General Services Administration
HHS	Health and Human Services
ICANN	Internet Corporation for Assigned Names and Numbers
ILEC	Incumbent Local Exchange Carriers
IOS	International Organization for Standardization
IP	Internet Protocol
ISP	Internet Service Provider
IT	Information Technology
ITAR	International Traffic in Arms Regulation
ITPEA	Identity Theft Penalty Enhancement Act
LOI	Letter of Inquiry
MSBO	Manufacturers' Sales Branches And Office
MVPD	Multichannel Video Program Distributors
NIST	National Institute of Standards and Technology
NRC	Nuclear Regulatory Commission
OCC	Office of the Comptroller of the Currency
OMB	Office of Management and Budget
PICC	Presubscribed Interchange Carrier Cost
RFT	Request For Tender
SCPA	Semiconductor Chip Protection Act
SOX	Sarbanes-Oxley Act of 2002
SSL	Secure Sockets Layer
TSM	Teaching, Suggestion, or Motivation
UCC	Uniform Commercial Code

UCITA	Uniform Computer Information Transactions Act
UDRP	Uniform Domain Name Dispute Resolution Policy
UETA	Uniform Electronic Transactions Act
USPTO	United States Patent and Trademark Office
USSS	United States Standards Strategy
VoIP	Voice-over-Internet Protocol
WTO	World Trade Organization

List of Abbreviations

General Introduction

Chapter 1. General Background of the Country

1. The U.S. declared independence from Great Britain in 1776, and after the Revolutionary War, adopted the U.S. Constitution in 1787. Originally only thirteen states, the U.S. acquired nearly twice as much land in 1803 by way of the Louisiana Purchase from France. The Constitution established a government of dual sovereignty in which the federal government was accorded limited powers under the Constitution and each individual state retained those powers not expressly given to the federal government. The Constitution also established three co-equal federal branches of government, the legislative, executive, and judicial branches. Each branch serves as a check on the other two. Because the legislative, judicial, and executive branches of government derive their power from the U.S. Constitution, they cannot act in opposition to it.

2. Generally speaking, the legislative branch drafts and enacts law, the judicial branch interprets law, and the executive branch enforces the law, although in practice all three branches generate binding rules and law. Through executive orders and administrative rules, the executive branch is perhaps the most prolific generator of binding law. Both the federal government and several states have hundreds of agencies that are housed within the executive branch but that often have rulemaking authority granted by the respective legislative branches.

3. The Constitution is viewed as the ultimate legal authority in the U.S. and has the force and effect of law. The only way to avoid a requirement under the Constitution is to amend the Constitution itself. The amendment process is articulated in the Constitution and requires two-thirds of the states (or Congress) to propose an amendment and three-fourths of the states to ratify a proposed amendment. The Constitution has been amended twenty-seven times in its 200 -plus-year history. The first ten amendments, created and ratified shortly after the Constitution was created, are known as the Bill of Rights, as they include several individual rights or liberties that government cannot violate. Several amendments followed the U.S. Civil War, which was fought in the period 1861–1865, and the effort to eradicate slavery. The remaining amendments have dealt with issues such as voting rights, prohibition (and repeal), and continuity of government.

4. Each of the fifty state governments also adopted state constitutions. Although states are sovereign entities with authority to generate self-governing law, state laws must operate in accord with both the U.S. Constitution and with federal law. The U.S. Constitution includes a provision that states that federal law is "supreme" when it conflicts with state or local law.[1]

5. The U.S. is a common law legal system, deriving from the United Kingdom's common law system. As a result, the creation of binding law is not relegated to the legislative process. In common law systems, like the U.S., judges, by deciding cases, create positive law.

6. According to the U.S. Census Bureau, the U.S. had a population of 331.9 million as of 2021. During the twentieth century, the American population more than tripled with a growth rate of approximately 1.3% a year, from about 76 million in 1900 to 281 million in 2000. The U.S. Census Bureau estimates the population reached the 300 million mark in October 2006. The fastest rates of population growth are among minority groups in the U.S. According to the Census Bureau's estimation for 2012, 50.4% of American children under the age of one belonged to racial and ethnic minority groups.

---

1. U.S. Const. Art. VI, § 2.

Chapter 2. Telecommunications Infrastructure

§1. General

7. Telecommunications infrastructure in the U.S. is well-developed. Landline voice telephone revenues have been declining for several years and will likely continue to do so. As smartphones and mobile telephony proliferate, fixed-line telephony declines. In 2004, more than 90% of households in the U.S. had an operational landline telephone. According to data provided by the Centers of Disease Control and Prevention, less than 45% have a landline telephone as of 2017. If the trend continues at the current pace, and there is little reason to believe it won't, landline telephones could soon become an irrelevant market force.

8. Additionally, the U.S. telecommunications structure shows a trend from voice telephony to Voice Over the Internet Protocol (VOIP) services. The U.S. VOIP market is strong and growing with VOIP subscriptions increasing 32% since 2013, increasing at a compound annual growth rate of 10%. The Federal Communications Commission (FCC) reports that VOIP subscribers outstrip wire line access lines for the first time ever.[2] In approximately twenty years since the advent of IP-based telephony, VOIP has captured the majority of subscriptions. The trend will likely continue with tens of millions of customers that can shift from legacy to VOIP solutions, including small and medium businesses that are still largely stuck on obsolete TDM (Time Division Multiplexers) systems.

I. The Telephone Market

9. This FCC is an agency of the federal government created by federal statute. It is the primary regulator of interstate communications, including television, cable, radio, and satellite. The FCC maintains records regarding subscribership of varying telephony services. Since 1999, the FCC collected such data from incumbent local exchange carriers (ILECs), competitive local exchange carriers, and mobile voice providers. Beginning in 2008, the FCC maintained subscribership data from interconnected VOIP service providers.[3] In addition, in 2014 the FCC distinguished "over-the-top" interconnected VOIP subscriptions from other interconnected VOIP subscriptions. The FCC used this data to compile a report that summarizes telephone usage as of December 31, 2016. The following data largely stems from this report.

10. Generally speaking, the U.S. telephone market demonstrates continued expansion of subscribership to mobile services and interconnected VOIP services. There is a concomitant recession in subscribership to traditional wired telephone

---

2. *See* (at 47 C.F.R. § 9.3).
3. *Ibid.*

services. Wire line technologies include “end-user” switched access lines and interconnected VOIP subscriptions. The FCC reports that as of 2016, there were 341 million mobile subscriptions in the United States, 58 million end-user switched access lines, and 63 million interconnected VOIP subscriptions. All told, there were 463 million retail voice telephone service connections. Figure 1 demonstrates the growth of interconnected VOIP subscriptions over a three-year period. Such subscriptions increased at a compound annual growth rate of 10%, while mobile voice subscriptions increased at a compound annual growth rate of 3%. Retail switched access lines declined at 12% per year.[4]

Figure 1 Retail Voice Telephone Service Connections, 2013–2016 (in Thousands)

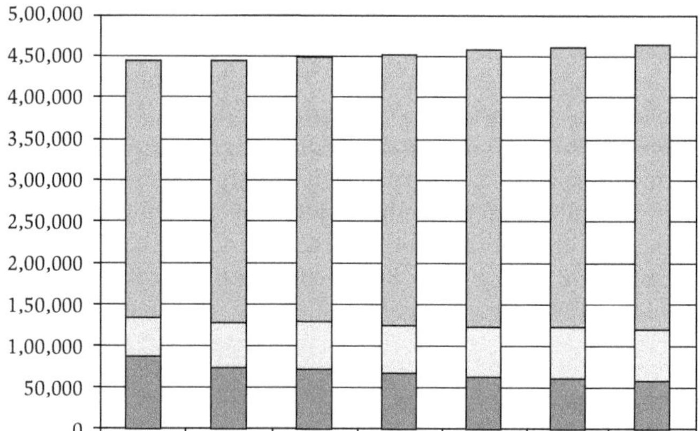

	Dec 2013	Jun 2014	Dec 2014	Jun 2015	Dec 2015	Jun 2016	Dec 2016
Mobile Voice Subscriptions	310,698	314,489	322,527	326,591	334,589	337,789	341,352
Interconnected VoIP Subscriptions	47,950	50,984	54,238	56,747	59,112	60,343	63,165
Retail Switched Access Lines	85,175	76,967	72,605	68,088	64,559	62,276	58,166

Note: Some previously published data have been revised.

11. Residential connections accounted for 53% of the 121 million wire line retail voice telephone service connections (including both switched access lines and interconnected VoIP subscriptions). Business connections accounted for 47% of the wire line retail voice telephone service connections. With regard to residential connections, there were approximately 64 million connections as of December 2016. Of those, 47% were non-ILEC interconnected VoIP subscriptions, 35% were ILEC switched access lines, 15% were ILEC interconnected VOIP subscriptions, and 2%

4. The compound annual growth rate is a smoothed rate of growth calculated by dividing the ending value by the beginning value, raising the result of that division to a power equal to one divided by the number of years in the period, and subtracting the number one from the result of the second step.

were non-ILEC switched access lines. With regard to commercial or business connections there were approximately 57 million wire line connections as of 2016. Of those, 40% were ILEC switched access lines, 35% were non-ILEC interconnected VoIP subscriptions, 20% were non-ILEC switched access lines, and 5% were ILEC interconnected VoIP subscriptions.

12. Overall, revenues for U.S. telecommunications companies are declining and have been declining since 2011. Although the decline is gradual for some telecommunications companies, perhaps due to long-term contracts that forestall customer defection, telecommunication companies have not succeeded in monetizing the data streaming through their networks. Traditional revenue streams all indicate decline: 30% drop in revenues for SMS messaging, 20% drop in international voice, and 15% drop in roaming. Increased competition also reduces normative telecommunications revenue. The FCC report shows an increase in providers from 1,644 to 1,691. Of those providers, 62% offer VOIP, which is an additional ninety-one providers from the previous year. The trend demonstrates continued growth for VOIP providers and increased competition in that market. As of 2016, there were 58 million end-user switched access lines in service and 63 million interconnected VOIP subscriptions, making VOIP 52% of wire line total.

§2. Fixed-Line Voice Telephone Networks

13. Throughout the past half-century, almost all U.S. commercial organizations have subscribed to telephone service. Over 90% of U.S. residents have subscribed to telephone service since 1970, but the number of lines provided by wire line carriers has declined since 2000, as costumers dispense with wire line service in favor of wireless. Similarly, the trend away from dial-up Internet access in favor of broadband service has reduced wire line lines. Before 2000, line growth averaged about 3% per year, reflecting growth in the U.S. population and the economy.

14. Local telephone businesses derive a portion of their revenue from entities that provide long-distance telephone service. Long-distance service requires usage of the switches and transport facilities maintained by local telephone companies. The access charges levied by local telephone companies have varied significantly over the years.

15. The historically dominant telephone provider in the U.S. is American Telephone and Telegraph Company (AT&T). In the late 1970s and early 1980s, AT&T furnished almost 75% of the nation's local telephone service and nearly all long-distance service. This confluence allowed AT&T to charge inflated prices for long-distance calls. The company then distributed a portion of those revenues to local telephone companies. Artificially high costs for long-distance telephone calls reduced demand and ultimately induced larger companies to avoid or otherwise circumvent the public switched network. As AT&T's monopoly over both long-distance and local service subsided, a more competitive market emerged.

16. The inefficiencies generated by AT&T's dominance in the U.S. telephone market subsided in 1985 after the FCC, in conjunction with state regulators, instituted meaningful changes in the way local telephone companies charged consumers. Instead of the subsidy remitted by AT&T to local companies generated by inflated long-distance charges, a uniform method of monthly access charges enabled local telephone companies to stabilize pricing. Long-distance charges were substantially reduced, and a marked increase in long-distance calls followed. The rebalancing of prices between local service and interstate long-distance calls during the mid-1980s restructured the telephone industry.

17. U.S. Congress and the FCC again reformed the U.S. telephone industry through the 1996 Telecommunications Act. The law introduced presubscribed interchange carrier costs (PICCs), which allowed local companies to recover their fixed costs from long-distance carriers on a per-line basis rather than a per-minute basis. Prior to the law, local companies recovered their fixed costs partly from monthly subscriptions directly billed to end users, and partly from per-minute long-distance carriers.

18. In 2000, the FCC restricted PICCs by consolidating them with monthly subscriber charges. The changes sought to align the access rate structure with the costs incurred to provide the service. A primary goal was to move away from per-minute access charges in favor of cost-based charging.

19. The Telecommunications Act of 1996 also sought to spur increased telecommunications access nationwide. Section 706 of the Act provides:

> (a) In general
>
> The Commission and each State commission with regulatory jurisdiction over telecommunications services shall encourage the deployment on a reasonable and timely basis of advanced telecommunications capability to all Americans (including, in particular, elementary and secondary schools and classrooms) by utilizing, in a manner consistent with the public interest, convenience, and necessity, price cap regulation, regulatory forbearance, measures that promote competition in the local telecommunications market, or other regulating methods that remove barriers to infrastructure investment.[5]

20. In order to determine how and whether telecommunications access was growing, the FCC in 2000 created a formal data collection program. The program standardizes data about subscribership to terrestrial wireless service providers, satellite service providers, cable operators, high-speed Internet access services from telephone companies,[6] and other facilities-based providers of telecommunications capability. Starting in 2005, the FCC required reporting from all facilities-based companies that high-speed connections, including data about types and numbers of

---

5. Telecommunications Act of 1996, 47U.S.C. § 1302 (2015).
6. For reporting purposes, "high-speed" Internet access connections are faster than 200 kilobits per second (kbps) in at least one direction.

customers and service offerings. The reporting requirement also extended to ILECs and cable operators. These companies must report the availability of digital subscriber lines (DSL) or cable high-speed connections, even if the consumer does not actually subscribe to a high-speed Internet access service. Even if the consumer only uses local telephone service or only cable TV, for example, the company must report whether high-speed Internet access is available.

§3. Mobile Telephone Networks

21. The U.S. has a high smartphone penetration rate with over 68% of the population using a smartphone as of 2017. The U.S. is also among the largest markets for smartphones worldwide. In 2018, an estimated 257.3 million people used smartphones, a dramatic increase from 2012, when less than 40% of the population used smartphones. As a result, mobile service is increasingly indispensable to businesses and individuals alike.

22. The U.S. is also a dominant provider of mobile telephone services worldwide, prompting some controversy. In 2018, AT&T and Verizon combined commanded nearly 70% of the wireless market. T-Mobile and Sprint are the closest competitors, with a combined market share of 32%. The consolidation of these four providers in the U.S. has strengthened U.S. market share worldwide, making it difficult for providers in other countries to gain significant ground.

23. Even so, there are over eighty facilities-based wireless service providers in the U.S. There are close to fifty virtual service providers that use one of the top four networks to provide service. As noted above, the top four wireless telecommunications service providers command the lion's share of the market, with AT&T servicing 155.7 million subscribers, Verizon Wireless with 153.1 million, T-Mobile with 81.3 million, and Sprint Corporation with 53.5 million subscribers. All four providers offer standardized 4G LTE, which is available wherever there is coverage, although the LTE bands each company uses are largely incompatible with each other. Smaller providers, outside the big four companies, usually provide native coverage over selected areas of the U.S. These companies offer nationwide coverage via roaming agreements with other carriers. The FCC reports that the telecommunications industry had more than 268,000 employees as of 2008, as compared to about 3,500 employees in 1986. The average monthly bill dropped from USD 96.83 at the end of 1987 to USD 50.07 as of December 2008.

24. As noted above, the nationwide trend to mobile and wireless services that accompanied the expanded use of the Internet, prompted a reduction in the fixed-line market. This can be seen in the digression of the copper wire infrastructure in the U.S. Since 2000, over 100 million copper lines have been disconnected, with cable and fiber optic increasingly replacing copper lines.

25. In the wake of these technological advancements and the FCC's regulations, the four largest providers have adopted differing strategies in their competition for larger market share. Verizon has invested over USD 20 billion to enhance basic telephone service with Internet, bundled video, and other functionalities. These services depend on a fiber optic system, which Verizon has implemented while simultaneously terminating its copper lines. In so doing, Verizon optimizes new FCC regulations that allow companies to own and operate several media, while also excusing Verizon from the legal obligation to share access to its old-fashioned copper lines with competitors.

26. AT&T, by contrast, invested in an IP-based network in order to provide Internet, TV, and VOIP services. Providing these services from an IP-based network allows AT&T to avoid traditional telephone state regulations and pricing regulations. The trend away from fixed-line telephony to technologies like VOIP have prompted AT&T to abandon – like Verizon – traditional landlines. AT&T's new objective, called Project Velocity, accelerates this trend by expanding VOIP, DSL, and fully jettisoning the landline system altogether. The FCC has signaled its assent to this plan.

27. These investments by the largest mobile telephone providers reflect the changing market, as smartphones become more and more critical to individuals and companies alike. Almost every relevant measurement tool indicates growth in mobile wireless subscribers. The FCC mandates that providers report subscribership as well as wireless numbers. From 1984 to 2008, the number of wireless subscribers increased from 92,000 to 270 million.

28. The telecommunications infrastructure in the U.S. is complicated by the quick pace of technological advancement and the concomitant insufficiency of traditional legal structures. Historical categorizations, like TV, telephone, and computing have proven less useful as cable companies offer video programs, as well as data and voice services in addition to traditional television service. Telephone type services occur through Internet computing, and Internet access can occur through telephone services. As a result, the traditional distinctions among these services no longer apply. Many of the federal regulations, likewise, turn on these traditional distinctions, making application of those regulations unclear. The large-scale move to IP-based networks and the overwhelming consumer embrace of advanced mobile devices has disrupted traditional telecommunications infrastructure.

Chapter 3. The Information and Communications Technologies Market

§1. GENERAL

29. There is a robust information and communications technologies market in the U.S., although the U.S. has fallen behind other countries in the availability of broadband service. In 2020, the U.S. ranked twenty-sixth globally, according to the Organization for Economic Cooperation and Development.[7] The FCC reports that 94% of U.S. residents had access to terrestrial broadband as of December 2017. The broadband speeds were at least 25Mbps/3Mbps, and responsive to the FCC's mandate to extend telecommunications capability "to all Americans in a reasonable and timely fashion." The FCC is authorized to take "immediate action" to comply with the mandate.[8]

30. The U.S. Congress defined advanced telecommunications capability as "high-quality" capability that allow users to "originate and receive high-quality voice, data, graphics, and video" services. At the direction of the U.S. Congress, the FCC maintains an existing speed categorizer of 25 Mbps download/3 Mbps upload (25 Mbps/3 Mbps) for fixed services. For mobile services, the FCC identifies the minimum speeds of 5 Mbps/1 Mbps, and a median speed of 10 Mbps/3 Mbps or higher. While 94% of Americans had fixed terrestrial broadband access at speeds of 25 Mbps/3 Mbps as of the end of 2017, over 24 million residents still lack fixed terrestrial broadband at speeds of 25 Mbps/3 Mbps. Access, however, is improving with 89.4% accessing in 2014 and 81.2% accessing in 2012, according to the FCC's 2018 Broadband Deployment Report (Table 1).[9]

31. An ongoing concern centers on the lack of broadband access to poor and rural communities. Internet access is increasingly vital for education, employment, and general economic opportunity. Rural areas without access struggle economically. In rural areas only 62% of U.S. residents had high-speed fixed Internet access as of 2015, whereas 97% of Americans had access in urban areas. Tribal lands in particular suffer, with 58% of those living on tribal lands without access as of 2015. Recent survey data from the Pew Research Center show that populations continuing to lag behind in Internet adoption include those with the elderly, uneducated, poor, and households in rural areas. In total, nearly 30 million people in the U.S. lack meaningful access to the digital age.[10]

---

7. *Coverage and Geography (National Broadband Maps)*, OECD, https://www.oecd.org/sti/broadband/broadband-statistics/ (last visited Jan. 24, 2020).
8. Telecommunications Act of 1996, 47U.S.C. § 1302 (2015).
9. *See 2018 Broadband Deployment Report*, FCC, https://www.fcc.gov/reports-research/reports/broadband-progress-reports/2018-broadband-deployment-report (last visited Jan. 24, 2020).
10. Cong. Research Serv., *Broadband Internet Access and the Digital Divide: Federal Assistance Programs*, CRS Report (updated Oct. 25, 2019) https://fas.org/sgp/crs/misc/RL30719.pdf.

Table 1 Percentage of Americans with Access to Fixed Terrestrial Broadband at Minimum Speed of 25 Mbps/3 Mbps

	2013	2014	2015	2016	2017
All U.S.	83.6%	89.4%	89.9%	91.9%	94.0%
Urban	92.3%	96.4%	96.7%	97.7%	98.5%
Rural	47.6%	60.4%	61.5%	67.8%	75.7%
Tribal	37.1%	57.2%	57.8%	63.1%	68.0%

Source: FCC, *Communications Marketplace Report*, p. 132.

§2. Market for Varying Types of Broadband Technologies

32. Prior to the broadband boom, Americans accessed the Internet by dialing up an Internet Service Provider (ISP) using the same copper telephone lines used for traditional telephone voice service. In the 1970s and 1980s U.S. residents using dial-up service enjoyed maximum speeds of approximately 56 kilobits per second. Although there was a cadre of businesses that used a dedicated line in conjunction with the local telephone company, a meaningful market shift did not occur until cable television companies in 1990 began offering modem broadband service to businesses and residences. Around the same time, telephone companies began to offer DSL service that allowed broadband over existing copper wire line. The growth in the market for broadband service has been significant. There were 2.8 million high-speed lines as of the end of 1999 and 409 million connections as of the middle of 2017. Approximately 353 million connections serve homes in the U.S., according to the FCC.

33. The FCC, in its 2017 report on Internet access, published Table 2. The data shows the rates of deployment of several types of broadband services. As indicated below, download and upload speeds reflect sophistication of the system providing the service as well as potential value.

Table 2 Percentage of Broadband Technologies by Types of Connection

	Connections over 200 kbps in at least one direction (%)	Residential connections over 200 kbps in at least one direction (%)	Fixed connections at least 10 Mbps downstream and 1 Mbps upstream (%)	Residential fixed connections at least 10 Mbps downstream and 1 Mbps upstream (%)	Fixed connections at least 25 Mbps downstream and 3 Mbps upstream (%)	Residential fixed connections at least 25 Mbps downstream and 3 Mbps upstream (%)
Cable modem	15.7	16.9	71.0	71.4	80.3	80.8
DSL	6.2	6.5	13.0	12.9	3.7	3.7
Mobile wireless	74.0	72.5	—	—	—	—
Fiber	3.2	3.3	13.7	13.4	15.2	14.8
All other	0.9	0.8	2.4	2.2	0.8	0.6

Source: FCC, *Internet Access Services: Status as of June 30, 2017*, pp. 16–22.

34. Census data from the 2016 American Community Survey states that 81.4% of U.S. households have a broadband Internet subscription. Broadband adoption differs from broadband availability. Broadband availability addresses whether broadband service is offered; broadband adoption identifies those in the U.S. who actually subscribe to and use broadband. Several studies indicate that U.S. residents increasingly are accessing the Internet, and doing so through diversifying devices, rather than primarily through a personal computer. In 2016, 52% of Americans leveraged at least two devices in order to connect to the Internet, including but not limited to smartphones, laptops, tablets, smart TVs, and gaming consoles.

35. As indicated by the data above, the market for fixed broadband services in the U.S. is capable of categorization by technology. Cable companies, for example, compete with those using copper and/or fiber optic systems. As of mid-2018, the U.S. had 111.7 million high-speed Internet subscribers, indicating a very strong market.

36. As of 2018, this market is currently led by cable network companies, which provide approximately 62% of all U.S. connections. The largest of these cable network companies is Comcast, which is the largest provider of fixed broadband service in the U.S. With 26.5 million customers, Comcast boasts approximately 23.7% market share. Comcast's 2018 cable revenues hit USD 13.8 billion, with broadband products significantly impacting the growth in revenues. Comcast's sales of broadband products increased by 9% annually. The company recently bid for control of the UK broadband provider Sky.

37. Charter Communications, which bought Time Warner Cable in 2016, is the second largest broadband provider in the U.S. As of 2018, Charter Communications had 24.6 million customers, up from 5.7 million before the Time Warner merger. The company now commands 22% of the U.S. broadband market.

38. The third largest provider of broadband service is AT&T, although AT&T is the largest provider of copper and fiber optic connectivity. The company has 14% share of the market with approximately 15.8 million subscribers as of 2018. Twelve years earlier, AT&T launched an initiative to replace much of its copper network with fiber. Fiber-based networks are currently servicing close to 9 million building across seventy cities. In addition to growing the coverage of its optic network, AT&T is upgrading some of its copper legacy lines to increase download/upload speeds.

39. The fourth largest provider of broadband services is Verizon Communications, about 7 million subscribers and 6.2% of the market as of mid-2018. Like AT&T, Verizon plans to enlarge its fiber-based network, with 6 million of its subscribers currently using the fiber-based system.

Chapter 4. E-Commerce: Facts and Figures

§1. General

40. The U.S. is a dominant player in the area of e-commerce worldwide. The e-commerce market in the U.S. has been continually evolving over the past decade. Generally understood, e-commerce is the buying and selling of services or goods entirely through electronic means. One can further define e-commerce by breaking it into three basic transactions. Business to consumer transactions, like online shopping allow individuals to buy assorted products or services and pay for the same online. Business-to-business transactions involve companies, like wholesalers and retailers exchanging products and services online. Consumer-to-consumer transactions allows individuals to buy and sell goods and services to each other through entities like eBay and other such websites.

The U.S. Census Bureau conducts four separate surveys that measure economic activity via e-commerce, including wholesale sales, retail sales, revenue for services industries, and shipments for manufacturing. Measures of e-commerce activity vary by economic sector. The Census Bureau also uses the collected e-commerce data to estimate the value of goods and services sold online. Much of the data in this section stems from the Census Bureau's 2016 report that summarizes statistics on sales and revenues from four sectors of the economy: manufacturing, wholesale, services, and retail.

Already healthy, retail e-commerce in the U.S. is projected to grow quickly in the coming years, going from USD 505 billion in 2018 to over USD 735 billion in 2023. The largest e-retailer in the U.S. is Amazon, generating over USD 235 billion through retail e-commerce in 2018. Walmart, Apple, Target, and eBay also generate significant revenue through retail e-commerce.

With regard to manufacturing and e-commerce, e-commerce shipments of U.S. manufactures were USD 3,469.6 billion in 2016, down 0.7% from a revised USD 3,495.3 billion in 2015. Total shipments were also down from 2015 to 2016, with USD 5,354.7 billion in 2016 and USD 5,519.0 billion in 2015. Notably, e-commerce shipments were almost 65% of all U.S. manufacturing shipments in 2016. Using the North American Industry Classification System, transportation equipment manufacturing reported 83.6% of their shipments occurred via e-commerce, beverage, and tobacco product manufacturing reported 75%, and paper manufacturing reported 70.5%.

Figure 2 E-Commerce Total Shipments/Sales/Revenues: 2015–2016

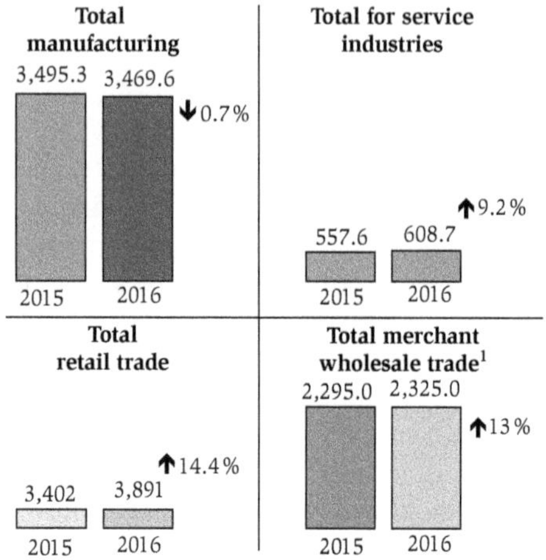

1 Total merchant wholesale, trade including manufacturers' sales branches and offices.

Note: For the estimates of e-commerce total shipments, sales, and revenues, measures of sampling variability can be found at www.census.gov/data/tables/2016/econ/e-stats/2016-e-stats.html.

Source: U.S. Census Bureau, 2016 Annual Survey of Manufactures; 2016 Annual Wholesale Trade Survey, 2016 Annual Retail Trade Survey; and 2016 Service Annual Survey.

With regard to the wholesale market, total e-commerce sales for merchant wholesalers in the U.S., increased 1.3% to USD 2,325.0 billion in 2016 from USD 2,295.0 billion in 2015. In 2015, e-commerce sales of merchant wholesalers, including manufacturers' sales branches and offices (MSBOs), were 32.4% of total sales in 2016, an increase from the revised 31.5% in 2015. According to the U.S. Census Bureau, e-commerce sales accounted for 27.2% of total sales of merchant wholesalers, excluding MSBOs in 2016, while e-commerce sales were 46.2% of the sales of MSBOs.

With regard to services, e-commerce revenues for service industries in the U.S. were USD 608.7 billion in 2016. This was up 9.2% from USD 557.6 billion in 2015. Total revenues were USD 14,591.1 billion in 2016, up 4.4% from USD 13,970.7 billion in 2015. E-commerce revenues were 4.2% of total revenues in 2016, an increase from the 4% in 2015.

Figure 3 E-Commerce as a Percentage of Total Shipments/Sales/Revenues: 2015–2016

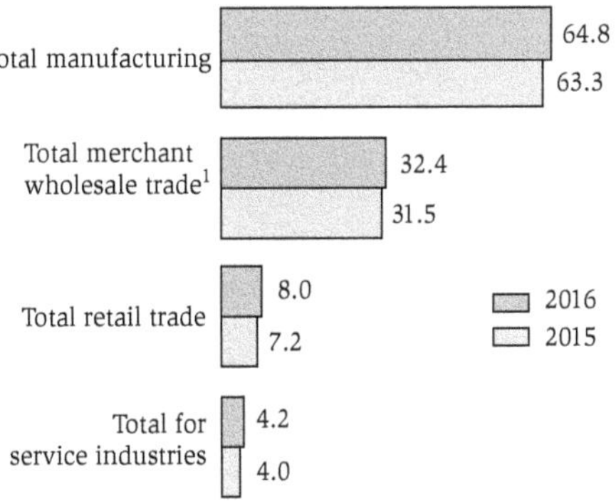

1 Total merchant wholesale, trade including manufacturers' sales branches and offices.

Note: For the estimates of e-commerce as a percentage of total shipments, sales, and revenues, measures of sampling variability can be found at www.census.gov/data/tables/2016/econ/e-stats/2016-e-stats.html.

Source: U.S. Census Bureau, 2016 Annual Survey of Manufactures; 2016 Annual Wholesale Trade Survey; 2016 Annual Retail Trade Survey; and 2016 Service Annual Survey.

And finally, with regard to sales from e-commerce, U.S. retailers generated USD 389.1 billion in 2016, an increase of 14.4% from USD 340.2 billion in 2015. According to the U.S. Census Bureau, total sales increased by 2.8% to USD 4,856.3 billion in 2016 from USD 4,726.0 billion in 2015. E-commerce sales were 8% of total sales in 2016, up from 7.2% in 2015.

While the clear trend favors e-commerce and online sales, online sales still constituted a relatively small percentage of all U.S. retail sales, with less than 10% by the end of 2018. The commercial trend, however, indicates growth of online sales, with 32% of Internet users buying items over the Internet at least once a month in 2017. In that same year, an estimated 78% of Internet users bought products online at least once during the year. Moreover, the massive increase in use of e-commerce to obtain staple goods and discretionary items during the pandemic has increased the use of e-commerce vendors and the increased usage of these vendors will likely continue into the foreseeable future.

Likewise, the proliferation of smartphones has spurred increases in mobile shopping. Mobile shopping allows for a customer to buy a service or a product from a mobile device, using an application such as Amazon, or over a web app. Mobile retail revenue in the U.S. is expected to grow from USD 156 billion in 2017 to about USD 420 billion in 2021. The incidents of mobile-only online shippers have been growing as retailers improve the mobile shopping experience.

Chapter 5. e-Government Initiatives

§1. General

41. Both federal and local governments in the U.S. extensively rely on the Internet and digital technology to deploy government goods and services. Generally, this online interaction is deemed "electronic government" or "e-government." More specifically, e-government assumes several discrete functions. Leveraging the Internet to assist the citizenry in finding and using government data and services and to allow feedback to the government from users serves a public outreach and public service function. Another function of e-government involves online presence as a revenue generator. The federal government – like private entities – originate revenue by advertisements on their websites, or by assessing fees for use of electronic portals. Yet another function of e-government involves streamlining the administration of government services. Whether it is the process of vetting private contracting or choosing which software IT to implement, the U.S. government contains hundreds of agencies and departments that generate large inefficiencies that could be reduced through e-government initiatives.

Of course, transitioning analogue government services to online government services increases concerns regarding data security and informational privacy. The many data breaches both in public and private sectors, demonstrate the need for adequate and evolving security protocols across the many departments and agencies of the U.S. government. As a result, several laws and concomitant policies require the adoption and enforcement of security and privacy measures as they relate to the sensitivity of the information and services at issue.

After the Internet boom, governmental portals and websites emerged during the Clinton administration, allowing more people in the U.S. to access government data and programs online, including significant amount of government data that was not previously available. The E-Government Act of 2002 requires federal agencies to use the Internet and other technologies to enhance citizen access to government information and services, improving government transparency and decision-making.[11]

In the U.S., the Office of Management and Budget (OMB) has led federal efforts to increase citizen-centric services through the Internet and other emerging technologies. The OMB is tasked with promoting electronic government services, particularly across the several federal agencies that face the public in one way or another. Pursuant to the Federal Funding Accountability and Transparency Act of 2006, the OMB is tasked with instituting and report to Congress on the creation of a website through which the public can access information about grants and contracts with federal agencies.[12]

In conjunction with the OMB, the Office of the Federal Chief Information Officer identified three principal objectives to provide better e-services across the varied federal agencies: (1) decrease duplication and inefficiencies within IT budgets and

11. 44U.S.C. § 3601
12. 31U.S.C. § 6101

IT investments, (2) assist agencies in delivering IT investments to increase government productivity and citizen access, and (3) increase the use of data across agencies to support IT management. Additionally, the Office of E-Government and Information Technology (IT) helps develop policies that promote the use of Internet-based technologies to make it easier for individuals and organizations to interact with the federal government, streamline taxpayer dollars, and incentivize citizen participation.

The election of Barack Obama as President of the U.S. increased governmental emphasis on the effective use of Internet technologies. One of President Obama's first memorandums, early in 2009, sought to leverage the Internet and other technologies to grow transparency in government. The memo, titled, Memorandum for the Heads of Executive Departments and Agencies on Transparency and Open Government, instructed federal agencies to "ensure the public trust and establish a system of transparency, public participation, and collaboration," and directed the Chief Technology Officer and OMB "to coordinate the development by appropriate executive departments and agencies [and] to take specific actions implementing the principles set forth in the memorandum." As a result, public websites like data.gov and recovery.gov sought to meet the president's goal of increased transparency across various federal agencies. These efforts are monitored pursuant to the E-Government Act, which requires federal agencies and the OMB to report annually on their progress.[13]

The following data largely derives from OMB's 2016 annual report to Congress regarding e-government initiatives. The objectives supported by OMB include:

- make federal government information and services more readily available to members of the public;
- make it easier for the public to apply for benefits, receive services, pursue business opportunities, submit information, and otherwise conduct transactions with the federal government; and
- enable federal agencies to take advantage of IT in sharing information and conducting transactions with each other and with state and local governments.[14]

§2. Particular e-Government Initiatives

42. The Federal Source Code Policy: achieving efficiency, transparency, and innovation through reusable and open source software has a long name and simple objective, to mitigate wasteful spending attending duplicative software purchases. With USD 6 billion in annual federal government spending on new software use, this policy aims to identify efficiencies across technologies and agencies. In addition, custom or tailored software that is created especially for the federal government must now be available – in most cases – across all federal agencies. The policy

13. 44U.S.C. § 3606
14. FY 2016 Annual Report to Congress: E-Government Act Implementation, https://www.whitehouse.gov/sites/whitehouse.gov/files/omb/egov/documents/omb-fy-2016-egov-act-report.pdf.

also encourages use of open-source software, including training and a pilot program. Indeed, mandatory code sharing applies to 20% of custom code purchased by the federal government as part of a three-year pilot program designed to maximize the economic benefits that attend code sharing and reuse.

43. With regard to cybersecurity efforts, the Federal Information Security Modernization Act of 2014 contains provisions effecting e-government initiatives. Under that Act, the OMB must facilitate and is accountable for the information security practices of federal agencies. The OMB is also responsible for developing policies and guidelines related to information security practices of the federal agencies. The division of the OMB responsible for cyber security collaborates across governmental departments in identifying and developing cyber security programs, including the federal government's response protocol for cyber breaches.

44. With regard to data center optimization, the Federal Data Center Consolidation Initiative was instituted in 2010 by the OMB. The primary objective of the Data Center Consolidation Initiative is to promote the use of green IT by reducing the overall energy and real estate footprint of government data centers; reduce the cost of data center hardware, software, and operations; increase the overall IT security posture of the Federal Government; and shift IT investments to more efficient computing platforms and technologies. This initiative spurred closure of over 1,900 data centers, with an estimated cost saving of nearly USD 1 billion. In December 2014, the Federal Information Technology Acquisition Reform Act (FITARA) was enacted. The Act adds to the requirements of the Data Center Consolidation Initiative. It mandates annual reports from federal agencies that most include the following: multiyear strategies to consolidate and optimize data centers, performance metrics and a timeline for agency activities, comprehensive data center inventories, and yearly calculations of investment and cost savings.[15]

45. Even so, well over 8,700 data centers remained in the federal inventory, and the Data Center Optimization Initiative of 2016 recognized this fact and set an objective of closing close to 52% of those data centers as well as optimize the remaining data centers using five key measurements, and reduce data center spending by USD 2.7 billion by the end of FY 2018.[16] Although this objective as well as other outlined above and required by the FITARA were supposed to be completed by October 1, 2018, The FITARA Enhancement Act of 2017 extended the data center requirements of FITARA until October 1, 2020.[17]

46. With regard to open government initiatives, open government has long been a hallmark of democratic participation of the citizenry in the U.S. Principles of transparency facilitate an accountable, responsive government, and are required

15. Title VIII, Subtitle D of the National Defense Authorization Act (NDAA) for Fiscal Year 2015, Pub. L. No. 113-291.
16. *See* OMB Memorandum on Data Center Optimization Initiative, https://datacenters.cio.gov/policy/.
17. FITARA Enhancement Act of 2017, Pub. L. No. 115-88, https://www.congress.gov/115/plaws/publ88/PLAW-115publ88.pdf.

under federal law, most prominently in the 1966 Freedom of Information Act (FOIA), which was one of the first such laws in the world. The FOIA is a federal law that generally provides that any person has a right, enforceable in court, to obtain access to federal agency records. Unless the records are protected from disclosure by one of nine FOIA exceptions identified in the statute, all federal agencies must make requested records available. Notably, FOIA does not apply to the courts, records held by Congress, or by state or local government agencies.[18]

47. On January 14, 2019, the Foundations for Evidence-Based Policymaking Act (Evidence Act), was signed into law. The Evidence Act includes the OPEN Government Data Act, in conjunction, these laws generally require the OMB, the Office of Government Information Services, and the General Services Administration (GSA) to collaborate in the development and maintenance of an online repository of best practices, standards, and tools to enable the adoption of open data practices across federal government departments and agencies. The Project Open Data Dashboard provides publicly accessible evaluations of each agency's performance in implementing of the Open Data Policy. A concurrent goal seeks to improve how data are used to generate evidence about policies and programs in the federal government, including increased use of evidence in a draft bill improving the use of evidence for drug policy and providing funding for "Pay For Success" grants, in addition to numerous provisions in a budget agreement in early 2018.[19]

48. Select federal employees and government contractors participate in biweekly meetings regarding implementation of Project Open Data, connecting over 800 federal data officers, in the hope of identifying and implementing best practices as they relate to data policy and data governance. Finally the OMB, through the third Open Government National Action Plan, focused on public feedback. The plan required select federal agencies to open communications with data users for feedback purposes, primarily feedback relating to the effectiveness of open government data. User-friendly feedback mechanisms have been implemented across the relevant federal agencies as a result.

Several concerns attend e-government initiatives. As indicated above, a significant portion of the population lacks access to broadband and/or the ability to use such service even when it is accessible. That population tends to be poor, rural, and elderly. Government services and programs available only online truncates these populations. More traditional, access points to government data and programs are increasingly inferior even when they are offered off-line. In addition, the federal government, in contrast to the private sector, has largely failed to efficiently harness new technologies. Due to poor management of technology investments, IT projects too often cost hundreds of millions of dollars more than they should, taking years longer than necessary to deploy, and deliver technologies that are obsolete by the time they are completed. As noted above, the federal government has recognized these inefficiencies and moved to mitigate them.

18. 5 U.S.C §552 et seq. (1966).
19. H.R. 4174 – 115th Congress: Foundations for Evidence-Based Policymaking Act of 2017.

The United Nations E-Government Survey measures how well a country applies e-government practices. In 2018, the U.S. moved up from twelfth to eleventh, even though the U.S. topped the list when it was first contrived in 2003. This is the second time over nine UN surveys in which the U.S. was listed outside the top 10. Other nations have developed significantly more robust e-government programs, including Estonia, which uses a universal electronic identification system that enables government offices to facilitate tax collection and basic business functions. Other nations, including Estonia, promote open government through use of open-source materials, open standards, and universal broadband access. These efforts garner international recognition as world leaders in the e-government efforts.

§3. State e-Government Initiatives

49. Notably, each of the fifty states in the U.S. fund and operate their own e-government initiatives. For example, each state has its own public access laws that should be consulted for access to state and local records. Some states are far more effective than others in providing online access to data, services, and programs offered by that state. Most states attempt to follow or mirror the initiatives implemented by the federal government, and as a result, the federal government often provides the template from which to start when state policy makers address e-government initiatives.

Part I. Digital Market Regulation

Chapter 1. Legal Status of Standards and Technical Specifications

§1. General

50. As opposed to other nations, the U.S. approach to standardization reflects an organic partnership of the private and public sectors. The standardization landscape in the U.S. reflects the nation's market-driven and diversified society. Due to its decentralized architecture, the standardization "system"' is sectoral or industrial in nature, with many standards developed by private entities that respond to market demand within the industry, whether the demand derives from consumers, government or businesses. The standardization framework in the U.S. is often described as "voluntary" because the government does not superimpose standardization through mandatory law. Instead, more often than not, standards derive from voluntary participation by both private stakeholders, sometimes with input from government experts and regulators.

Because standardization largely derives from voluntary participation by private entities, and because standardization often is industry-specific, the standards themselves do not have the force and effect of law. Voluntary participation traditionally refers only to the manner in which the standard was developed. Just because a standard that was adopted by a private accrediting entity was not adopted with the voluntary participation of all businesses within that industry does not necessarily mean that compliance to a consensus standard is optional or whether a government entity or market sector has endorsed the standard for mandatory use. Trade organizations, for example, often police their membership's infractions outside of government enforcement.

Even so, compliance with an industry standard can have evidentiary impact in a judicial proceeding. A business that complies with industry standards is less likely to be held liable under tort law from a consumer plaintiff than a business that fails to comply with industry standards. Also, federal agencies often look to and sometimes formally adopt standards generated by the private sector.

Of course, defining standardization includes a broad outlook. It includes the process of developing standards, acceptance of those standards, as well as implementation. Evaluating whether companies conform to the standards, certification processes, measurement and testing and more are often included in the standardization inquiry. Regardless, standardization in the U.S. has played a key role in gaining access to those markets which have developed and enforced sectoral standards. As economies become more global and less regional, standardization will likely play an increasingly instrumental role.

Direct involvement and payment of the associated expenses when creating standards depends upon the perceived interests of the industries that may be affected by resultant standards. Initially, the entities and organizations that seek to develop industry standards bear the costs of doing so. If the standards succeed, however, those costs are eventually borne by consumers that benefit from standardization. Often consumers, or end users, pay for standardization through application fees and the like. The benefits are seen to equalize or exceed the costs, and entities that invest in the process, hiring experts, and conducting testing, often develop their expertise through the process and illicit "buy-in" for future compliance.

The U.S. standardization approach, developed over several decades, arguably reflects a belief that innovation and progress derives from decentralized government, except where government intervention is essential. The voluntary creation of standards differentiates the U.S. from other standardization practices across the globe. Most other countries adhere to a "top-down" approach featuring government entities or appointees generating standards to be widely applied to interested stakeholders.

§2. The American National Standards Institute

51. The American National Standards Institute (ANSI) is one of the leading nongovernmental organizations that facilitates U.S. standardization. ANSI supervises the generation, drafting, and implementation of hundreds of diverse norms that have material impact on a wide range of businesses and trades, "from acoustical devices to construction equipment, from dairy and livestock production to energy distribution, and many more."[20]

In the wake of World War I, a need for uniformity was recognized spurring a handful of private companies in conjunction with three governmental agencies to form the American Engineering Standards Committee (AESC) in October 1918. In the following year, AESC vetted its first standard on pipe threads. Thereafter, AESC focused on accident protection, approving standards in 1921 that helped protect the heads and faces of industrial workers. AESC expanded thereafter, creating standards to guide safety practices in mechanical engineering, mining, and construction. The AESC continued to diversify and grow, eventually becoming ANSI.

Today, ANSI continues to serve as a nongovernmental, not-for-profit third party that coordinates industry leaders, government officials, and outside experts to generate a diverse range of guidelines. ANSI is now also actively engaged in accreditation, which is loosely defined as assessing the competence of businesses to determine conformance to standards. Thousands of voluntary standards have

20. *See About Ansi*, Ansi, https://www.ansi.org/about_ansi/overview/overview?menuid=1 (last visited Jan. 27, 2020).

resulted from ANSI's efforts and processes. Due to the centrality of ANSI's historical experience, the organization reduces overlapping and duplicative standards across industries.

Importantly, a cadre of private organizations have joined ANSI in facilitating the creation of guidelines, norms and standards, most of which are supported by the industries subject to the standards. For example, trade associations often create their own standards entity to promote and stabilize goods or services within that trade. The Aerospace Industries Association generate standards that apply to their members rather than the industry itself. Moreover, the Aerospace Industries Association performs promotional functions like advocating for federal investment and lobbying for policies and laws that enhance the market for the association's membership.

Along with standardization developed by an established entity like ANSI, and along with standardization established by trade or industry players like Aerospace Industries Association or the Telecommunications Industry Association (TIA), standards also develop at times through a more ad hoc process. Particularly with rapid technology developments and the creation of new markets, de facto standards arise from usage of trade. Although such loose standards benefit from quick creation, they do not cultivate the consensus-based, voluntary participation among interested stakeholders, and are therefore of more limited value.

§3. Telecommunications Industry Association

52. The TIA is similar to the Aerospace Industries Association and other trade groups, in that it develops voluntary, consensus-based standards for an array of industry players. The TIA, while originally operating under a different name, has been helping to develop standards in the field of information and communications technology for over ninety years. The guidelines promulgated by TIA include norms that cover cellular towers, satellites, accessibility, data terminals, VOIP devices, mobile device communications, multimedia multicast, data centers, vehicular telematics, machine to machine communications, and smart utility networks, among others.

Government agencies, academic organizations, consumers, equipment manufacturers, and other stakeholders participate with the member businesses in crafting standards. The TIA is not limited to standard creation, often advocating before Congress and federal agencies on behalf of its membership. In 2011, TIA advocated for the award of over USD 8 billion to the FCC for modernization of broadband programing through the FCC's Universal Service Fund. In the following year TIA successfully lobbied for increased spectrum auctions and the creation of a nationwide public safety broadband network—FirstNet.

Standards promulgated by TIA have not always attracted universal adoption by industry players. The most popularly adopted standards by the telecommunications industry include: (1) the telecommunications cabling standards, which is used by virtually all voice, video, and data networks, (2) fiber optic color-coding standards, (3) data transmission systems and equipment standards, and (4) telecommunications infrastructure standard for data centers.

In light of increased globalization of the telecommunications market, TIA also collaborates with the International Telecommunication Union, the International Organization for Standardization, and the International Electrotechnical Commission. In 2017, TIA integrated through a merger with an international entity—QuEST Forum. QuEST Forum specialized in promoting the ICT industry internationally, and the merger signaled TIA's attempt to increase its global reach, which includes more than 500 members, and partner organizations across the Americas, Europe-Middle East, and Asia-Pacific as of 2019.

§4. Government Involvement in Standardization

53. While the private sector plays a meaningful part in standardization, the U.S. government also has a long history of involvement in standardization. The U.S. Constitution charges the federal government with establishing standardized weights and measurements.[21] Moreover, various federal agencies, often cooperating with private sector standardization efforts, codify such standards into enforceable statutory or regulatory law.

As the nation's largest employer, the U.S. federal government is the largest single user of standards and norms. Regulations and standards within the federal government include an estimated 44,000 provisions that perform the same function as voluntary standards generated by the private sector. Although there have been movements to harmonize standards across the federal government, typically each federal agency retains discretion regarding adoption of application standards for that agency. Increasingly, federal agencies cite to and rely on standards created by voluntary consensus by the private sector.

As of 2018, over 6,000 organizations generate standards in the U.S. ANSI supervises 200 of those organizations through accreditation processes, but the array of entities generating standards has spurred the U.S. government to coordinate this decentralized approach. In 1995, the U.S. Congress passed the National Technology Transfer and Advancement Act with the primary goal of bringing technology and industrial innovation to market more quickly. But the Act also directly addressed new the development of new standards across federal agencies by requiring agencies to cooperate with each other and private standards developing organizations. The entity responsible for facilitating that process among the many federal agencies was the National Institute of Standards and Technology (NIST), a nonregulatory federal agency within the Technology Administration of the U.S. Department of Commerce. NIST was already the federal agency responsible for weights and measurement standards in the U.S. and had already collaborated extensively with ANSI.[22]

---

21. U.S. Const. Art. 1 § 8.
22. Public Law 104-113, 110 Stat. 775 (1996).

I. National Institute of Standards and Technology

54. NIST does not have rulemaking authority, but it is a federal agency under the supervision of the Department of Commerce in charge of standardization for federal agency purposes. NIST states that its mission is to "promote U.S. innovation and industrial competitiveness by advancing measurement science, standards, and technology in ways that enhance economic security and improve our quality of life."[23] In developing standards for federal agencies, NIST also works closely with private sector companies, including ANSI. Hosting one of the oldest physical laboratories in the U.S., NIST was founded in 1901. In large part, Congress created the agency to address inferior measurement standards and to promote U.S. competitiveness with industrialized countries that boasted more universal standards like Germany and the UK.

The industries that NIST has focused on have changed over time. As of 2019, the onsite laboratories and programs at NIST include a Communications Technology Laboratory, an Engineering Laboratory, an Information Technology Laboratory, a Material Measurement Laboratory, a Center for Neutron Research, and a Physical Measurement Laboratory. In May 2019, NIST conducted a workshop aimed at developing new standards for a specific emerging technology entitled: Federal Engagement in Artificial Intelligence Standards Workshop. NIST continues to address technology advances in this way.

II. U.S. Standards Strategy

55. Standardization across the U.S., as mentioned above, is an amalgamation of private and public undertakings without a central top-down mandate. In light of the disparate groups engaged in standard-setting and the varying levels of compliance such standards demand, the public and private sectors have historically collaborated in efforts to identify more generalized strategies.

In 2005, government officials and private standardization organizations used ANSI to help identify a strategy for future standardization in the U.S. The summit eventually created the United States Standards Strategy (USSS). The strategy confirmed the existing system of private, voluntary, and sectoral approach to standardization but included recommendations on improving the framework. Tactical initiatives operating within this framework were developed to facilitate diverse interests to meet their own national and individual organizational objectives. For example, ANSI recognized the service industry as a sector that has been rapidly growing in the global economy and workforce, amounting to about 78% or USD 10.3 trillion of the U.S. GDP in 2012. ANSI stated that difficulties arise because the service industry is very diverse, ranging from utilities, IT, finance, tourism, education, to retail. A one-size-fits-all strategy was rejected by ANSI, which noted that each of these areas has different needs and priorities for standardization for services, systems, and personnel. ANSI emphasized that "the United States must

23. *See NIST Mission, Vision, Core Competencies, and Core Values*, NIST, https://www.nist.gov/about-nist/our-organization/mission-vision-values (updated Jan. 26, 2017).

devote more attention to understanding the needs of the service industry sector and establishing service standards initiatives to meet those needs."[24]

The USSS builds off its predecessor, the National Standards Strategy, which was negotiated over two years and approved in 2000. This forerunner also focused on the diversified society, transparency, and voluntary nature of standards development in the U.S. and relied on a wide variety of constituents over the two years in developing the strategy. The USSS, approved in 2005, focuses more than its predecessor on globalization and the need for standards designed to meet stakeholder needs irrespective of national borders.

The global economy has raised the stakes in standards development. Competition for the advantages that accompany a widespread adoption of technology has reached a new level, and the impetus to develop globally accepted standards is greater now than ever before[25]

The new name also reflects a standardization environment that incorporates new types of standards development activities, more flexible approaches, and new structures. The strategy lays out general guidelines for future U.S. standardization that attempts to incorporate globally accepted principles for standards development:

- Transparency: essential information regarding standardization activities is accessible to all interested parties.
- Openness: participation is open to all affected interests.
- Impartiality: no one interest dominates the process or is favored over another.
- Effectiveness and Relevance: standards are relevant and effectively respond to regulatory and market needs, as well as scientific and technological developments.
- Consensus: decisions are reached through consensus among those affected.
- Performance Based: standards are performance-based (specifying essential characteristics rather than detailed designs) where possible.
- Coherence: the process encourages coherence to avoid overlapping and conflicting standards.
- Due Process: standards development accords with due process so that all views are considered, and appeals are possible.
- Technical Assistance: assistance is offered to developing countries in the formulation and application of standards.[26]

§5. International Standardization

56. With varied and significant worldwide interests, both private and public, the U.S. is heavily involved in international standardization efforts and institutions. Concerted international standardization developed in the early 1900s and is often

24. *See* United States Standards Strategy, ANSI (2015), https://www.ansi.org/standards_activities/nss/usss.
25. *See* United States Standards Strategy, ANSI (2005), http://www.strategicstandards.com/files/U.S.pdf.
26. *Id.*

marked by the founding of the International Electrotechnical Commission. Development of international standards in the west, however, did not take off until after World War II and the creation of the United Nations Standards Coordinating Committee.

The UN Standards Coordinating Committee eventually spawned the International Organization for Standardization (ISO) in 1946. In 1946, the ISO had delegates from twenty-five countries and met at the Institute of Civil Engineers in London with the goal of facilitating "the international coordination and unification of industrial standards."

Through the 1950s and 1960s, international efforts attempted to standardize screw threads, pipe sizing, couplings, bearings, and power transmissions. The immediate goal was to harmonize interchangeability among western developed nations, including standards for units, symbols, and vocabularies. With the emergence of new information and communication technologies in the 1980s and 1990s, international standardization expanded efforts to address telecommunications.

Today, the ISO is an independent, nongovernmental international organization with a membership of approximately 164 national standards bodies. As economies flatten as a result of global trade, the ISO seeks to provide standards applicable to global commerce. As of 2019, the ISO has 783 technical committees and subcommittees and has published 22,738 international standards, covering almost thousands of industries from agriculture, to health care, manufacturing, and technology.

The ISO lists the key principles that drive its standardization process:

(1) ISO standards respond to a need in the market.
(2) ISO standards are based on global expert opinion.
(3) ISO standards are developed through a multi-stakeholder process.
(4) ISO standards are based on a consensus.[27]

Although private standards companies in the U.S. participate in international efforts and although private companies participate in international efforts as well, the U.S. is a signatory of the World Trade Organization (WTO). Under U.S. law, international treaties enjoy superior status over standards developed by private entities—when the two conflict. Under the WTO, the U.S. is obligated to seek standards that comply with the WTO Agreement on Technical Barriers to Trade. This obligation is enforceable against private standards as well. The obligation also promotes internationally accepted standardization principles and honors the stated objectives of impartiality, relevance, openness, consensus, and transparency. The U.S. also pushes for flexibility and timeliness in developing international standards pursuant to WTO obligations.

U.S. Government departments and agencies such as the Department of Commerce and its agencies (e.g., NIST and the International Trade Administration); the Office of the U.S. Trade Representative, the Department of State; and other regulatory agencies throughout the federal government work closely with each other,

27. ISO Homepage, ISO, https://www.iso.org/home.html (last visited Jan. 27, 2020).

with ANSI, and with others in the private sector on issues affecting U.S. competitiveness in the global marketplace. With regard to private sector involvement in international standardization, ANSI accredits organizations to serve as U.S. Technical Advisory Groups to ISO and other organizations approved by ANSI's National Committee.

Chapter 2. Legal Status of Standard Terms and Conditions

57. Owing to its common law development, the U.S. does not provide specific legal status for standard terms and conditions. Instead, when contracts are litigated, the contract terms are evaluated on their merits without reference to any preapproved standard terms. Moreover, contracts are generally governed by state law in the U.S. and so a national standardization approach would face significant hurdles in the U.S. system.

Although the common law does provide for nonenforcement of unconscionable contract terms, it does not provide for automatic enforcement of standardized terms on the other end of the spectrum. Nevertheless, the terms of contracts in the U.S. are generally upheld unless some type of fraudulent or other impermissible behavior led to the formation of the contract. This includes contracts that are formed in the online context, sometimes referred to as "clickwrap" or "browsewrap" agreements. The terms of these types of online contracts are generally enforced, although courts may take a skeptical view towards terms like mandatory arbitration provisions that would cause an individual to waive substantive legal rights in a context where they have not had specific notice of the provision.

At least partially because contracts are generally enforced by their terms, there has not been significant effort to reform the contracts system in the U.S. or any individual states. Accordingly, it is unlikely that the U.S. will adopt a standard terms and conditions regime in the near term, either at the state or federal level.

Chapter 3. International Private Law Applied to the Online Environment

§1. General

58. Nonjudicial conflict resolution has materially impacted and continues to impact dispute resolution in the U.S. Over the past two decades the U.S. government and the private sector have largely favored alternatives to dispute resolution that avoids the traditional court-based litigation and trial. While the judicial system historically offered independent and principled dispute resolution using established processes for rules of evidence and rules of procedure, court-based litigation had become costly, time-intensive, and unwieldy. Several jurisdictions report a long backlog of cases, which delayed litigation for years and stunted resolution.

Although alternatives to court-based dispute resolution in the U.S. have been around for 100 years, a significant trend toward "Alternative Dispute Resolution" (ADR) began in earnest in the 1990s. The popularized term, ADR, is a general term that represents a number of methods for dispute resolution that avoid judicial determination. Mediation, arbitration, and mock trials are all included in ADR.

Resort to ADR continues to trend in both the public and private sectors in the U.S. as it is perceived as a quicker, more predictable, and more cost-effective form of dispute resolution. Court-based litigation is also widely perceived as slower and more traumatic. Indeed, the vast majority of civil cases filed in the U.S. are settled before a trial court can determine the merits of the conflict. As a result, the disputing parties often spend considerable resources litigating the dispute, only to settle the dispute without clear judicial resolution on the underlying conflict.

Although all ADR methods seek to avoid judicial determination, ADR methods differ. Mediation is a formal negotiation among the disputing parties that is coordinated by a neutral, nonjudicial facilitator. Mediation can be voluntary or mandated by statutory law or by a judge. It can also be required if the disputing parties previously agreed by contract to mediate future disputes. Arbitration, by contrast, often resembles a private lawsuit. Instead of a negotiating process like mediation, arbitration involves a more contentious process whereby the parties select an arbitrator or group of arbitrators to hear the arguments presented by the disputing parties and render a binding decision.

Resolution through ADR can be a voluntary decision after the dispute arises, it can be a contractually agreed upon method before the dispute arises, or it can be statutorily required. For example, in the ICT industry, the Telecommunications Act of 1996 expressly contemplates state regulatory commissions to use arbitration to resolve interconnection-related disputes.

A. Agreements Arrived at Through Negotiation

1. Voluntary Negotiations

Upon receiving a request for interconnection, services, or network elements pursuant to section 251 of this title, an ILEC may negotiate and enter into a binding agreement with the requesting telecommunications carrier or carriers without regard to the standards set forth in subsections (b) and (c) of section 251 of this title. The agreement shall include a detailed schedule of itemized charges for interconnection and each service or network element included in the agreement. The agreement, including any interconnection agreement negotiated before February 8, 1996, shall be submitted to the State commission under subsection (e) of this section.

2. Mediation

Any party negotiating an agreement under this section may, at any point in the negotiation, ask a State commission to participate in the negotiation and to mediate any differences arising in the course of the negotiation.

B. Agreements Arrived at Through Compulsory Arbitration

1. Arbitration

During the period from the 135th to the 160th day (inclusive) after the date on which an ILEC receives a request for negotiation under this section, the carrier or any other party to the negotiation may petition a State commission to arbitrate any open issues.[28]

Contractual clauses requiring arbitration are binding, and a court of law will seldom allow disputing parties to avoid ADR when a contractual clause requires it and where the dispute arises under the contract, although the online contracting context is placing increasing pressure on this approach. Although ADR clauses in contracts are binding, parties cannot waive the right to administrative process in most instances. Of course, contracts formed through fraud or misrepresentation are not binding.

Although the judiciary initially resisted and devalued attempts to bypass judicial review through ADR, judges and courts have now generally embraced ADR. In large part, courts view ADR as a mechanism to help reduce the congested court docket. Many judges across the U.S. strongly encourage or even require disputing parties to mediate their disagreement before the court will hear it. These mandates by individual judges are often buttressed by legislation. Both the federal government and state governments have enacted laws of varying types to encourage or mandate ADR. The American Arbitration Association (AAA) reflects the interrelationship among state and federal laws encouraging ADR and the private sector. The AAA is a nonprofit organization that provides arbitration services.

Due to its long history and robust offerings, the AAA also offers specialized arbitration services tailored to particular industries. For example, the Cellular TIA, a nonprofit trade association, asked the AAA to administer an arbitration program for the wireless industry and its customers in the U.S. The rules pertaining to wireless industry arbitrations through the AAA contain three tracks: Regular Track Procedures; Expedited Procedures for cases involving claims of less than USD 75,000; and Large/Complex Case Track Procedures for cases involving claims of at least USD 500,000. An identification to the specific arbitration procedures attending each

28. 47U.S. Code §252 (1996).

track through the AAA for wireless industry conflicts has been published by the AAA and illustrates how arbitrations have been tailored to some aspects of the ICT market.[29]

§2. Enabling Legislation

59. The trend in the U.S. favoring ADR is reflected in statutory law both on the federal level and through state legislation. More than two-thirds of the states have laws encouraging some form of ADR, whether arbitration, mediation or other ADR. Several states, including Texas,[30] Virginia,[31] and Florida[32] have statutory schemes that mandate ADR in certain circumstances, or provide uniform processes for ADR. These statutes do not typically turn on the subject matter of the dispute. Instead, the statutes require mediation of most lawsuits filed in a state court prior to summary judgment.

The Uniform Arbitration Act is an attempt to unify state law as it relates to arbitration. Counterintuitively, the Uniform Arbitration Act was created by a nongovernmental entity in an attempt to entice states to adopt it and thereby unify arbitration law across state lines. In 2000, the Act was updated by the Uniform Law Commission. The new Act, called the Revised Uniform Arbitration Act has been adopted by eighteen states, with thirty-five states having adopted some version of the Uniform Arbitration Act as of 2018.

With regard to federal legislation, the U.S. Congress enacted the Federal Arbitration Act (FAA) in 1925. In large part Congress used the FAA to confront judicial resistance to ADR. The FAA embodies a national policy favoring ADR. It ensures that contracts that require parties to resolve disputes through binding arbitration will be upheld in most cases.

> A written provision in any maritime transaction or a contract evidencing a transaction involving commerce to settle by arbitration a controversy thereafter arising out of such contract or transaction, or the refusal to perform the whole or any part thereof, or an agreement in writing to submit to arbitration an existing controversy arising out of such a contract, transaction, or refusal, shall be valid, irrevocable, and enforceable, save upon such grounds as exist at law or in equity for the revocation of any contract.[33]

The FAA allows contracting parties to customize many components of the arbitration itself, including which issues are subject to arbitration, how arbitrators are chosen and what their qualifications must be. Even rules of evidence, rules of procedure and choice of substantive law may be specified by contract. Although the question of whether the FAA preempts a state law is a subject of frequent litigation,

---

29. See Wireless Industry Arbitration Rules, amended July 1, 2016, available at https://www.adr.org/sites/default/files/AAA_Wireless_Rules%20%283%29.pdf.
30. Tex. Civ. Prac. & Rem. Code, Ch 154, § 154.002 (2019).
31. *See* Va Code. Ann. Title 8.01, Ch 20.2 (2019).
32. *See* Fla. Stat. § 44.102 (2005).
33. 9U.S. Code § 2 (1947).

the courts routinely hold that the FAA supersedes state requirements that restrain the enforceability of mandatory arbitration agreements.

Importantly, arbitration determinations are final. No appeal can be made to the court system, except for exceptional and limited circumstances. The FAA provides that an arbitration conclusion or determination may be confirmed by filing the arbitration award in a court of law within one year of the arbitration award. Once confirmed by the court, the arbitration award is actionable by law officers as an enforceable judgment. The FAA applies in both state courts and federal courts, and has been upheld in the face of a constitutional challenge.[34]

The deference that the FAA commands requires that state and federal courts accept arbitration awards without modification. In a few prescribed instances, a court may vacate an entire award under the FAA or even modify it, although courts are admonished to give deference to the arbitration award, including questions about the scope of the contractual arbitration agreement, with ambiguities resolved in favor of arbitration.

The U.S. federal government also favors ADR to facilitate dispute resolution among federal agencies and to facilitate disputes between a government agency and the public. This commitment to ADR is illustrated in the legislative history of the Administrative Dispute Resolution Act of 1992,[35] which was reauthorized by the Administrative Dispute Resolution Act (ADRA) of 1996.[36] The ADRA authorizes and encourages U.S. federal agencies to use mediation, conciliation, arbitration in the following circumstances:

(1) There is mutual consent by the parties to participate in the ADR process (with consent being obtained either before or after an issue in controversy has arisen).
(2) Prior to the submission of a claim. and
(3) In resolution of a formal claim. Use of ADR shall be coordinated with counsel.[37]

The ADRA reflects the current federal policy promoting ADR across U.S. agencies and for disputes that such agencies have with private entities and individuals. Indeed, every federal agency is required to analyze whether and how ADR could apply within each agency, including intra-agency disputes as well as external disputes with the public and contracting parties. This policy has been extended to disputes arising within the executive branch as demonstrated through Executive Order 12778, which encourages nonjudicial conflict resolution:

> in order to facilitate the just and efficient resolution of civil claims involving the United States Government, to encourage the filing of only meritorious civil

34. *See* 9 U.S.CA §§ 1 et seq.
35. 5 U.S.CA §§ 571 et seq.
36. 48 CFR § 1233.214.
37. *Id.*

claims, to improve legislative and regulatory drafting to reduce needless litigation, to promote fair and prompt adjudication before administrative tribunals, and to provide a model for similar reforms of litigation practices in the private sector and in various states.[38]

§3. ADR in Intellectual Property and Technology

60. Mediation, and to a lesser extent, arbitration have only recently been applied in disputes stemming from IP and technology claims. Before the mid-1980s IP disputes and patent claims in particular were resolved almost exclusively through the judiciary. Few alternatives were available to patent claimants because courts had long held that patent issues were of public concern and the open court system was the only avenue to resolve such disputes in a way that served the public interest. Addressing such disputes through ADR was ruled as contrary to public policy.

This public policy rationale was reversed with the enactment of several federal laws favoring ADR and arbitration in particular. The Patent Act was amended to specifically support patent disputes through ADR:

> (a) A contract involving a patent or any right under a patent may contain a provision requiring arbitration of any dispute relating to patent validity or infringement arising under the contract. In the absence of such a provision, the parties to an existing patent validity or infringement dispute may agree in writing to settle such dispute by arbitration. Any such provision or agreement shall be valid, irrevocable, and enforceable, except for any grounds that exist at law or in equity for revocation of a contract.
>
> ***
>
> (c) An award by an arbitrator shall be final and binding between the parties to the arbitration but shall have no force or effect on any other person … .[39]

Notwithstanding the relative novelty of ADR as an option to resolve patent and other IP disputes, ADR has become an increasingly popular method of resolving legal disagreements including technology, intellectual property, and related matters. Because arbitrators can be experts in the field, courts are often less well equipped to adjudicate complex issues related to emerging technologies and the untested claims that arise therefrom.

An interesting issue, however, arises in IP arbitrations due to the fact that the private dispute resolves issues as they relate to the arbitrating parties alone. To partially alleviate the narrow precedential value, notice of an arbitration award may be filed with the Commissioner of Patents and Trademarks. This notice could prompt independent actions by other claimants. Such independent challenges could ultimately lead to a finding of invalidity or unenforceability. Such a finding would not

38. Exec. Order No. 12778, 56 C.F.R. 55195 (1991).
39. 35 U.S.C. §294.

bind the earlier arbitrating parties, unless they had agreed that the arbitration award may be amended by a subsequent determination of validity or enforceability.

§4. ADR in the International ICT Sector

61. The global telecommunications sector is transforming. Privatization and liberalization confront increasing technological change. A diffuse market characterized by multiple providers of information and communications technology (ICT) services using Internet protocol (IP), wireless, and broadband technologies is replacing a relatively stagnant market characterized by regional telephone monopolies that provided simple telephone service.

Some disputes arising from these changes have prompted policy makers to evaluate effective dispute resolution. With regard to the telecommunications industry, failure to resolve disputes effectively can:

- restrict needed capital from investors;
- delay new services and infrastructure;
- generate higher prices by limiting competition; and
- reduce liberalization, including social and technical development.

Although these issues have been exacerbated by recent and increased globalization, they are not new. The Convention on the Recognition and Enforcement of Foreign Arbitral Awards, also known as the "New York Convention,' is one of the key instruments in international arbitration. The resolutions generated at the New York Convention were adopted by a United Nations diplomatic conference in 1958 and mandates that courts of contracting states enforce private agreements to arbitrate and recognize and enforce arbitration awards made in other contracting states. Article V of the Convention provides that recognition and enforcement of the award may be refused by the courts in the country where enforcement is sought only for the following reasons:

(1) incapacity of a party to conclude the arbitration agreement or invalidity of the arbitration agreement under the governing law of the agreement (if no governing law is specified, the law of the place where the award was made governs);
(2) lack of proper notice of the proceedings to the respondent as well as respondent's inability to present his case;
(3) the arbitrator has exceeded his authority and decided on matters not subject to arbitration;
(4) irregularity in the composition of the tribunal or in the arbitral procedure; and
(5) the award has not yet become binding on the parties, or has been set aside or suspended under the law under which the award was made.[40]

---

40. Convention on the Recognition and Enforcement of Foreign Arbitral Awards, signed at New York, June 10, 1958, 330 U.N.T.S. 38, No. 4739 (1959).

The New York Convention was very successful in promoting the use and validity of arbitration-based resolution. One recent international arbitration involved a group of Swedish technology entrepreneurs arbitrating a claim that musician will.i.am's company improperly backed out of a USD 25 million deal to buy a wireless headphones start-up. In May 2020, a California federal judge enforced a USD 228,438 costs award to the Swedish tech group, which had initiated arbitration in Sweden before the Stockholm Chamber of Commerce. Both parties were obligated to pay half the costs of the proceeding, amounting to more than €420,000 (approximately USD 455,570), but I.Am.Plus neglected to do so. By enforcing the arbitration award levied in Sweden, the California judge relied specifically the New York Convention, the international treaty relating to the enforcement of international arbitration awards.

Among multinational companies in the U.S., including ICT organizations, international arbitration has become a preferred method for resolving disputes arising in connection with transnational business transactions. When conducting business with parties from different countries international arbitration has certain advantages compared to litigation, particularly because of the ability to enforce awards internationally and because it provides for a neutral process for resolving disputes outside of the courts of one of the parties. Indeed, international arbitration awards are generally more enforceable outside the country where they are rendered than court judgments. Moreover, the parties have the ability to choose the place of arbitration, the number and type of arbitrators, the procedural rules and timetable, and the substantive law to be applied. However, arbitral tribunals typically have less flexibility to consolidate multiple proceedings into one and have difficulty determining the propriety of considering claims that arise from different agreements, or that involve non-contracting parties.

The World Intellectual Property Organization's (WIPO) Arbitration and Mediation Center designed an International Survey on Dispute Resolution in Technology Transactions. The survey analyzed the effectiveness of ADR as compared to court litigation, including a qualitative evaluation of these dispute resolution options. The results of the survey provide a statistical basis to identify trends in the resolution of technology-related disputes, including a comparison of cost between ADR and litigation. Those surveyed spent more time and incurred significantly higher costs in court litigation than in arbitration and mediation.

- Respondents estimated that court litigation in their home jurisdiction took on average approximately three years and court litigation in another jurisdiction took on average three and a half years.
- Respondents estimated that legal costs incurred in court litigation in their home jurisdiction amounted on average to USD 475,000, and legal costs of court litigation in another jurisdiction amounted to slightly over USD 850,000.
- Respondents indicated that mediation took on average eight months, and 91% of respondents stated that costs of mediation typically did not exceed USD 100,000.

– Respondents indicated that arbitration took on an average slightly more than one year and cost on an average slightly over USD 400,000.[41]

Relative Time and Costs of Resolving Disputes Through Court Litigation, (Expedited) Arbitration, Mediation, Expert Determination

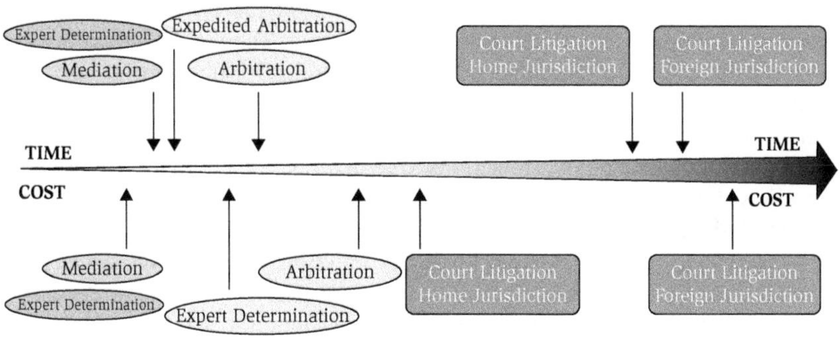

41. *Results of the International Survey on Dispute Resolution in Technology Transactions*, WIPO, https: //www.wipo.int/amc/en/center/survey/results.html (last visited Jan. 28, 2020).

Chapter 4. Competition Law Applied to the Digital Market

§1. General

62. Regulation of competition in the ICT Market in the U.S. has a long history. Promotion of competition and the prohibition of constructs that restrict competition represent a foundational economic principle in the U.S. U.S. competition law promotes competition, not competitors, such that healthy competition encourages rivalry among businesses and organizations to fight for consumers by producing higher-quality products and services at lower prices. The theory of healthy competition permeates U.S. economics, although it is strangely subverted in several manifestations of telecommunications law.

In the U.S., competition law is colloquially termed antitrust law, and consists of varied federal and state government laws, regulating both conduct and organization of entities within the U.S. for the primary purpose of benefiting consumers. With regard to federal statutes, the primary laws are the Sherman Act of 1890,[42] the Clayton Act of 1914,[43] and the Federal Trade Commission Act of 1914.[44] Taken together, these laws target three anticompetitive behaviors. They prescribe cartels and collusion among businesses that restrain trade. They monitor and prohibit mergers of large organizations when the combination of such organizations would substantially reduce competition in a particular market. And they restrict monopolies and the abusive pricing that attends monopolistic markets.

In the late 1800s, for example, Standard Oil Company was the largest oil company in the U.S. Standard Oil Company leveraged its market share to threaten competitors and to secure extremely favorable transportation deals with railroads, which were the primary transportation method at the time. This continued behavior harmed the economic environment of its competitors and lead to Standard Oil's near monopoly of the oil industry in the U.S. The U.S. Supreme Court in 1911 held that Standard Oil violated the Sherman Antitrust Act. The court required the company to be broken up into several independent companies. The effects of the Court's ruling remain impactful today, with Standard Oil of New Jersey becoming Exxon, Standard Oil of Indiana becoming Amoco, Standard Oil Company of New York becoming Mobil, which later merged with Exxon to form ExxonMobil, and so on.

More recently, the U.S. Congress as well as international regulators have moved to investigate whether U.S. tech giants are violating antitrust law. Many argue that digital markets and the tech industry have been dominated by a handful of companies such as Facebook, Google, and Amazon and that these companies are so large that they have generated competition problems and anticompetitive conduct. Under an agreement with the Department of Justice (DOJ) in 2019, officials from the Federal Trade Commission (FTC) are reportedly preparing to investigate any practices

42. Sherman Act of 1890, 51 Cong. Ch. 647, 26 Stat. 209.
43. Clayton Act of 1914, 63 Cong. Ch. 323, 38 Stat. 730.
44. Federal Trade Commission Act of 1914, 63 Cong. Ch. 311, 38 Stat. 717,.

at Facebook that may harm competition in the digital market. In addition to identifying anticompetitive conduct, the policy makers and investigators will assess whether existing antitrust laws, competition policies, and current enforcement levels are adequate to address these issues.

While federal departments and agencies, like the DOJ and the FTC, typically police and prosecute infractions of antitrust law, private parties in many instances may bring lawsuits in federal court to enforce these statutory protections.

Early U.S. regulatory efforts focused on outlawing collusive agreements among rival companies. These under-the-table agreements fixed prices, supply, and market share. The companies participating in the collusion did so through pools, and later through trusts, which provides the moniker for this area of law in the U.S., antitrust law. Big trusts first emerged in the U.S. railroad industry due to scarce capital and seemingly endless territory. The need to develop wide swaths of wild country with limited resources justified the creation of trusts, which in turn allowed railroad companies to discriminate on rates in such a way as to prevent introduction of any new competitor.

Notable exemplars that illustrate the U.S. government's enforcement of antitrust law include dismantling of the giant telephone company AT&T. The Sherman Act provided the legal grounds to identify AT&T as a monopoly and then break up the company into one long-distance company and seven regional companies, in the name of promoting consumer welfare and the economy as a whole. Business mergers became increasingly common, culminating in the 1990s.

By then, the FTC required preapproval of large mergers and acquisitions before consummation. Negotiations typically required conditions to mergers, like the sale of satellite and subsidiary companies to avoid monopolistic behavior in discrete markets.

In another highly publicized exemplar, the federal DOJ and nineteen states sued Microsoft for antitrust violations in 1999. The trial court determined that Microsoft had unfairly exerted its influence over several companies to block competition with Microsoft's Internet browser. In the ensuing settlement negotiations, Microsoft agreed to stop the anticompetitive practices identified by the government.

The prosecution and application of antitrust laws in the U.S. has varied over time, as different constituencies argue the merits and scope of such laws. The freedom of a business to innovate and grow is balanced against obstacles to market entry for smaller businesses and the overall economy as it relates to individual consumers. Some argue that the antitrust laws should primarily protect consumers and efficiencies while others cite more nuanced roles for antitrust laws and the scope of their application.

In the telecommunications sector, antitrust law is somewhat aberrant because of the need to secure interconnection among different entities that are often competitors. Whether it is interconnection of fixed telephone lines, mobile network facilities, or net neutrality for ISPs, cooperation among companies rather than competition often attends the telecommunications sector, a phenomenon not shared in other U.S. industries.

Additionally, U.S. antitrust laws have diminished effect where such laws conflict with free speech principles. The Newspaper Preservation Act of 1970, for example, provides some immunity from antitrust law by allowing newspaper organizations to cooperate under joint operating contracts.[45] Even so, several statutes have overcome the free speech hurdle to effectively prohibit certain media cross-ownership. The Communications Act of 1934 and the Telecommunications Act of 1996 contain media ownership restrictions.

§2. Competition and the Telecommunications Act of 1996

63. The Telecommunications Act of 1996 contained several objectives including an objective to grow the telecommunications sector by decreasing regulatory restraints to increase competition. Congress sought to spur private ownership and increased competition, thereby growing advanced telecommunications technologies and increased access to all Americans. The Act significantly restructured the local telephone market by breaking up the monopolies that several states had awarded to local exchange carriers. By imposing on established local exchange carriers an obligation to allow competitive local exchange carriers to connect with established networks, the Telecommunications Act truncated the competitive advantage attending an established carriers' ownership of the physical infrastructure needed to supply telecommunications services. The law required the established local exchange carriers to share their networks with competitors, among other obligations, aimed at eroding barriers to entry in the telephone market. Such barriers were often imposed by state and local government, and the Telecommunications Act materially reduced those barriers.

Requiring incumbent carriers to share infrastructure in order to reduce barriers to entry for new competitors includes interconnection obligations on all carriers. Pursuant to the Telecommunications Act, ILECs are subject to a host of duties intended to facilitate market entry over and above the obligation on carriers to interconnect with equipment and technology of competing carriers. The obligation to allow interconnection includes doing so at any feasible point that is, at minimum, of the same quality used by the established or incumbent exchange carrier, or its subsidiary. The rates and contractual terms negotiated by incumbent providers and newcomers must be reasonable and nondiscriminatory. Incumbent carriers are prohibited under the Act from installing certain capabilities or functions that would reduce effective interconnection. Broken down more acutely, each local exchange carrier must provide:

- reasonable resale of its services;
- number portability;
- dialing parity;
- access to ducts, poles, and rights of way;
- reciprocal compensation arrangements;
- duty to negotiate agreements for interconnection;
- duty to allow nondiscriminatory interconnection;
- duty to provide unbundled and nondiscriminatory access to its network elements;
- duty to offer all telecommunications services for resale at wholesale rates;

45. Newspaper Preservation Act of 1970, Pub. L. No. 91-353, 84 Stat. 466.

- duty to provide reasonable public notice of any changes affecting the interoperability of its facilities and networks;
- duty to provide for physical or virtual collocation of any equipment necessary for interconnection.

With regard to numbering, all telecommunications carriers have legal obligations to pay the costs associated with numbering. While carriers bear the cost, a third party designated by the FCC typically administers and maintains numbering largely due to the fact that the FCC has exclusive jurisdiction over the same. The Telecommunications Act also addresses the legal obligations attending number portability, access to rights of way and telephone poll, and dialing parity.

The Act also requires that established exchange carriers must offer wholesale rates for telecommunications services in certain instances to counter state-sanctioned monopolies. The great majority of the new obligations foisted on established exchange carriers do not apply to rural telephone entities until another carrier formally requests interconnection and the state public utilities authority concludes that the request is not economically destructive to the rural provider and that it is reasonably implemented. The goal of universal access drives the state public authority's determination.

The Telecommunications Act also authorizes the FCC to require state utility authorities to set the same rates charged by established local exchange carriers to competing carriers. These rates apply irrespective of the established carrier's past investment into facilities and infrastructure. The rates set by the FCC for newly competing providers are based on forward-looking cost by reference to a hypothetical involving the most efficient functionality rather than the actual network element being provided. The FCC deemed the determination of actual cost and service charges unnecessarily complicated and an added burden to new competitors. The FCC, in its published Regulatory Fees Fact Sheet summarizes these obligations:

> As required under the Communications Act of 1934, as amended, the Commission has established, in a series of separate proceedings, procedures to finance interstate telecommunications relay services, universal service support mechanisms, administration of the North American Numbering Plan, and shared costs of local number portability. To accomplish these Congressional directed objectives, contributions are collected from all telecommunications carriers providing interstate telecommunications and certain other providers of telecommunications.[46]

In order to facilitate this wide-scale restructuring of the telecommunications market, the Telecommunications Act includes procedures for arbitration and dispute resolution. An interconnection agreement is a contract between an established local exchange carrier and a telecommunications carrier linking their two networks

46. Fed. Commc'ns Comm'n, *Regulatory Fees Fact Sheet* (Sept. 11, 2015), https://docs.fcc.gov/public/attachments/DOC-335228A1.pdf.

together for mutual exchange consistent with the duties set out in the Telecommunications Act. Interconnection agreements are often contentious as competitors are forced to collaborate, and the Act's negotiation procedures, which include pricing standards, help alleviate that tension.

Those pricing standards are mandatorily based on costs, irrespective of revenue projections. The cost of interconnecting must be reasonable and nondiscriminatory. A reasonable profit often factors into negotiations and settlements.

The Act also includes authority to forbear. The overarching goals of universal access and increased competition in the telecommunications market supports the FCC's authority to withhold enforcement of statutory provisions or FCC regulations when those legal precepts undermine the legislation's principal objectives. No geographically discrete market analysis is required before the FCC may choose to forbear. Instead, the FCC's decision to forbear is context driven. If the market conditions that originally prompted the promulgation of a regulation no longer exist, the FCC will conduct biennial review of those regulations to determine whether they should be modified or terminated.

The dual goals of universal access and increased competition has manifested in a drive to provide service in all geographic areas that are reasonably comparable to services provided in large metropolitan areas. Similarly, the FCC has indicated that rates charged for similar services in urban areas should approximate rates in rural areas. Because schools, health care institutions, and libraries have greater public impact, the Telecommunications Act focuses on ensuring access to these institutions, at times requiring preferential rates for basic services.

I. FCC Implementation

64. The authority of the FCC to implement the required interconnection and facilitate broader competition by imposing diverse obligations on established local exchange carriers has been challenged several times in federal courts. For the most part, the courts have upheld the FCC's authority to implement local competition requirements, including the FCC's jurisdiction in designing pricing methodology for unbundled services and interconnection, more generally.

For example, the FCC required established local exchange carriers to provide competing exchange carriers with access to "entrance facilities" at cost-based rates. When this FCC policy was challenged, the court in *Talk America, Inc. v. Michigan Bell Telephone Co.* held that cost-based rates for entrance facilities access was reasonable and that the FCC was owed deference in determining that entrance facilities were part of the established local exchange carrier's network. The 2011 decision held that ILECs must provide interconnection facilities to competitors at cost-based rates. Because such rates are normally significantly lower than the tariff rates most ILECs have been charging, this ruling provided a material economic benefit to competitive local exchange carriers.[47]

In another dispute regarding implementation of pro-competition policy, a state public utilities commission imposition of a USD 25 million penalty was upheld. An

47. 564U.S. 50 (2011).

established local exchange carrier failed to file an interconnection agreement that was subject to the Telecommunications Act. The agreement memorialized switching and shared transport services between an established exchange carrier and a competitor.

The courts have also weighed in on the FCC's "pick and choose" rule, concluding that the rule was a reasonable interpretation of the interconnection requirement in the Telecommunications Act. The court again confirmed the legality of requiring ILECs to make any interconnection, service, or network element provided under an approved agreement available to any other requesting carrier upon materially similar terms and conditions.

Even so, the FCC does not have limitless authority when regulating competition in the ICT market. In October 2004, the Washington, D.C. Circuit Court of Appeals vacated the FCC's Triennial Review Order. The court's decision *in United States Telecom Ass'n v. FCC* was based on the Telecommunications Act of 1996 section 251 and that section's characterization of unbundled network elements for established local exchange carriers and competitive local exchange carriers. The court's decision invalidated FCC rules that required established local exchange carriers to lease certain network elements (such as local switching or the high-frequency portion of the loop) at a cost-based wholesale price to competing local exchange carriers.[48] Proponents of this ruling maintain that the rates set by the government were too low and gave the competition an unfair advantage, whereas opponents argue that without the regulated rates, they could not compete in the local phone business in several geographical areas because the established companies' rates would be too high. Instead of pursuing further court adjudication, the FCC in late 2004, released a set of rules which phase out, over a year, all leasing of established local exchange carrier local switching, while preserving access to most copper local loops and interoffice facilities.

Similarly, the FCC's standard when requiring established local exchange carriers to provide unbundled services have been successfully challenged. The FCC maintained an "open-ended" standard when determining whether to require unbundling, a standard that was rejected by the courts. In response, the FCC implemented a new standard, the "reasonably efficient competitor" standard, which the FCC justified in its 2004 order:

> In our Triennial Review Order, we recognized the marketplace realities of robust broadband competition and increasing competition from intermodal sources, and thus eliminated most unbundling requirements for broadband architectures serving the mass market. Our efforts there made it easier for companies to invest in equipment and deploy the high-speed services that consumers desire. The Triennial Review Order had the effect of limiting unbundled access to next-generation loops serving the mass market. In this Order, the Commission takes additional steps to encourage the innovation and investment that come from facilities-based competition. By using our section 251 unbundling authority in a more targeted manner, this Order imposes unbundling obligations only in those situations where we find that carriers genuinely are

48. United States Telecom Ass'n v. FCC, No. 15-1063 (D.C. Cir. 2016).

impaired without access to particular network elements and where unbundling does not frustrate sustainable, facilities-based competition.[49]

In another implementation ruling, the FCC's decision to use wire centers and business line density to assess high-capacity loops was upheld, noting that such variables were objective and reasonably reflected potential facilities-based competition.

Finally, many have questioned whether the Telecommunications Act of 1996 and subsequent regulations stemming therefrom violate the U.S. Constitution. The argument is that the U.S. government through the Act's requirement of forced sharing privately owned property, the U.S. government has "taken" the private property in violation of Article V of the U.S. Constitution. The courts have held, however that a statute requiring telephone companies to make a physical connection does not constitute a taking of property under Article V of the U.S. Constitution.

II. State Regulation and Preemption

65. While much of the regulation regarding telecommunications and competition within the telecommunication sector stems from the Telecommunications act of 1996 and the FCC's subsequent policies, state law plays a large part in regulation competition in the ICT market. Federal statutes and the FCC set outer boundaries, allowing state regulation to provide further legislation within those outer boundaries. The Telecommunications Act itself embraces the federalism inherent in dual sovereigns – state government and the federal government. In this cooperative system, there is room for state government to set policy consistent with FCC regulations. As a result, state Public Utilities Commission's retain significant power regarding interconnection agreements and the effect such policies have on competition.

III. Bell Operating Companies

66. As briefly noted above, the market for telecommunication services in the U.S. has varied over time – ever since Alexander Graham Bell invented the telephone. As early as the 1920s, AT&T had secured ownership or control over a large majority of telephone exchanges. With the Telecommunication Act of 1934, the U.S. federal government joined state governments in regulating telephony. In 1974, AT&T lost a major lawsuit brought by the U.S. DOJ.

The federal government alleged that AT&T monopolized the long-distance telephone market through its near monopoly of the infrastructure required to make long-distance calls. The DOJ asked the court to divest long-distance services from local services and manufacturing. In the ensuing settlement agreement, AT&T broke

49. In the Matter of Unbundled Access to Network Elements Review of the Section 251 Unbundling Obligations of Incumbent Local Exchange Carriers, Order on Remand, (Dec. 15, 2004), https://docs.fcc.gov/public/attachments/FCC-04-290A1.doc.

off seven regional operating companies, sometimes referred to as Regional Bell Operating Companies (RBOCs), with each RBOC consisting of an assortment of local telephone companies that were previously owned by AT&T. At the time, RBOCs remained regulated monopolies, each with an exclusive franchise in its region. As a result, the settlement agreement disallowed RBOCs from providing long-distance service. The justification for that prohibition was that each RBOC was a monopolist in its own region, and there was a threat that RBOCs could engage in a number of anticompetitive actions with regard to long-distance service.

In 1996 when the Telecommunications Act was enacted, RBOCs had approximately 89% of telephone access lines, while competitive access providers had less than 1% of the access lines. The Act attempted to move all telecommunications markets toward competition, and includes an entire section dedicated to Bell Operating Companies (BOCs). As noted above, the lawsuit and settlement that broke the Bell monopoly prohibited RBOCs from offering long-distance service. The Telecommunications Act, however, provides that RBOCs would be allowed to offer long-distance services once they made a showing that their local markets had been opened up to competition.

The FCC determines whether local markets have sufficiently opened to increased competition using a complex formula. Even if the BOC demonstrates compliance with the formula, it may only provide long-distance service through a separate affiliate. Moreover, the Act limits BOCs from manufacturing telecommunications equipment until the BOC demonstrates sufficient in-region long-distance service.

Of course, these particularized constraints on BOCs did not go unchallenged. By singling out one particular company for detrimental treatment in the market, the U.S. government opened itself to challenge as an illegal Bill of Attainder. But because the business restrictions imposed on BOCs were not deemed to be "punishment," no bill of attainder occurred. Similarly, the courts noted that many of the restrictions were not perpetual, that the provisions were implemented to ensure fair competition rather than to punish, and that the restrictions were part of a comprehensive plan to reduce restrictions on BOCs as competition materialized. Courts have also held that the restrictions on BOCs did not violate the Equal Protection Clause of the U.S. Constitution. First, no fundamental right to provide long-distance service has been recognized and as such, the U.S. government need only prove that the restrictions were a rational way to achieve a legitimate governmental purpose – increased competition.

IV. Enforcement and Judicial Review

67. The Telecommunications Act of 1996 confers jurisdiction to federal courts over state agency decisions affecting the country's telecommunications market. Because state public utility commissions often promulgate rules that are inconsistent with FCC regulations, federal court jurisdiction is appropriate. If a federal court concludes, as a threshold matter, that the state commission acted within the purview of the Telecommunications Act, the federal court will next apply a deferential standard to the state action. Only if the state acted arbitrarily or capriciously will the court invalidate the state action. A state commission's finding of fact, for example, is reviewed under that deferential standard.

The U.S. Supreme Court has supported antitrust laws, maintaining that competition is critical to a free-enterprise system?

> Every violation of the antitrust laws is a blow to the free-enterprise system envisaged by Congress. This system depends on strong competition for its health and vigor, and strong competition depends, in turn, on compliance with antitrust legislation. In enacting these laws, Congress had many means at its disposal to penalize violators. It could have, for example, required violators to compensate federal, state, and local governments for the estimated damage to their respective economies caused by the violations. But, this remedy was not selected. Instead, Congress chose to permit all persons to sue to recover three times their actual damages every time they were injured in their business or property by an antitrust violation.[50]

With regard to FCC actions, exclusive jurisdiction lies with U.S. federal appellate courts. The FCC also enjoys wide discretion, as the appellate court will only invalidate FCC rules and actions if they are deemed arbitrary and capricious. In other words, the appellate court may believe the FCC rule is unwise or inefficient, but the court will nevertheless uphold the FCC rule unless it is arbitrary.

When the FCC issues an order affecting a particular individual or business, the judicial review under the Administrative Procedure Act requires the court to presume the validity of the FCC's order unless the claimant can show manifest error and injustice. Importantly, the exhaustion of administrative processes may be a precondition to court adjudication.

Remedies for violations of competition law are not limited to money damages or fines. Indeed, allowing private parties to sue for antitrust violations broadens the field of potential prosecutors and thereby strengthens the application of antitrust law. Under the Sherman Antitrust Act, damages for violations may be trebled, which further promotes private litigation and thereby antitrust enforcement. Other statutory provisions allow courts to award penalties commensurate with the financial power of the offending company.

Apart from money damages and penalties, public enforcement and prosecution plays a large role in antitrust law given the complexity involved in such cases and the power wielded by defendants, which are typically large corporations. The DOJ and the FTC are primarily responsible for prosecuting antitrust enforcement actions, although only the DOJ has jurisdiction to bring criminal antitrust lawsuits.

Federal courts have the authority to break up large companies into competing parts with independent ownership. The courts, however, are loath to use this remedy and have done so only in a few instances. AT&T Corporation, Standard Oil, and Microsoft have all faced court decisions mandating fragmentation. Additionally, the federal government preemptively analyzes proposed mergers. This preventative function seeks to avoid market concentration before it happens. The Hart-Scott-Rodino Antitrust Improvements Act requires that large companies attempting to

---

50. Hawaii v. Standard Oil Co. of California, 405U.S. 251, 262 (1972).

merge must first give notice to the FTC and the DOJ before merging. The notice to the DOJ and FTC includes a detailed filing outlining the anticipated market impact of the merger. Companies required to file may not take any steps to integrate the merger until notified by the federal officials.[51]

In 2019, the U.S. federal government lost its court challenge to prevent the USD 85.4 billion merger of AT&T and Time Warner. This merger has already impacted the media market, which parallels the arguments made by lawyers for the DOJ who claimed that the merger would materially reduce competition and harm consumers. The U.S. Court of Appeals for the District of Columbia Circuit rejected the Justice Department's bid to divest some of Time Warner's assets as a precondition to merger. The court instead agreed with AT&T's argument that Time Warner was essentially a wireless provider that is considered a content distributor, and as such does not compete with AT&T's central business model. Because the companies do not compete, AT&T argued the merger would benefit consumers in the form of lower bills and increased entertainment provided on mobile devices.

The court's decision allowing the merger combined one of the biggest wireless providers with a media business that includes HBO, Warner Bros., and CNN. These media groups were added to AT&T's 154 million wireless subscribers, in addition to satellite and DirectTV. AT&T plans to morph Time Warner into a streaming video entity as the television market continues to trend in that direction. AT&T now controls Turner Broadcasting, which U.S. lawyers argued should be sold as a condition to merger. Turner Broadcasting includes the cable networks TNT and TBS, CNN, and rights to broadcast games of major sports leagues like the National Basketball Association and Major League Baseball.

Similarly, the wireless industry is dominated by the nation's four major carriers—AT&T, Verizon, T-Mobile, and Sprint. Although four is a relatively few number of major carriers, these companies have been engaged in a price war for several years.

Given the borderless flow of data in the ICT market, international competition laws have had an increasing effect on U.S. ICT providers. European officials issued a €1.5 billion antitrust fine against Google in 2019. The fine is the third major penalty the EU has levied against Google in as many years. Google was fined €4.3 billion last year for abusing its market dominance in mobile, and €2.4 billion the year before for manipulating shopping search results.

51. 15U.S.C. § 18a, title II.

Chapter 5. Regulation of the Electronic Communications Market

§1. General

68. The regulatory framework for telecommunications has not kept pace with convergent technology. The flow of content, including mobile telephone calls, Internet use, and digital entertainment originally generated for cable disbursement are all delivered to one device via varying technologies. Services and content offered through such multimedia devices are often regulated differently. Telecommunications media are more heavily regulated than print media in the U.S. Government regulations dictate terms of ownership of telecommunications, physical operation of facilities, and sometimes the transmitted content, itself. Government regulation of the telecommunications sector is justified by two principles: (1) for wireless media, the electromagnetic spectrum, as a finite resource, should operate in the public interest; and (2) for wired media, transmission lines and equipment occupy public land and public rights of way.

The starting point, however, is the U.S. Constitution and the First Amendment to that Constitution, which states that "Congress shall make no law. . . abridging the freedom of speech, or of the press; or the right of the people peaceably to assemble, and to petition the Government for a redress of grievances."[52] Codified in the Constitution, the country's foremost legal document from which all U.S. jurisprudence stems, the fundamental right to "free speech" has had widespread impact. The fundamental right to free speech continues to shape the regulation of the telecommunications sector. Arguably, no other country in the world is more protective of free expression than the U.S.

Even so, free speech and free expression are not absolute rights. Over the course of two centuries, varying levels of free speech protection apply in varying contexts, including but not limited to, different media, regulations dealing with content of expression as opposed to time, place, and manner of expression, and private versus public restrictions of expression. More specifically, the fundamental right to free expression generates distinctions from other countries in areas like defamation law, hate speech law, obscenity, and political speech restrictions.

Although the right to free expression is articulated as fundamental, it is not limitless. A common misunderstanding is that the right protects all expression, allowing Americans to say anything at any time. In truth, the right only protects against government suppression or restriction of expression. This extends to federal, state, and local government, but does not include private suppression of expression. If, for example, YouTube refused to upload a video that denigrated a local politician, free expression protections would not apply because no government action or actor suppressed the expression. If an employee of a private company posts negative comments about the employer on Facebook, no free expression right will protect the employee from the negative consequences stemming from the employee's expression.

52. U.S. Const. amend. I.

One of the most direct applications of free expression to the telecommunications sector is through the doctrine of prior restraint. Often associated with censorship, a prior restraint is a governmental prohibition of a particular instance of expression prior to the expression taking place. A prior restraint can occur in a number of ways, but with regard to print and electronic news media, it often occurs through a court's issuance of an injunction that prohibits the defendant from publishing certain material.

Another direct application of free expression to regulation of the telecommunications sector involves government regulation of content, as opposed to content-neutral regulations. The government cannot require private operators of television programing to refrain from denying climate change or to promote U.S. combat efforts abroad. The government can, however, legally prescribe the time, place, and manner in which private television broadcasters provide services. This distinction will be addressed more fully below.

The FCC regulates most telecommunications media in the U.S. As noted above, the FCC asserts control over broadcast media through the granting, renewing, and revoking of operator licenses to use the electromagnetic spectrum. The FCC asserts control over satellite media by bootstrapping this concept to direct broadcast satellite systems. The FCC's authority over cable and telephone service is more attenuated, and entities providing cable and telephone service are not exclusively regulated by the FCC. State and city governments typically grant cable companies a quasi-monopoly through a franchise agreement to operate within particular areas. Most states have a separate department – Public Utilities Commissions – that principally regulate telephony within the state's jurisdiction. Finally, the Internet does not technically come within the FCC's scope of authority. Even so, the FCC required network neutrality for the Internet, arguing that it was ancillary to its authority to regulate telephone services, cable, and satellite.

A further source of regulatory authority stems from state and local government's ability to legally circumscribe telecommunications providers to ensure consumer protection and public safety, and to promote competitive telecommunications markets in the state. That said, state laws targeting telecommunications providers typically apply only to common carriers. A private telecommunications business that does not provide services to the general public is not generally regulated by state law. Of course, state regulatory authority is not absolute. The Telecommunications Act of 1996, while maintaining state authority over telecommunications facilities and operations within each state, also identifies discrete exceptions to that authority.

§2. Regulation of Legacy Telecommunications Providers

69. The history of broadcast regulation is long and complicated. The legacy networks, including basic telephone service, broadcasting, and cable video service, emerged at different times and were each regulated differently. Although all are were governed by the 1934 Communications Act, each nevertheless has historically been regulated differently. Each technology was considered to provide separate functions and fulfill distinct societal needs, and that underlying presumption has proved problematic today. As a result, policies applying to telephone providers differ from those governing cable video providers and digital broadcast providers. Understanding the policies or values driving each area of regulation informs the current debate regarding Internet and broadband regulation.

With regard to historic regulation of broadcasting, at a high level, broadcast regulation sought to facilitate the public interest. Of course, government regulation of the electromagnetic spectrum preceded any regulation of telecommunications via cyberspace. Prior to 1912, the U.S. government was the dominant user of the electromagnetic spectrum. In that year, the government offered licenses to private entities for radio broadcasting. Without regulations prescribing use, private radio operators broadcast over each other, prompting Congress to pass the Federal Radio Act in 1927. That law called for a federal commission to distribute discrete frequencies and assign the use for each. Moreover, radio operators were prescribed to broadcast only in the "public interest, convenience, and necessity."[53]

The Radio Act was superseded by the Communications Act of 1934.[54] The Communications Act of 1934 consolidated federal regulatory authority over fixed-line communications under the authority of the FCC and was an expansive framework for the regulation of interstate communication generally. In the name of uniformity of regulation, the Act sought to protect both the public interest and individual consumers. It is important to note that although the U.S. congress retains dominant authority to regulate interstate commerce as it relates to telecommunications, state and local governments have authority to create additional regulations affecting localized interest.

Telephone service providers were much more heavily regulated than broadcast providers. Again, the government sought to promote society's interest in efficient, fair, and equitable distribution of a public good. Ensuring public access was a key goal of early regulation, and communications systems were viewed as a utility that was critical to society and economy. The most prominent private organization in the history of telecommunication regulation was the Bell Telephone Company, later known as the AT&T. The company had been in the business of building a telecommunications network and infrastructure long before 1934. Absent regulation, competition over infrastructure development and service was fierce, with AT&T refusing to interconnect with competitors. This created poor quality service in many areas and very little long-distance service. After the Great Depression, public sentiment turned away from laissez-faire capitalism, allowing the federal government to regulate the telephone industry as a means of building a national telephone system.

Cable video service regulation, by contrast, began as a service called Community Antenna Television (CATV). It sought to provide video programing to rural areas of the U.S. that could not receive broadcast signals. CATV captured local broadcast signals and transmitted them via coaxial cables to local communities. The U.S. government did not regulate cable operations because they did not directly compete with broadcast stations. But when cable operators began importing distant broadcast signals, which competed directly with local broadcast stations in the 1960s, the FCC concluded that cable regulation fell under its jurisdiction. By importing distant broadcast channels, according to the FCC, cable operators were threatening the

53. Radio Act of 1927, ch. 169, 44 Stat. 1162.

54. Communications Act of 1934, Pub. L. No. 98-549, 48 Stat. 1064.

existence of local broadcast stations. In 1968, the U.S. Supreme Court ruled in favor of the FCC's bid to regulate cable operators.

The U.S. Congress altered the regulatory landscape for telecommunications when it passed the Telecommunications Act of 1996. Among the first digital media laws, the Act attempted to catch up to digital technology. The Act dispensed with traditional ownership rules that restricted communications companies from owning entities in more than one media sector. The Act explicitly sanctioned local telephone companies to offer long-distance calls. It allowed traditional broadcasters to operate and own cable communications systems. More generally, the Act promoted the movement away from analogue and toward digital telecommunications. Even so, the Act retained (or did not formally eradicate) the fundamental policies that distinguish differential regulation depending on media, which continues to complicate contemporary regulatory efforts.[55]

§3. The Federal Communications Commission

70. Congress created the FCC through the Communications Act of 1934 as an agency responsible for supervising and enforcing the provisions of the Act. The FCC is composed of five commissioners who are appointed by the President of the U.S. The commissioners' five-year appointments must be confirmed by the U.S. Senate. One commissioner is selected to serve as chairperson by the President of the U.S. The Chair sets the agenda and designates leaders of the FCC's various departments. Commissioners have final decision-making authority on all FCC matters.

The FCC is characterized as an administrative agency under the executive branch and it is staffed by experts with experience in the telecommunications sector. Over the years, the agency's primary goal has been to ensure provision of telecommunication service throughout the nation.

The FCC retains jurisdiction over all forms of electric communication. It has expansive powers and discretion both with general rulemaking as it pertains to fair dissemination of telecommunication services, but also with regard to prosecuting infractions that undermine the same. It has the power to preempt local government measures when they conflict with federal powers, which includes but is not limited to, regulation of rates and services. Indeed, classifications, fees and charges, and other practices related with communication services fall within the FCC's ambit. Not only does the FCC have authority to create binding rules, it may also prosecute infractions of them. Beyond that, the FCC may even declare a particular event or practice unlawful upon a finding that the practice is an unfair trade practice.

The discretion afforded the FCC includes authority to forbear from enforcing discrete provisions of the Act itself, if necessary to protect consumers or prevent unfair discrimination consistent with public interest. In the same vein, the FCC has discretion to waive a rule if the application in a given context contravenes public interest. The circumstances for waiver must be sufficiently unique to merit waiver.

55. Telecommunications Act of 1996, Pub. L. No. 104-104, 110 Stat. 56 (codified as amended in scattered sections of 47U.S.C.).

That said, federal agencies in the U.S. created by statute and therefore by congressional mandate. The FCCs powers, as a result, derive from Congress and can be rescinded by congressional amendment. Further, the FCC's power is limited to the authority Congress delegated to it by statute. For example, the FCC does not have the power to regulate currency prices or enforce securities laws. Although it has discretion in some instances to forbear from enforcing certain communications regulations, generally speaking, it is obligated to enforce its own rules.

I. The FCC Structure

71. The Communications Act of 1934 is divided into "titles" that lay out the FCC's obligations and authority as they relate to specific media. Title I outlined general provisions, including the responsibilities and structural organization of the FCC. Title II authorizes FCC rulemaking with regard to telephone and telegraph common carriers. Title III authorizes the FCC to license and regulate radio communications that use the electromagnetic spectrum. Title IV described procedural and administrative provisions for FCC decision-making. Title V identified the range of civil and criminal penalties, including forfeitures, for noncompliance with the Act and with FCC regulations. Title VI outlines requirements for ownership and operation of cable stations, and Title VII includes miscellaneous provisions, such as protections for the disabled.

With the advent of new media and technology, Congress has added new titles, bringing these new media under the original Act's regulatory purview. For example, the FCC currently has the authority to generate binding rules as they relate to cellular media, Wi-Fi, and satellite, in addition to the broadcast spectrum and traditional wire line telephony. DSL, cable, and broadband service technology also fall within the FCC's regulatory authority.

There are seven bureaus that make policy and handle day-to-day decisions:

(1) The Media Bureau develops and administers rules for cable television, broadcast television, radio, and satellite.
(2) The Wireline Competition Bureau develops policies and rules for telephone companies.
(3) The Wireless Telecommunications Bureau oversees mobile telephones, personal communications services, pagers, and two-way radios.
(4) The International Bureau oversees satellite and policy matters related to international telecommunications services.
(5) The Consumer and Government Affairs Bureau informs consumers about telecommunication products and services, coordinates telecommunications policy with over government agencies, and handles matters related to disability rights.
(6) The Enforcement Bureau enforces the Communications Act and the FCC's rules.
(7) The Public Safety and Homeland Security Bureau recommends and administers telecommunications policy related to public safety and emergency management.

The following is taken from the FCC official website and depicts the organizational chart of the FCC as of August 2019.

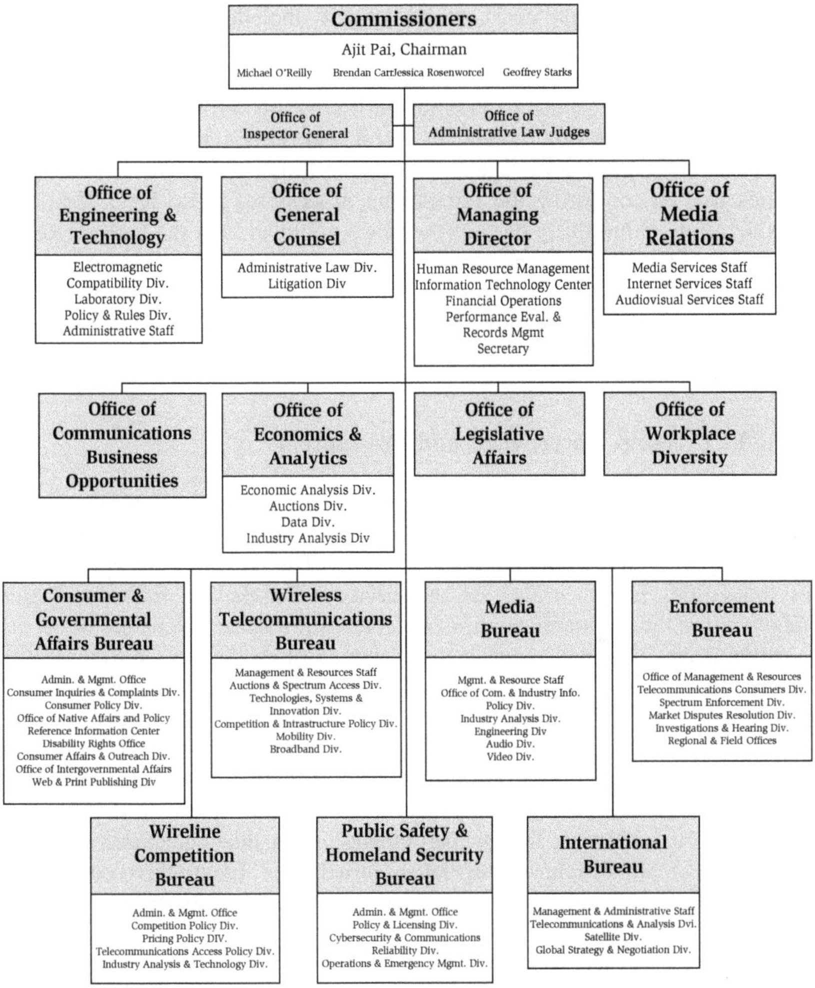

Within the scope of the authority granted to it by Congress, the FCC has authority to promulgate rules, which have the force and effect of law. To do so, the FCC uses a notice and comment procedure that is also used by other U.S. agencies with rulemaking authority. When proposing a new rule or modifying an existing rule, the FCC posts a "Notice of Proposed Rulemaking" in the U.S. government's official digest of administrative actions – the Federal Register. At minimum, the public has thirty days to comment on the proposed rule before the FCC takes substantive action on the proposed rule. The FCC may opt to withdraw, revise or maintain a proposed rule after analyzing the public commentary. If the FCC revises the proposed rule, it must reissue the proposal as a "Further Notice of Proposed Rulemaking."

When the time period lapses and no revisions ensue, the FCC issues a Report and Order, which details its final decision and typically includes a thorough rationalization of the new rule as it relates to FCC jurisdiction. This rationalization buttresses the rule from invalidation. The Administrative Procedures Act provides that agency rules (including the FCC) can be invalidated if they are "arbitrary and capricious." The rationalization that often attends a report and orders attempts to identify the rational basis undergirding the agency's decision to issue the rule.

Entities that object during the rulemaking process may also file a Petition for Reconsideration within thirty days of the rule's publication in the Federal Register. Typically, the FCC will respond to such petitions with a Memorandum and Order denying the petition, at which point the petitioner may challenge the FCC rule in federal court. After considering the petition, the FCC will respond with a Memorandum and Order.

II. The FCC, Local Governance, and Preemption

72. The Communications Act of 1934 applies to interstate and foreign communication, including communication through television and radio, when that communication originates or is received within the U.S. The Act does not apply, in most cases, to facilities, practices, charges, and services when they are intrastate. In determining whether the communication is interstate or intrastate, the nature of the communication drives jurisdiction rather than location of facilities used to disseminate or receive the communication. This holistic inquiry serves to broaden the FCC's jurisdiction.

Importantly, with regard to interstate communications and foreign communications, the FCC's jurisdiction is exclusive. State and local regulations that conflict with FCC regulations relating to interstate commerce are preempted. As a result, where a local transmission facility participates in an interstate transmission network, the FCC retains exclusive regulatory jurisdiction. Even where one interstate connection attends several services and facilities that are solely intrastate, the FCC may have exclusive jurisdiction.

The Telecommunications Act of 1996 also impacted the regulatory framework of the FCC as it relates to the state and local government jurisdiction. The Act generally preserved the traditional authority of state and local governments to regulate construction, location, and modification of communications facilities like phone towers. State utility commissions maintained authority under the Act to control pricing and zoning matters in most instances. But where state regulations conflict with FCC regulations, the prior are preempted and invalid. Whether an FCC rule or policy preempts state telecommunications law depends on a finding that a specific state law is inconsistent with the FCC's rule, or that the state law interferes with the FCC's ability to achieve a distinct and articulated federal goal.

The Telecommunications Act also removed the ability of state governments to regulate local telecommunications competitions in many instances. The Act created a federal framework to govern discrete functions of telecommunication competition. As a result, no state or local government may prescribe any entity from providing interstate or intrastate telecommunications service. If the FCC determines that a state or local government has violated the Telecommunications Act of 1996 by prohibiting an organization from providing interstate or intrastate telecommunications service, the FCC must preempt the state action. Indeed, preemption does not occur absent FCC action.

§4. Enforcement

I. FCC Proceedings

73. As noted above Congress granted broad discretion to the FCC, both in rulemaking and in prosecuting and enforcing FCC rules and the relevant telecommunications statutes. With regard to enforcement proceedings, the FCC is guided by the twin objectives of fair and just results as well as ensuring appropriate business practices. All matters that concern issues arising under the Communications Act of 1934 or relating to its enforcement fall within the FCC's enforcement jurisdiction, including investigations aimed at preventing telecommunications practices that are contrary to the public interest. The FCC may initiate proceedings itself, or proceedings may be initiated pursuant to the petition or application of an interested person or entity.

The Enforcement Bureau is the primary department within the FCC responsible for enforcing the provisions of the Communications Act, the FCC's rules, orders, and various licensing obligations. The primary objectives undergirding the Enforcement Bureau are to investigate potential unlawful conduct to ensure:

(1) consumer protection in an era of complex communications;
(2) a level playing field to promote robust competition;
(3) efficient and responsible use of the public airwaves; and
(4) strict compliance with public safety-related rules.[56]

The Enforcement Bureau prosecutes and enforces FCC rules and the Communications Act in two primary ways: (1) by initiating investigations, and taking appropriate action if violations are found; and (2) by mediating disputes between industry participants. The Enforcement Bureau has substantial discretion as to whether to proceed by rulemaking or adjudication. It can determine questions of prosecutorial procedure, whether to allow oral argument, and whether the investigation will be conducted publicly or privately. Its enforcement conclusions can be submitted as generally applicable rules, similar to common law judicial precedent. But the Enforcement Bureau may also prescribe narrow rules for specific parties to a specific investigation.

---

56. *Enforcement*, Federal Communications Commission, https://www.fcc.gov/enforcement (last visited Jan. 27, 2020).

In most cases, the Enforcement Bureau opens an investigation after receiving information about a potential violation from several sources. If deemed meritorious, the Enforcement Bureau pursues more information through a Letter of Inquiry (LOI). The LOI requires the alleged offender to answer questions and produce documents relevant to evaluating whether a violation of FCC rules, deceptive trade or practice, or other statutory violation has occurred. The Enforcement Bureau also has discretion to investigate through physical inspection of facilities, and it may compel the production of information and testimony through administrative subpoenas.

The Enforcement Bureau is not restrained by the strict rules as to the admissibility of evidence that prevail in U.S. federal courts. Even so, enforcement proceedings hew to the essential policies undergirding the rules of evidence to ensure a fair process. The burden of proof to justify the FCC's rules and decisions lies with the entity asserting injury or rule invalidity.

The Enforcement Bureau may delegate prosecutorial functions, but petitioners typically have a right to appeal from the delegated body's decision. The Bureau may delegate enforcement duties to a panel of commissioners, an individual commissioner, an employee board, or an individual employee. Any person aggrieved by any order, decision, or action made pursuant to such delegation may file an application for review by the Commission, itself. The person or group conducting the hearing generally must prepare and file an initial, or recommended decision subsequent to the hearing. Any party to the proceeding may file exceptions to the initial or recommended decision, which must be reviewed by the Commission as provided by statute.

After an order, decision, or action has been made in any proceeding by the FCC, any party adversely effected by it may petition for reconsideration. A petition for reconsideration must be filed within thirty days from the date upon which public notice is given of the order, decision, or action at issue. However, the FCC may consider late-filed petitions for reconsideration.

If an investigation reveals that an entity violated a legal obligation that the FCC is responsible for enforcing, the FCC has several remedial options. It may fine or penalize the entity by handing down a Notice of Apparent Liability for Forfeiture, or NAL. This notice informs the offending entity or person how that entity or person violated the law and the amount of the penalty resulting from the violation. The entity or person may file a response, which the FCC will evaluate and will typically address in a subsequent order.

The FCC does not have unbridled discretion in imposing penalties. The Communications Act prescribes the maximum amount that the FCC may levy against an offender. The Act also identifies several factors the FCC must take into account before imposing a penalty.

If a potential offender seeks to address a potential violation outside of the NAL process, it may request settlement negotiations with FCC personnel. If these negotiations are successful, the FCC will typically issue a Consent Decree, which often includes a compliance plan designed to prevent recurrence of the alleged violation that prompted the enforcement action. Often the Consent Decree will include a voluntary financial contribution to the U.S. Treasury.

More serious violations may result in a forfeiture, however the FCC is generally precluded from issuing a forfeiture to an entity who is not a conventional subject of

FCC regulation. In other words, it is significantly more difficult for the FCC to issue a forfeiture notice to entities that are not engaged in broadcasting, cable system operations, satellite communications, or other telecommunication carriers. Outside of forfeiture, the FCC retains a number of enforcement tools, including nonmonetary enforcement tools like public admonishments, Notices of Violation, cease and desist orders, and, in extreme cases, license revocations.

The FCC has an obligation to address properly presented constitutional claims, especially those claims that challenge FCC rules rather than Congressional mandates that are simply carried out by the FCC. Notably, the FCC need not address every comment, but need only respond to those comments that raise significant problems.

II. Judicial Proceedings

74. Any grievance or petition within the jurisdiction of the FCC, typically, should first be adjudicated through the FCC's administrative process before the issue may be reviewed by a court of law. The rule requiring the exhaustion of administrative remedies before court review is not, of course, absolute. If the subject matter of the dispute is not within the exclusive jurisdiction of the FCC, the Communications Act allows court review without administrative exhaustion. For example, the FCC has concurrent, not exclusive jurisdiction regarding allegations of unfair competition in the telecommunications sector.

Administrative review as a precondition to federal court review requires that the FCC first have a meaningful "opportunity to pass" on the disputed issue. Just because the FCC discusses a particular legal issue does not always amount to an "opportunity to pass" on the issue. Petitioner must show that the FCC reviewed the legality of the issue through an adversarial process. It is not required that the party seeking federal court review of a particular issue was the party that handled the same issue before the FCC.

A party's failure to identify a particular statutory challenge through the administrative process typically precludes a federal court from later considering the issue after exhaustion of administrative remedies. In some instances, however, if the issue is necessarily implicated by an argument made during the administrative process, the federal court may legally review its validity.

While the filing of an application for administrative review is a condition precedent to judicial review of any order, decision or action made by the FCC, the filing of a petition for administrative reconsideration is not a condition precedent to judicial review. A petition for reconsideration is only a prerequisite to federal court review when the party seeking federal court review was not a party to the underlying administrative proceeding.

With regard to actions that challenge an order issued by the FCC, statutory provisions determine the adjudicatory process. Proceedings that seek to enjoin or suspend an FCC order must typically follow a uniform procedure used with most federal agencies set forth in the Hobbs Act, which provides the following:

> On the entry of a final order reviewable under this chapter, the agency shall promptly give notice thereof by service or publication in accordance with its rules. Any party aggrieved by the final order may, within 60 days after its entry, file a petition to review the order in the court of appeals wherein venue lies. The action shall be against the United States. The petition shall contain a concise statement of:
>
> (1) the nature of the proceedings as to which review is sought;
> (2) the facts on which venue is based;
> (3) the grounds on which relief is sought; and
> (4) the relief prayed.[57]

The Hobbs Act provides that the federal court of appeals where the alleged injury arose has exclusive jurisdiction to enjoin, suspend, or generally determine the validity of final FCC orders. The federal courts must afford deference to FCC final orders and must limit the court's review to discrete violations. With regard to standing, any party that can show injury or that it has been somehow aggrieved by the FCC final order may file a petition for review in the proper court of appeals within sixty days of the FCC's issuance of its final order.

The federal court is limited in its review of the FCC order, action, or decision. The court may only set aside the FCC ruling or action if it was arbitrary, capricious, an abuse of discretion, or otherwise contrary to constitutional right or express statutory provision. The reviewing court can also review FCC's underlying jurisdiction when the FCC executed the rule itself or when FCC took action, as well as the procedures followed by the FCC in coming to the complained of rule or action. In most cases, the FCC need only articulate a rational justification or explanation for its rule or action, including a mere rational connection between underlying facts and the FCC's rule or action. In sum, federal courts are legally obligated to afford deference to the FCC's rulings on matters that fall within the FCC's jurisdiction.

Indeed, the courts have recognized that the FCC's rulings must, at times, rest on judgment and estimations and cannot always be based on established data and demonstrable facts. Even if the court finds the FCC's action or ruling to be unwise, ill conceived, or inferior to alternative approach, the court will not overturn the action unless the FCC failed to consider clear relevant factors or made overt and unreasonable errors.

With regard to *state* government rulings – and in particular state agency rules affecting telecommunications – the federal courts have subject matter jurisdiction to review the same. The Telecommunications Act of 1996 recognized the need to harmonize telecommunications decisions that have interstate implications, and therefore provided for federal court review of state commission decisions that relate to interstate transmissions.

There is no implied private right of action under the Communications Act, such as an action for injunctive relief, but private enforcement actions are cognizable when the FCC order in question requires a particular action by an identified party.

---

57. Hobbs Act, 28U.S.C. § 2344.

Chapter 6. Regulation of Broadcasting Activities

75. The FCC has imposed licensing and owner restrictions, as well as content requirements, on broadcast media, based on a scarcity justification, which requires those entitled to leverage the electromagnetic spectrum to do so in the public interest. In the 1980s, the FCC backed away from the scarcity justification, although that justification continues to impact regulatory decisions in some instances today.

§1. Broadcast Content Requirements

76. Although the First Amendment restricts the government's ability to regulate the content of speech or expression, a handful of content regulations have been found valid. This recognition is illustrated by the rise and fall of the "fairness doctrine," which required broadcasters to present controversial issues of public importance in a manner that was equitable and honest, as determined by the FCC. Several First Amendment free speech challenges survived judicial scrutiny, but nevertheless, the FCC eliminated the policy in 1987, and removed the rule that implemented the policy from the Federal Register in August 2011.

The equal-time rule, however, remains good law. The equal-time rule requires U.S. radio and television broadcast stations to provide an equivalent opportunity to opposing political candidates who request it. If a station gives prime time to a candidate, the station must do so for another candidate who requests it, at the same or similar price, if feasible. A related regulation requires that broadcasters offer time to candidates at the same rate as their "most favored advertiser." The equal-time rule stemmed from concerns that broadcast stations could unduly affect the outcomes of popular elections by only broadcasting one viewpoint or candidate. There are several exceptions to the rule, including news events, which have been broadly interpreted to include some political debates as well as talk shows.

In addition, broadcast stations must identify those who sponsor them. Stations must provide routine reports that illustrate that programming meets community needs and that some programming is dedicated to children. Specific content limitations for cigarette advertising, on-air hoaxes, and indecent or obscene material have been upheld in many instances and not violating the First Amendment Free Speech protections.

§2. Broadcast Ownership Restrictions

77. The common ownership of multiple media sources by a single entity has been regulated by the FCC, Congress, and subject to First Amendment scrutiny by the judiciary. In recent years, beginning with the Telecommunications Act of 1996, the U.S. has deregulated ownership requirements. The concomitant increase in media merging and concentration of ownership has correlated with a decrease in public trust in large media outlets. The ongoing debate has focused on the ownership of broadcast stations, newspapers, and cable stations. No specific regulation constrains the number of television broadcast stations that one entity can own, but the cumulative national reach of such stations cannot exceed 39% of U.S. households. No such limits constrain satellite or fiber optic providers. In a similar vein, duopolies are allowed only if sufficient number of independent television stations remain to ensure a diversity of views and news. A duopoly normally occurs in television and radio broadcasting in which two or more stations in the same city or community share common ownership.

With regard to broadcast and cable cross-ownership, one entity may own a television station and a cable television service in the same market, as long as the cable operator faces effective competition in the market. In the realm of network ownership, major VHF networks, like ABC, CBS, FOX or NBC cannot merge, but a single entity may own a major VHF network and an Ultra High Frequency network. With regard to broadcast and newspaper cross-ownership, the FCC attempted to lift the bar that prevents one entity from owning both a newspaper and a television station in the same media market. A federal court, in *Prometheus Radio Project v. FCC* invalidated the FCC's attempt to lift the restriction on procedural grounds.[58] Finally, some legal limitations disallow television and radio co-ownership as well as limit the number and scope of national radio ownership, although these legal restrictions have been relaxed in the most recent decade. Clear Channel, for example, has owned as many as 1,200 radio stations.

§3. Broadcast Licensing Restrictions

78. Broadcast licensing, as noted above, stems from the scarcity principle, and involves the federal government's permission to use a portion of the radio frequency spectrum in a particular geographical area for broadcasting purposes. The scarcity theory historically served as justification for a variety of rules governing licensing, but also including ownership and sometimes content restrictions. Prior to 1993, the FCC awarded licenses through a competitive process. The competitor that best demonstrated broadcasting service for the public interest was favored. Stations are licensed for eight years only and must petition for renewal before the eight-year term expires. Renewal petitions must show compliance with federal laws and FCC regulations and that the station operated in the public's interest.

In *Bechtel v. FCC*, a federal appellate court prohibited that process,[59] and the FCC now distributes licenses by auction. The FCC awards licenses only to U.S. applicants, as the Communications Act prohibits the FCC from granting a broadcast or common carrier license to a non-U.S. citizen, which includes organizations of which one-fourth of the stock is foreign-owned. The prohibition does not apply to cable, but does apply to television stations, radio stations, and telephone companies that use a satellite or radio link.

58. 652 F.3d 431 (2011).
59. 10 F.3d 875 (D.C. Cir. 1993).

§4. Regulatory Framework for Multichannel Video Program Distributors

79. The regulations that specifically apply to broadcast media alone are becoming less significant due to the fact that most people in the U.S. access broadcast programing through cable or satellite. Broadcast media providers, sometimes called multichannel video program distributors (MVPD), are regulated under a different framework from other communications media. MVPD's broadcast television service to approximately 90% of U.S. residents. Broadcast media, as opposed to cable and satellite, have traditionally faced more restrictions and public service obligations. In large part, this distinction stems from a subscription rationale. Because consumers purposely subscribe to cable and satellite programing, they are presumably aware of the content offered. Broadcast media, by contrast, is both more pervasive and uninvited by the individual consumer. This justification remains despite the fact that 90% of television consumers watch broadcast programing through paid services offered by cable and satellite companies.

I. Must Carry Rules

80. A demand for carriage is commonly referred to as "must-carry." In the U.S., the government has required cable television providers to carry locally licensed television stations. Smaller, local broadcasters struggled as cable providers increased their market share. Cable providers preferred local affiliates of major broadcast networks, many of which were co-owned by the cable providers. Local, nonaffiliated broadcasters argued that the emerging system unfairly captured and controlled advertising revenue. The requirement that cable companies must carry local broadcast channels was challenged as violating the First Amendment Free Speech safeguard. In *Turner Broadcasting System, Inc. v. FCC*, the U.S. Supreme Court ruled that First Amendment free speech protections apply to cable providers. The FCC's must-carry rule burdens cable providers, the court held, but because the provision did not identify which content the cable operators must include, the FCC's rule was content-neutral. The must-carry rule did not differentiate between "favored" and "disfavored" speech; it only required cable operators to carry local broadcast programming – regardless of content.

As a result, if a broadcast station asserts its must-carry rights, the broadcaster cannot demand compensation from the cable operator. With regard to cable television, the FCC originally lacked regulatory jurisdiction because cable did not use public airwaves to distribute programming. This changed when the FCC recognized how cable could undermine broadcast television programming. To promote the public welfare, the FCC in 1965 required cable companies to carry local broadcast channels. The FCC also barred cable companies from importing broadcast signals that replicated local broadcast programming.

As of 2016, approximately 50% of U.S. households rely on cable, compared to less than 10% that still rely on over-the-air broadcasting. According to Nielsen, a global measurement and data analytics company, 14% of U.S. households watch television over the air as of 2019. Tellingly, only a fraction of that 14% consume television by broadcast over the air, while the larger—and growing—segment of the 14% has at least one subscription video service like, Hulu, Netflix, or Amazon Prime, for example. Those in this group tend to be younger, with a median age of thirty-six. They also tend to be more affluent, and more device-connected, according to Nielsen.

II. Franchising Authorities

81. Unlike broadcast stations, the FCC does not issue licenses to cable companies. Instead, companies must obtain a franchise agreement to conduct business in a local market. These are essentially contracts that state and local governments enter into with cable providers permitting cable companies to build and operate a cable network that services a particular area. Typically, municipalities and county governments enter into these franchise contracts, and as a result, these companies are subject to local regulation in several regards. Absent permission from local government, cable companies may not construct cable lines across public rights of way.

III. Access Channels

82. State and local governments have been authorized by the U.S. Congress to require cable companies to carry a set number of local, public-oriented programming. As a result, most cable providers are required to set aside channels for public interest, local government, and/or education purposes. In addition, the FCC requires cable companies to set aside some channel capacity for lease in order to facilitate local programming. A cable operator with twelve or fewer channels must set aside up to three channels for local commercial television stations and at least one channel for a local noncommercial educational television broadcast station. Cable operators with more than twelve channels must set aside one-third of their channel capacity for local commercial stations, and cable systems with between thirteen and thirty-six channels must carry at least one, but need not carry more than three, local noncommercial educational television stations. Cable systems with more than thirty-six channels must carry all local noncommercial educational television stations requesting carriage with some exceptions for duplication of signals. The law forbids cable companies from modifying the content on these set-aside channels, but cable companies may set production quality standards.

IV. Content Regulation

83. As distinguished from broadcast television, the FCC does not regulate obscenity and indecency with regard to cable programming. Again, the distinction stems from subscribership. Some subscribers want channels that offer sexually oriented programming. Regardless, subscribers are presumed to know of indecent cable programming whereas indecency in broadcast is arguably imposed against a viewer's will and knowledge.

V. Direct Broadcast Satellite Service

84. In 1962, Congress overtly gave the FCC regulatory authority of direct broadcast satellite service through the Communications Satellite Act of 1962.[60] Despite the FCC's authority over direct broadcast satellite service, the FCC's regulatory approach remains somewhat unclear due to the hybrid nature of direct broadcast satellite service. Direct broadcast satellite service is both a subscription-based service like cable and a broadband-like service because it uses the electromagnetic spectrum to disseminate programming. While federal courts in the U.S. are split as to the characterization of direct broadcast satellite service, the FCC currently regulates direct broadcast satellite service like cable. For example, the FCC has not imposed the content-based restrictions on obscenity to direct broadcast satellite services. This is important because direct broadcast satellite service is the second most popular paid programming service. It services about 30% of U.S. residents.

VI. Channel Set-Asides

85. In the 1992 Cable Act, Congress required direct broadcast satellite providers to set aside at least 4% channel capacity for informational programming, educational programming, or other such public service programming. Like cable, direct broadcast satellite providers may require such channels to meet minimum technical standards, but providers may not impose editorial or content requirements.

VII. Carry One, Carry all Provisions

86. While cable companies were able to supply local programming to their customers, direct broadcast satellite providers had to pay additional monies for local programing. Congress attempted to address this discrepancy in 1999 through the Satellite Home Viewer Improvement Act. This law allowed direct broadcast satellite providers to transmit local broadcast signals without first getting permission from copyright holders. The Satellite Home Viewer Improvement Act has a catch, however. The Act contains a "carry one, carry all" provision, which requires direct broadcast satellite providers that want to carry a station to also carry all local stations in the same market that request to be carried.

---

60. Communications Satellite Act of 1962, Pub L. 87-624, 76 Stat. 419.

Chapter 7. Regulation of Online Interactive Services

87. In contrast to the telecommunications sectors outlined above, the Internet is more informally regulated in the U.S. No federal agency is directly tasked with overseeing or regulating the Internet, including the licensing of service providers, regulating prices, ensuring access, or monitoring content. This is due, in part, to the rapid technological convergence as well as the Internet's global reach and fluid architecture. Even so, the Internet is not immune to regulation. While not a government entity, the Internet Corporation for Assigned Names and Numbers (ICANN) facilitates the Internet's functionality. ICANN, once a U.S. government operation, was transitioned into a nonprofit corporation after sustained pressure from the United Nations. Although the U.S. developed the Internet, the U.S. is no longer the Internet's majority user.

Use of the Internet in the U.S. is also affected by international laws that have transnational reach. The General Data Protection Regulation (GDPR) is an EU regulation addressing data protection and privacy.[61] The scope of the GDPR not only includes data processed on the Internet that derives from Member States, it also includes data processed or transmitted over the Internet that derives from other countries, including the U.S. Indeed, the U.S. previously negotiated a "Safe Harbor" exception with the EU, that diluted the data privacy restrictions for U.S. businesses and Internet users. As discussed in Part IV, the Safe Harbor exception no longer applies and U.S. Internet users must comply with the data privacy restrictions provided in the GDPR, where applicable.[62] Moreover, the EU and the U.S. agreed to a set of principles to facilitate data processing of personal data from the EU. The EU-U.S. Privacy Shield Framework allows personal data from the EU to be transferred and processed by U.S. entities that certify compliance with the Privacy Shield Principles. If a U.S. company certifies but fails to comply, the FTC has the authority to enforce noncompliance as an unfair and/or deceptive trade practice.

Network Neutrality, has been, and will likely continue to be, a highly controversial issue. Network neutrality, or simply net neutrality, is the FCC policy requiring that ISPs treat all Internet communications equally. ISPs may not discriminate or charge differently based on user, content, platform, website, application, type of device, or method of communication. Although the Communications Act does not directly authorize the FCC to regulate the Internet, the FCC claims the authority to prescribe network neutrality as incident to its express authority under the Act to protect competition and consumers of telecommunications services, which now includes VOIP. As a result, the FCC instituted a policy requiring network neutrality, which requires network transparency, prohibits network blocking lawful content, and prohibits network owners from unreasonable discriminating against most online content or applications.[63]

According to the FCC, legitimate network management practices include: "ensuring network security and integrity, including by addressing traffic that is harmful to

---

61. Regulation (EU) 2016/679 on the protection of natural persons with regard to the processing of personal data and on the free movement of such data (2016).
62. *See Infra* Part IV, for Data Privacy.
63. 47 C.F.R. §§ 8.1–8.17.

the network; addressing traffic that is unwanted by users […] consistent with a user's choices regarding parental controls or security capabilities; and by reducing or mitigating the effects of congestion on the network."[64] Importantly, the FCC repealed its own net neutrality regulations in 2018. The U.S. Congress, as of April 2019, is considering the Save the Internet Act, which would reinstate net neutrality – this time by statute.[65] The proposed statute would restrict broadband companies from abusing their position as gatekeepers to the Internet. The proposed law would bar broadband providers from blocking or slowing access to the Internet, or charging for faster access. The proposed law would also expressly grant the FCC authority to regulate the Internet with regard to potential broadband abuses.

64. Preserving the Open Internet, 76 FR 59192 (Sept. 23, 2011) (codified in 47 CFR 0.111)
65. Save the Internet Act, H.R. 1644, 116th Cong. (2020).

Chapter 8. Regulation of Cryptography and Dual-Use Goods

§1. General

88. U.S. businesses and organizations have long distributed software and other technology components internationally. For over seventy years, the U.S. government has grappled with whether and how to regulate these technologies, including cryptography, in light of security concerns – especially as they conflict with economic growth and global technology convergence. As the technology capabilities have improved in countries with low labor and overhead cost, U.S. businesses have increasingly outsourced software development, including cryptography elements. Whether through a satellite office, or employment of foreign nationals who are not U.S. citizens, this development prompted further regulatory oversight over export controls, including licensing and reporting requirements.

World War II is often cited as a milestone in government regulation over cryptography export. The clear importance of uncompromised communication in wartime and the ability to break the codes of enemies emerged as a critical lesson. Up until 1992, cryptography was listed as a "munition" or as "Auxiliary Military Equipment," limiting the export of cryptographic technology like a weapon. Importantly, attempts to limit information regarding cryptography domestically were limited by the U.S. Constitution's protection of free speech. As a result, cryptography grew nationally, but businesses that sought to grow globally by exporting software and cryptography had to conform with strict federal regulations that include licensure for cryptography above a specific strength.

But the fluid nature of the Internet and the increasing commercialization of the Internet made it increasingly difficult to forestall the spread of cryptography knowledge and advances. One of the largest such advances came from a private company through Netscape's SSL technology in 1994. Secure Sockets Layer (SSL) technology employs a cryptographic system that uses two keys to encrypt data – a public key known to everyone and a private key known only to the recipient of the message. SSL facilitates authentication of the accessed website and bolsters the privacy and integrity of the exchanged data while it is in transit. Netscape's SSL technology was widely adopted as a method for protecting credit card transactions using public key cryptography, again illustrating how the commercialization of cryptography eroded military and security protocols meant to curtail dissemination.

Moreover, in the late 1980s and early 1990s, privacy advocates and others challenged restrictions that limited the widespread availability of encryption software outside the U.S. Commercial sales facilitated by the Internet were hamstrung by such policies and business groups increased lobbying pressure to relax the restrictions. On the other side of the argument, the National Security Agency argued that global dissemination of strong encryption technology would hamper the U.S. intelligence agencies from gathering intelligence through signal interception, including foreign terrorist operations. Further, communications among NATO intelligence communities and allied governments might become less secure. With secure encryption capabilities, criminal organizations, terrorists, and enemy spies could communicate more effectively.

The popularization of the personal computer in concert with e-commerce and rogue companies willing to flout the rules, however, drove encryption into the broader public market. This trend away from restricting dissemination of cryptography came to a head in 1996 when President Bill Clinton signed Executive Order 13026. The Executive Order included language that was geared towards security concerns, but the order ultimately transferred commercial encryption from the Munition List to the Commerce Control List. The order:

> determined that the export of encryption products described in this section could harm national security and foreign policy interests even where comparable products are or appear to be available from sources outside the United States, and that facts and questions concerning the foreign availability of such encryption products cannot be made subject to public disclosure or judicial review without revealing or implicating classified information that could harm United States national security and foreign policy interests.[66]

Even so, the Executive Order went on to state that "the software shall not be treated as "technology"" for purposes of Export Administration Regulations (EAR). The Executive Order clarified that encryption products must be controlled for foreign policy and national security interests and warned that if the new EAR regulations that facilitated reclassification as commerce do not provide adequate controls on encryption products, such products will be redesignated as defense articles. Encryption-related products designed for military applications remained on the Munition List, but otherwise encryption products moved to the commerce control list. With a commercial commodity classification, export of 56-bit encryption was sanctioned, and in 1999 the Export Administration Regulations allowed 1,024-bit RSA to be exported without any backdoors, including new SSL technologies to support the RSA. And one year later, in 2000, the Department of Commerce streamlined exportation of commercial software that included cryptography regardless of key length restrictions in certain instances.

§2. The Department of Commerce and Export Administration Regulations

89. Today, a distinction is made separating commercial from military cryptography. If the encryption product was originally designed for military use or military application, it is regulated under military rather than commercial protocol. All non-military cryptography exports are regulated through the Department of Commerce, particularly the Bureau of Industry and Security (BIS). Even commercial grade cryptography includes export restrictions in some instances, like exportation to terrorist organizations, and export software and other commodities with encryption surpassing 64 bits.[67] The process for relaxing exportation restrictions on encryption

66. Administration of Export Controls on Encryption Products, Exec. Order No. 13026, 61 Fed. Red. 224 (1996), https://www.hsdl.org/?abstract&did=799501.
67. 15 CFR § 742.15.

products involves agency rules. In particular, BIS petitions to amend the Export Administration Regulations to modify the requirements of License Exception, "Encryption Commodities, Software and Technology," and the requirements for qualifying an encryption item as mass market. BIS can also seek to modify specific license requirements for encryption items. Military cryptography includes cryptography that supports military equipment as well as specialized cryptographic consulting, which require licensure.

Nonmilitary encryption that has high functionality is regulated under a 5X002 export classification, which requires export licensure from the Department of Commerce. The process for acquiring such a license is laid out in an "encryption outline" on the BIS website.[68] Updates or modifications of the source code and changes in Internet location must be reported to BIS. Nonmilitary encryption items with lower encryption functionality are controlled less stringently and will generally be classified under a 5X992 classification. This includes software with low encryption functionality as well as digital techniques that enable digital signatures or authentication, and technology specially designed and limited for banking use or money transactions.

Some "mass market" encryption items can also be classified under 5X992 if they are already widely available to the public at retail selling locations. In some cases, the exporter must file an encryption registration or export report with the BIS. Additionally, some encryption components require export licensure if they are destined for one of the terrorism-supporting or embargoed regions, identified as Cuba, Iran, North Korea, Sudan, Syria, and the Crimea region of Ukraine. With regard to military encryption components, it is possible to export, but exporters must comply with the State Department's International Traffic in Arms Regulations (ITAR). ITAR is a regulatory regime that restricts and monitors the export of defense and military-related technologies with the purpose of protecting U.S. national security. ITAR implements the provisions of the Arms Export Control Act,[69] and the Department of State Directorate of Defense Trade Controls interprets and enforces ITAR.

As noted above, the Department of Commerce through BIS controls exports of encryption items and does so principally through regulations promulgated as the EAR. The regulations are divided into basic categories, with distinct ramifications.[70] The U.S. Commerce Control List (CCL) is broken in to ten Categories.[71] Encryption items fall under Category 5, Part 2 for Information Security, which covers:

(1) Cryptographic Information Security; (e.g., items that use cryptography);
(2) Non-cryptographic Information Security (5A003); and
(3) Defeating, Weakening of Bypassing Information Security (5A004).

68. *See* Encryption and Export Administration Regulations (EAR), Bureau of Industry and Security (2017), https://www.bis.doc.gov/index.php/policy-guidance/encryption.
69. 22U.S.C. Ch. 39.
70. 15 CFR §§ 740, 772, 774.
71. *See* Supplement No. 1 to part 774 of the EAR, https://www.bis.doc.gov/index.php/documents/regulations-docs/2345-774-10-24-18/file.

The following table provides a reference point and categorization of the aforementioned exportation regulations:

Quick Reference Guide *Category 5 Part 2 - Information Security: ECCN 5X*		
A	"END ITEMS," "EQUIPMENT," "ACCESSORIES," "ATTACHMENTS," "PARTS," "COMPONENTS," AND "SYSTEMS"	
I. CRYPTOGRAPHIC "INFORMATION SECURITY"		
5A002	NS AT EI	"Information security" systems, equipment and "components" ▪ **.a** – Designed or modified to use 'cryptography for data confidentiality' having 'in excess of 56 bits of symmetric cryptographic strength key length, or equivalent', where that cryptographic capability is usable without "cryptographic activation" or has been activated, as follows: o **a.1** Items having "information security" as a primary function; o **a.2** Digital communication or networking systems, equipment or components, not specified in paragraph 5A002.a.1.; o **a.3** Computers, other items having information storage or processing as a primary function, and components therefor, not specified in paragraphs 5A002.a.1. or 5A002.a.2.; N.B. For operating systems, see also 5D002.a.1. and 5D002.c.1. o **a.4** - Items, not specified in paragraphs 5A002.a.1. to a.3., where the 'cryptography for data confidentiality' having 'in excess of 56 bits of symmetric cryptographic strength key length, or equivalent' meets all of the following: ▪ **a.** It supports a non-primary function of the item; and ▪ **b.** It is performed by incorporated equipment or "software" that would, as a standalone item, be specified by ECCNs 5A002, 5A003, 5A004, 5B002 or 5D002.. • **.b** – designed/modified to enable, by means of "cryptographic activation," an item to achieve/exceed the controlled performance levels for functionality specified by 5A002.a that would not otherwise be met. ▪ **.c** – designed/modified to use or perform "quantum cryptography" (Quantum Key Distribution - QKD) ▪ **.d** – designed/modified to use cryptographic techniques to generate channelizing codes, scrambling codes or network identification codes, for systems using ultra-wideband modulation techniques and having a bandwidth >500 MHz; or "fractional bandwidth" of 20% or more ▪ **.e** – designed/modified to use cryptographic techniques to generate the spreading code for "spread spectrum" systems, not controlled in 5A002.d, including the hopping code for "frequency hopping" systems.
5A992	AT	Equipment not controlled by 5A002 ▪ **.c** – Commodities classified Mass Market – 740.17(b)
II. *NON-CRYPTOGRAPHIC "INFORMATION SECURITY"*		
5A003	NS	"Systems' "equipment" and "components," for non-cryptographic "information

	AT	security" ▪ **.a** – Communications cable systems designed/modified using mechanical, electrical or electronic means to detect surreptitious intrusion (See Note re: physical layer security) ▪ **.b** – "Specially designed" or modified to reduce the compromising emanations of information-bearing signals beyond what is necessary for health, safety or electromagnetic interference standards.
III. DEFEATING, WEAKENING OR BYPASSING "INFORMATION SECURITY"		
5A004	NS AT EI	"Systems," "equipment" and "components" for defeating, weakening or bypassing "information security" ▪ **.a** – Designed /modified to perform 'cryptanalytic functions' including by means of reverse engineering
B		TEST, INSPECTION AND "PRODUCTION EQUIPMENT"
5B002	NS AT	"Information Security" test, inspection and "production" equipment ▪ **.a** – Equipment "specially designed" for the "development" or "production" of equipment controlled by 5A002, 5A003, 5A004 or 5B002.b; ▪ **.b** – Measuring equipment "specially designed" to evaluate and validate the "information security" functions of equipment or "software" controlled by 5A002, 5A003 or 5A004, or 5D002.a or 5D002.c respectively
C		"MATERIAL" – [RESERVED]
D		"SOFTWARE"
5D002	NS AT EI	"Software" ▪ **.a** – "Software" "specially designed" or modified for the "development," "production" or "use" of **a.1** - equipment specified by 5A002 or "software" specified by 5D002 c.1; **a.2** – equipment specified by 5A003 or "software" specified by 5D002 c.2; **a.3** equipment specified by 5A004 or "software" specified by 5D002 c.3. ▪ **.b** – "Software" designed or modified to enable, by means of "cryptographic activation", an item to meet the criteria for functionality specified by 5A002.a, that would not otherwise be met; ▪ **.c** – "Software" having the characteristics, or performing or simulating the functions of **c.1** - the equipment controlled by 5A002.a, .c. .d or .e; , **c.2** – the equipment controlled by 5A003; **c.3** - equipment specified by 5A004. Note: does not apply to "software" limited to tasks of "OAM" implementing only published or commercial cryptographic standards
5D992	AT	"Information Security" "software" not controlled by 5D002 ▪ **.c** – Commodities classified Mass Market – 740.17(b)
E		"TECHNOLOGY"
5E002	NS AT EI	"Technology" ▪ **.a** – "Technology" according to the General Technology Note for the "development," "production" or "use" of equipment or "software" controlled by 5A002, 5A003, 5A004 or 5B002, or 5D002.a or 5D002.c

		respectively ▪ **.b** – "Technology" to enable, by means of "cryptographic activation," an item to achieve/exceed the controlled performance levels for functionality specified by 5A002.a that would not otherwise be met.
5E992	AT	"Information Security" "technology" according to the General Technology Note, not controlled by 5E002 ▪ **.b** – "Technology" for the "use' of Mass Market commodities or "software" controlled by 5A992.c or 5D992.c respectively

Flowcharts 1 and 2 are provided by the Bureau of Industry and Security, a department of the U.S. Department of Commerce:

*Flowchart 1: Items Designed to Use Cryptography Including Items Not Controlled under Category 5, Part 2 of the Ear**

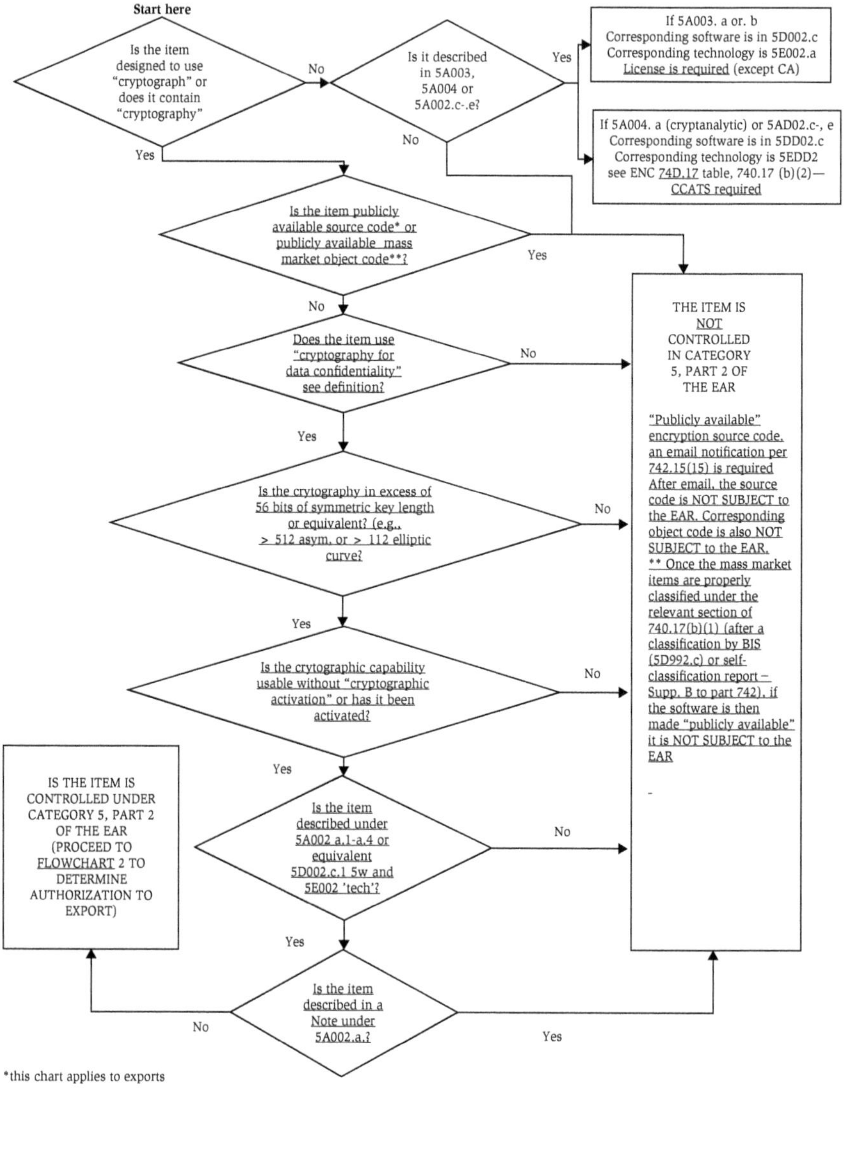

Flowchart 2: Classified in Category 5, Part 2 of the EAR

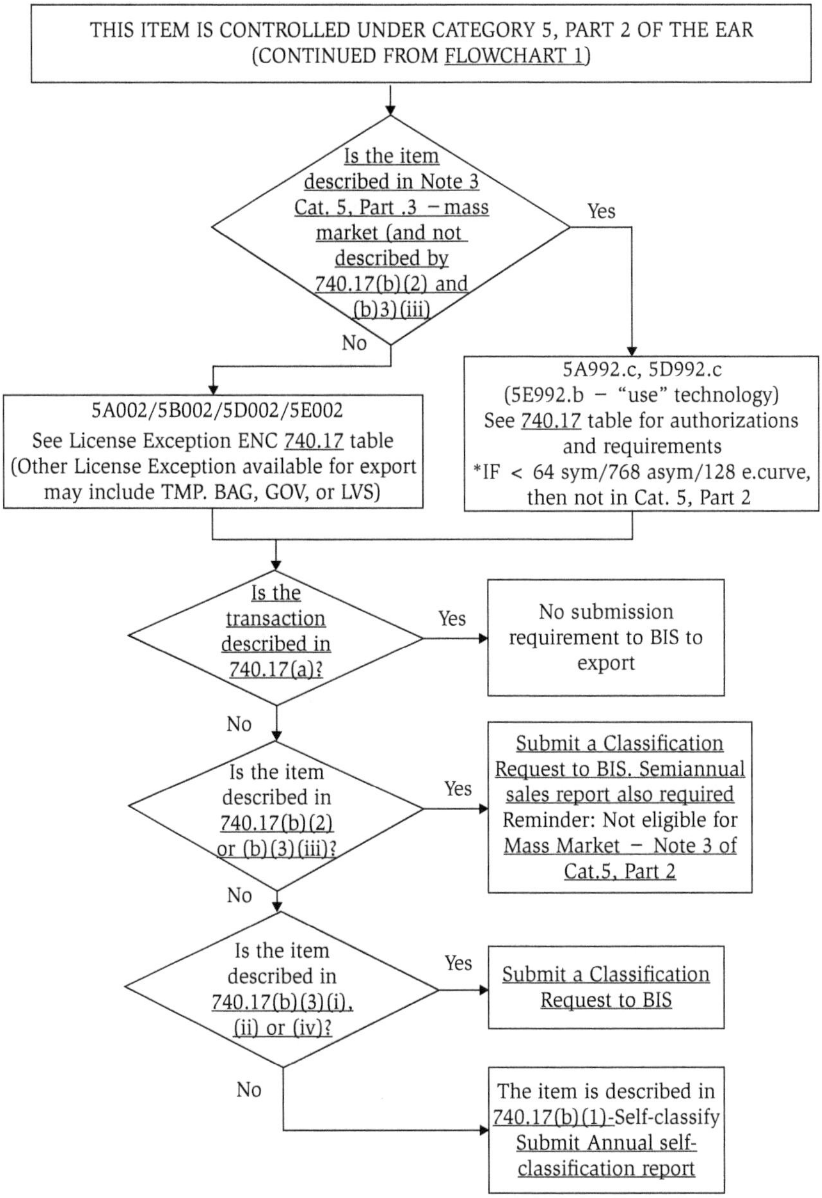

The controls affecting cryptology that are codified in category five of the EAR further delineate between multilateral and unilateral controls. The unilateral controls in category five (e.g., 5A992.c, 5D992.c, 5E992.b) are determined solely by U.S. authorities. The multilateral controls in category five (e.g., 5A002, 5A003,

5A004, 5B002, 5D002, 5E002) derive from the Wassenaar Arrangement List of Dual-Use Goods and Technologies. Changes to the multilateral controls are agreed upon by the participating members of the Wassenaar Arrangement.

§3. The Wassenaar Arrangement

90. Many of the above restrictions stem from the Wassenaar Arrangement. On August 15, 2017 the Wassenaar Arrangement Agreements were published in the Federal Register.[72] The arrangement is a multilateral export control regime with forty-two participating states including EU Member States, Russia, South Africa, and the U.S. Much of the agreement targets export of weaponry and armaments, with encryption technology incidental to the same.

Under the Wassenaar Arrangement, the forty-two participating states exchange information on transfers of conventional weapons and dual-use goods and technologies. A primary objective of the arrangement is to promote accountability among its members in exports of weapons and dual-use goods in an effort to restrict "destabilizing accumulations." Proposals for changes to items or technologies identified for reporting and control that achieve consensus are approved by participating states at annual plenary meetings. Participating states are charged with implementing the agreed list changes as soon as possible after approval.

On September 20, 2016, the BIS issued a final rule updating the EAR and the CCL pursuant to the Wassenaar Arrangement Plenary Agreement (2015) on Export Controls for Conventional Arms and Dual-Use Goods and Technologies. This final rule essentially implements changes agreed in the Wassenaar Arrangement and represents a relaxation of certain U.S. encryption controls. The Final Rule is thirty-eight pages of amendments, primarily made to harmonize the EAR with the Wassenaar Arrangement changes.[73]

With regard to cryptography, the Final Rule eliminated the need for certain subcategories of encryption, a limitation on mass market encryption regulation, authorization of export, and transfer without a license of certain encryption items to companies in countries listed in Part 740, creation of a new category entitled "less sensitive government end users," as a license exception, and the addition of technical performance parameters for "network infrastructure" components, like WAN, MAN, and Virtual Private Network.[74]

While the Wassenaar Arrangement has engendered some successful regulations among its members, there is lingering disagreement regarding Wassenaar's scope, and the lack of enforcement attending a body largely called to exchange and collect information. Without meaningful enforcement for participation states that fail to

---

72. 82 FR 38764, Wassenaar Arrangement 2016 Plenary Agreements Implementation (2016)
73. 81 FR 64655, Wassenaar Arrangement 2015 Plenary Agreements Implementation, Removal of Foreign National Review Requirements, and Information Security Updates (2016), https://www.federalregister.gov/documents/2016/09/20/2016-21544/wassenaar-arrangement-2015-plenary-agreements-implementation-removal-of-foreign-national-review.
74. *Id.*

comply, a few members have historically avoided full participation. Finally, disagreement about which nations constitute "states of concern" and what constitutes a "destabilizing" transfer undermines Wassenaar's effectiveness.

§4. Enforcement

91. The U.S. government continues to prosecute and enforce violations of cryptography and dual-use goods regulation. Across the U.S. and in seven embassies and consulates around the world, BIS Special Agents and other affiliated officials enforce U.S. export laws using criminal and administrative investigative tools. Export Administration Regulations (Title 15 of the Code of Federal Regulations Parts 730 through 774) Code of Federal Regulations (CFR) determines which enforcement tool applies. In particular, "Enforcement and Protective Measures" are laid out in Part 764:

> §764.1 Introduction.
>
> In this part, references to the EAR are references to 15 CFR chapter VII, subchapter C. This part specifies conduct that constitutes a violation of the Export Administration Act (EAA) and/or the Export Administration Regulations (EAR) and the sanctions that may be imposed for such violations. Antiboycott violations are described in part 760 of the EAR, and the violations and sanctions specified in part 764 also apply to conduct relating to part 760, unless otherwise stated. This part describes administrative sanctions that may be imposed by the Bureau of Industry and Security (BIS). This part also describes criminal sanctions that may be imposed by a United States court and other sanctions that are neither administrative nor criminal. Information is provided on how to report and disclose violations. Finally, this part identifies protective administrative measures that BIS may take in the exercise of its regulatory authority.[75]

Part 764 identifies the several ways in which violations occur, including but not limited to "engaging in prohibited conduct, conspiracy, solicitation and attempt, possession with intent, and misrepresentation." Part 764.3, however, identifies the range of sanctions that accompany rule violations:

> §764.3 Sanctions.
>
> (a) Administrative. Violations of the EAA, the EAR, or any order, license or authorization issued thereunder are subject to the administrative sanctions described in this section and to any other liability, sanction, or penalty available under law. The protective administrative measures that are described in §764.6 of this part are distinct from administrative sanctions.

---

75. 15 CFR § 764.1.

(1) Civil monetary penalty. (i) A civil monetary penalty not to exceed the amount set forth in the EAA may be imposed for each violation, and in the event that any provision of the EAR is continued by IEEPA or any other authority, the maximum monetary civil penalty for each violation shall be that provided by such other authority.

***

(2) Denial of export privileges. An order may be issued that restricts the ability of the named persons to engage in export and reexport transactions involving items subject to the EAR, or that restricts access by named persons to items subject to the EAR.

***

(3) Exclusion from practice. Any person acting as an attorney, accountant, consultant, freight forwarder, or in any other representative capacity for any license application or other matter before BIS may be excluded by order from any or all such activities before BIS.

(b) Criminal—(1) General. Except as provided in paragraph (b)(2) of this section, whoever knowingly violates or conspires to or attempts to violate the EAA, EAR, or any order or license issued thereunder, shall be fined not more than five times the value of the exports or reexports involved or $50,000, whichever is greater, or imprisoned not more than five years, or both.

(2) Willful violations. (i) Whoever willfully violates or conspires to or attempts to violate any provision of the EAA, the EAR, or any order or license issued thereunder, with knowledge that the exports involved will be used for the benefit of, or that the destination or intended destination of items involved is, any controlled country or any country to which exports or reexports are controlled for foreign policy purposes, except in the case of an individual, shall be fined not more than five times the value of the export or reexport involved or $1,000,000, whichever is greater; and, in the case of an individual, shall be fined not more than $250,000, or imprisoned not more than 10 years, or both.

***

As noted above, the U.S. government has relaxed much of the post-World War II cryptography export restrictions over the past two decades, but it has not shied away from enforcing those regulations that continue to have the force and effect of law.

The government, under the law, may impose steep penalties and impose injunctive relief for noncompliance. Per violation, civil fines and penalties can reach as high as USD 300,000, or twice the value of the offending transaction, whichever is larger. Criminal infractions, by contrast, can result in twenty years in prison and up to USD 1 million in penalties per violation. With regard to injunctive relief, an offending company's export privileges may be revoked as a result of a violation. A denial of export privileges prohibits an entity or person from participating in any way in any transaction subject to the EAR. Officials may ban U.S. companies from exporting certain items and government officials may ban foreign entities from receiving specified U.S. technologies.

In 2013, Computerlinks FZCO, a business based in the UAE, settled a dispute brought by the Department of Commerce, which alleged that Computerlinks FZCO reexported controlled network devices and software to Syria without having a license to do so. The settlement included a USD 2.8 million penalty. In 2014, a California company paid a USD 115,000 penalty based on allegations that the company facilitated unauthorized disclosures to a Russian engineer who had been hired by the company. The engineer was given access to controlled technology without a license. Also, in 2014 an Intel subsidiary paid a USD 750,000 fine based on allegations of exporting encryption software in violation of the EAR.

In the BIS 2018 annual report, the agency states that "the year was again a record-breaking year for export enforcement in the Bureau of Industry and Security (BIS)," including the largest regulatory penalty in BIS history. The penalty produced a settlement in which the Chinese telecom giant, ZTE, paid USD 1.761 billion in combined criminal and civil penalties. Only USD 400 million was suspended and placed in escrow by ZTE. ZTE faced multiple charges and violations of the International Emergency Economic Powers Act, false and misleading statements, and obstruction of the administration of justice. The criminal charges were related to the illegal shipment of telecommunications equipment to Iran in violation of the EAR.

The BIS 2018 annual report goes on to compare enforcement efforts to the previous year:

> BIS investigations resulted in the criminal conviction of thirty individuals and companies for export violations, as compared to thirty-one convictions in Fiscal Year 2017. The penalties for these convictions came to $618,500 in criminal fines, $9,642,496 in forfeitures, and more than 506 months of imprisonment, compared to $287,102,532 in criminal fines, more than $166,234,123 in forfeitures, and more than 576 months of imprisonment in Fiscal Year 2017.[76]

In 2018, BIS investigations resulted in the imposition of a total of USD 1,101,431,225 in civil penalties. Even so, BIS emphasized in its report that enforcement activities should focus on prevention and compliance. As such, BIS issued Administrative Enforcement Guidelines in 2018 to promote greater transparency and predictability to the administrative enforcement process.[77]

---

76. U.S. Department of Commerce, Bureau of industry and Security, *Annual Report to the Congress for Fiscal year 2018* (2018), https://www.bis.doc.gov/index.php/documents/pdfs/2401-2018-bis-annual-report/file.
77. *See Administrative Enforcement Guidelines*, 83 Fed. Reg. 5 (2018), https://www.bis.doc.gov/index.php/documents/pdfs/1567-administrative-enforcement-guidelines/file.

Part II. Online Public Services

92. Other than as set forth in Chapter 5 of the introductory section above with respect to access and efficiency initiatives, the United States does not have a strong framework for online public services. At least partially due to the federal system of governance, key governmental functions are distributed between and among both the federal government and the state governments. Accordingly, there is not one single entity that would be responsible for implementing and maintaining robust online public services.

An additional challenge in the current political environment in the U.S. is the existence of significant political polarization. Because the two primary political parties (the Democrats and the Republicans) have staked out conflicting positions on issues related to online public services, significant advancement in the availability of online public services has not been achieved in the U.S. This issue is further exacerbated by the lack of significant control at the federal level by either party in the recent past. Although one party or the other may have raw numerical control (i.e., a bare majority in the Senate and House of Representatives coupled with control of the presidency) from time to time, the lack of a super-majority has prevented any significant legislation from being enacted that would fundamentally alter the status quo in the public services space. The most recent exception to this situation was in the period from 2008 to 2010, in which the Democrats held a significant majority and were able to pass the Affordable Care Act, which was intended to address significant issues in the provision of health care in the U.S.

In view of these challenges, the U.S. system for online public services is fairly minimal but will be discussed in the context of the overall framework, eHealth (or telemedicine), and online voting in the following chapters.

Chapter 1. e-Government Legal Framework

93. The U.S. does not have a substantial regulatory environment for overall online public services. One of the primary challenges to erecting such a system in the U.S. is the bifurcated nature of overall governance, with the states having primary regulatory authority over some aspects of public services, the federal government having authority over others, and the state and federal governments having joint or overlapping authority in others. In view of this environment, there is little reason for either states or the federal government to build a significant regulatory framework addressing e-government issues, and instead online public services are addressed on an ad hoc basis. There are currently no significant efforts to change the status quo in this regard.

Chapter 2. Legal Framework for eHealth

94. Telemedicine (or eHealth) is one area where the federal and state governments have been active recently. The situation in health care generally in the U.S. is complicated by the fact that the U.S. does not have a public health system that covers all Americans. Instead, a system of overlapping options exists, with most options being regulated at both the state and federal levels. With respect to public options, the U.S. has Medicare, which primarily provides health care for older Americans, and Medicaid, which primarily provides health care for low-income Americans. Medicare is funded and regulated primarily at the federal level, while Medicaid is funded and regulated at both the federal and state levels. Aside from these two public options, most Americans obtain their health care utilizing private insurers, with the majority of this insurance being employer-provided (or subsidized). Accordingly, the most significant regulatory framework in the U.S. is with respect to regulation of private insurers.

Prior to the COVID-19 pandemic, there was little use of telemedicine services in the U.S., but the pandemic and the resulting easing of some regulatory restrictions has resulted in significant increases in the use of telemedicine services nationally. The most significant aspects of the regulatory environment for telemedicine are prescription medications (sometimes referred to as regulation of controlled substances), medical professional licensure, and reimbursement of telemedicine services. Each of these will be addressed in the following sections.

§1. Prescription Medications

95. In the U.S., prescription medications are primarily regulated at the federal level by the Controlled Substances Act (CSA) of 1970 and its many subsequent amendments. The primary enforcement authority in the U.S. is the Drug Enforcement Administration. Under the CSA, an in-person doctor visit is typically required in order to receive a prescription for controlled pharmaceuticals. In the past, this has placed significant restrictions on the ability of health care professionals from practicing telemedicine. However, there is an exception for national emergencies and the COVID-19 pandemic is considered such a national emergency. Accordingly, access to prescriptions without an in-person doctor visit have been permitted during the pandemic. However, there is currently no indication that this flexibility will necessarily continue after the pandemic.

At the state level, many states also have restrictions on the issuance of prescriptions and the associated controlled medications. Accordingly, the ability of health care providers to prescribe medications via telemedicine approaches may be limited in particular jurisdictions, irrespective of the permissive environment at the federal level.

§2. Medical Professional Licensure

96. Medical professionals in the U.S. are subject to licensure laws in the states in which they practice, rather than at the national level. Each state has its own licensing regulations and/or procedures and so licensure in one state neither guarantees the ability to become licensed in another state nor does it provide authorization to practice in any other states. In the telemedicine context, this means that medical professionals licensed in one state cannot normally provide telemedicine services to patients in other states. However, the pandemic and associated limitations on the availability of health care providers have caused many states to relax their licensing restrictions in order to try and shore up the availability of such services. This is most likely to be a short-term measure and is unlikely to address the availability of telemedicine services across state lines on a longer-term basis though.

§3. Reimbursement of Telemedicine Services

97. Although not strictly a regulatory regime, the policies for reimbursement of telemedicine services, particularly for Medicare, have the effect of regulating the availability of such services. In particular, if reimbursement is not available for telemedicine services through Medicare, health care providers are unlikely to provide such services (or alternatively, will only provide such services to patients whose insurance will cover such services).

Prior to the pandemic, Medicare reimbursement of telemedicine services was quite limited and particularly focused on general access issues (such as rural communities lacking reasonable access to health care providers). However, during the pandemic, the federal government has taken steps to increase access to telemedicine services, first in the Telehealth Services During Certain Emergency Periods Act of 2020 (part of the Coronavirus Preparedness and Response Supplemental Appropriations Act) and then in the Coronavirus Aid, Relief, and Economic Security Act or "CARES Act." Through this legislation, the federal government has provided increased reimbursement for telemedicine services during the pandemic, but it is not clear whether these policies will continue into the future.

At the state level, which is primarily relevant to Medicaid reimbursement, states have been slowly embracing telemedicine models over time and becoming more permissive on reimbursement of telemedicine expenses. However, in response to the pandemic, many states also issued emergency orders to increase patient access to telemedicine services, and particularly increasing access from home. It remains unclear how much of these temporary measures will continue after the pandemic, however.

Chapter 3. Online Voting

98. Although some states in the U.S. do allow a limited form of electronic submission of ballots, the U.S. does not participate in true online voting to any significant extent. Moreover, due to the current political climate in the U.S., it is unlikely that the U.S. will embrace online voting in the foreseeable future. In particular, voting access issues have become a significant political dispute over the last two decades and the two primary political parties are significantly at odds with respect to any changes to existing voting systems (primarily in-person or mail-in voting). Accordingly, it is unlikely that any legislation establishing a significant online voting mechanism will be forthcoming in the short term.

Chapter 4. Other e-Government Services

99. As discussed above, the U.S. does not have a significant system for online public services. Federal and state governments do have online portals that provide various specific services such as enrollment in public benefits, occupational or other licensing, and tax collection. However, these services are primarily augmentative to the existing in-person provision of these services. With the lack of an overarching framework for e-government services in the U.S., these specific services lack any tie to a comprehensive scheme of e-governance.

Part III. Online Transactions

Chapter 1. Electronic Contracting

§1. Hardware Contracts

100. U.S. contract law is predominately common law, it is not statutory in nature. Derived from judicial precedents and developing by accretion, early American contract law evolved from English property law, specifically real property law. Today, the law of contracts in the U.S. is largely a creature of state law and varies from state to state. A handful of federal statutes affect specific areas or industries as they relate to contract law.

Perhaps the most important and impactful effort to standardize contract law among the states deals with the law governing transactions involving the sale of goods. Through widespread adoption of the Uniform Commercial Code (UCC) at the state level,[78] contracts that involve the sale of goods have become standardized nationwide. The UCC represents the primary legal authority for the sale of goods in the U.S. As a result, it has largely fulfilled its purpose to make uniform, clarify, and modernize previously disparate state law as it deals with commercial transactions. Secondary benefits include predictability and stability and increased efficiency in the marketplace.

As a result of widespread adoption of the UCC across the U.S., contracts involving the sale of goods, including hardware contracts, are largely standardized. In particular, several implied warranties attend contracts for the sale of hardware in the U.S. Implied warranties, are not textually explicit, meaning the warranties exist even though they have not been expressly memorialized. A commercial seller does not have to inform the buyer or promise to the buyer that the product is guaranteed to work for its mutually intended purpose because the law itself implies or creates that warranty.

The implied warranty of merchantability is justified by the seller's superior bargaining position in certain contexts.[79] Because the seller is often in a better position to know how the product performs and whether it will work properly in any given context, the implied warranty of merchantability incentivizes sellers to ensure the quality of their product before taking it to market. Notably, the implied warranty of merchantability applies only to goods, not services. As discussed below, U.S. courts are mixed regarding whether the sale of software is the sale of a good or service. If

78. UCC § 1-103 (2001).
79. *See* UCC § 2-314.

software is deemed a good, the implied warranty represents a legally enforceable promise that the software meets the standards of performance expected by parties to the transaction.

Another implied contractual obligation may attend a contract for ICT hardware. The implied duty of good faith and fair dealing requires that neither party will do anything that will destroy or injure the right of the other party to receive the benefits of the contract. This doctrine is more amorphous and courts often exercise significant discretion when determining its reach and scope. Courts often address this implied obligation on a case-by-case basis, analyzing the facts to determine what is fair under the circumstances.

Importantly, the UCC allows sellers to disclaim any express and implied warranty.[80] Disclaimers must be specific and conspicuous. The law varies from state to state regarding the language and format required for such disclaimers.

§2. Software Contracts

I. General

101. As noted above, U.S. contract law is predominately common law and it is largely governed by each state within the U.S., rather than by the federal government. Having fifty states with fifty different laws relating to contract formation, contract interpretation, contractual presumptions, contractual breach, and contract enforcement creates sizable inefficiencies, which are exacerbated as traditional boundaries subside in the era of globalization. National and global supply chains and online goods and services often include scores of different states and foreign nationalities.

The UCC, is a comprehensive set of laws that address the legal dimensions of commercial transactions in the United States.[81] It is not a federal law, but a proposed legal framework for commercial transactions. Nearly every state has adopted large sections of the UCC, resulting in a much more harmonized legal landscape that facilitates interstate business transactions. While the UCC is the most important legal guide for software contracts in the U.S., a few discrete and specific federal statutes also impact software contracting in certain circumstances. Importantly, contracting parties are entitled to and often do specify the applicable state law that is to govern enforcement of the contract itself.

With regard to court interpretation of contracts when a dispute over the contract arises, modern courts will sometimes consider evidence and entertain presumptions that are not included within the four corners of the contract itself. For example, several promises will be implied by law as included in the contract, even if those promises are not actually written into the contract. Implied promises typically require the parties to act in "good faith" and to deliver products that meet a minimum quality standard. A commercial seller does not have to inform the buyer or promise to the buyer that the product is guaranteed to work for its mutually intended purpose

80. UCC § 2-316.
81. UCC § 1-103 (2001).

because the law itself implies or creates that warranty. Moreover, ambiguous contract language will be interpreted against the party that drafted the contract, particularly with regard to insurance contracts.

More often than not, for an unexpressed term may be implied, the implication must arise from the central purpose of the agreement in order to effectuate the intention of the parties, or it must be clear that the implied term was within the contemplation of the parties that they deemed it unnecessary to express or state it. In other words, an unexpressed provision will not be implied by a reviewing court just because the reviewing court believes the term should reasonably have been included in the written agreement. Material contractual terms are not typically left to implication. Finally, U.S. courts are ordinarily powerless to imply a term or provision that is against the express terms of the contract.

II. Federal Statutes

102. The law of contracts varies from state to state, with each state's common law often providing the relevant legal boundaries. Even so, contracts involving the sale of goods are largely standardized in the U.S. due to widespread adoption of the UCC. As a result, nationwide federal contract law is largely confined to discrete statutory schemes. Federal statutes that impact contract law generally, include the following:

- Wall Street Reform and Consumer Protection Act 2010.
- Fair Debt Collection Practices Act.
- Fair Credit Billing Act.
- Gramm-Leach-Bliley Act.
- Fair Credit Reporting Act.
- Truth in Lending Act.

III. Implied Contractual Obligations

A. *Duty of Good Faith and Fair Dealing*

103. The implied duty of good faith and fair dealing has been around as long as the U.S. It represents a general presumption that the parties to a contract will deal with each other honestly, fairly, and in good faith. Parties to a contract will not act so as to not destroy the right of the other party or parties to receive the benefits of the contract. Notably every contract contains an implied duty of good faith and fair dealing in the performance and enforcement of the contract. The New York Court of Appeals memorialized these precepts, stating: "In every contract there is an implied covenant that neither party shall do anything, which will have the effect of destroying or injuring the right of the other party, to receive the fruits of the contract. In other words, every contract has an implied covenant of good faith and fair dealing."[82]

Many organizations in the ICT industries in the U.S. are insufficiently apprised on their obligation to refrain from interfering with or failing to cooperate in a contracting party's performance. Such organizations overlook these obligations because their contracts do not explicitly require them to cooperate or explicitly state that they must not interfere with their contracting partner's performance under the contract.

Importantly, there is no specific definition of this duty outside of the general concept itself. Courts have discretion to determine its scope and courts often address this implied obligation on a case-by-case basis, analyzing the facts to determine what is fair under the circumstances. Even so, a majority of court decisions indicate that "good faith" amounts to honesty in a party's conduct during and under the agreement. "Fair dealing," by contrast, extends beyond honesty by requiring that a contracting party may not act in a way that is contrary to the "spirit" of the contract. A spate of cases from across the U.S. interpret these implied obligations in varying contexts.

The *Restatement of Contracts* is an aggregation of law across the U.S. that groups court decisions by subject matter and proposes general legal precepts based on a majority of those decisions. It often represents the majority law across U.S. jurisdictions. With regard to the implied duty of good faith and fair dealing. The Restatement (Second) of Contracts states:

> [B]ad faith may be overt or may consist of inaction, and fair dealing may require more than honesty. A complete catalogue of types of bad faith is impossible, but the following types are among those which have been recognized in judicial decisions: evasion of the spirit of the bargain, lack of diligence and slacking off, willful rendering of imperfect performance, abuse of a power to specify terms, and interference with or failure to cooperate in the other party's performance.[83]

The U.S. Supreme Court has held that the duty of good faith and fair dealing attaches to every contract unless it is expressly excluded.[84] The obligation is rarely excluded from government contracts and some states forbid parties from excluding it in certain contexts. While the obligation is often difficult to expressly exclude, it only applies to the party's reasonable expectations under the contract and does not extend to contract negotiation.

In the recent case, *Northern District of California, Weeks v. Google LLC*,[85] plaintiffs alleged that Google's Pixel phones were defective. Although the contract included an express warranty regarding the quality of the phones, Google reserved the right to either repair, refund, or replace defective phones at Google's discretion.

---

82. Kirke La Shelle Company v. The Paul Armstrong Company et al. 188 N.E. 163 (N.Y. App. 1933).
83. *See* Restatement (Second) of Contracts § 205, cmt d.
84. *See* Northwest, Inc. v. Ginsberg, 134 S. Ct. 1422 (2014).
85. Case No. 18-cv-00801 NC (N.D. Cal. Aug. 16, 2018).

Google chose to replace the allegedly defective phones, but plaintiffs refused the offer, claiming that Google was merely replacing defective phones with more defective phones, and that Google would continue to do so until the warranty expired. Reading the contract terms objectively, the court agreed with Google that the warranty language gave Google the right to respond exactly as it had:

> The Court understands plaintiffs' outrage at Google's being able to replace a defective Pixel with another defective Pixel for 365 days straight. . . . It beggars reason and would appear to make hash of the spirit of the warranty. But the warranty provided a remedy, and as far as the Court can tell, Google abided by its remedy. . . . The question of whether it was valid under the express warranty to replace a defective Pixel with another defective Pixel must be answered in the affirmative based on a plain reading of the Limited Warranty.[86]

The court, however, looked beyond the express language of the contract. Turning to the implied warranty of good faith and fair dealing, the court found that Google's conduct frustrated the central purpose of the contract. The court stated that the implied obligation of good faith and fair dealing precluded dismissal of the claimant's breach of warranty allegations.

B. *Implied Warranty of Merchantability*

104. The implied obligation of merchantability guarantees that a product sold by a merchant will work when used for its intended purposes. Under this implied warranty, the goods must reasonably conform to a typical buyer's expectations. The law justifies this added obligation imposed by the law on the idea that the seller is in a better position to know whether the seller's product will perform as anticipated under the contract. The implied obligation encourages sellers to ensure the quality of their products before taking them to market. Like the previous section, the warranty of merchantability is implied. It does not need to be expressly memorialized in the contract itself. While it can be expressly disclaimed by name, there are several states that disallow such disclaimers in certain contexts. For example, in the state of Massachusetts, it is illegal to disclaim this warranty on household goods sold to consumers.

Perhaps the most important and impactful effort to standardize contract law among the fifty states in the U.S. deals with the law governing transactions involving the sale of goods. Through widespread adoption of the UCC,[87] contracts that involve the sale of goods have become standardized nationwide. The UCC represents the primary legal authority for the sale of goods in the U.S. The UCC memorializes the implied warranty of merchantability.

UCC § 2-314. Implied Warranty: Merchantability; Usage of Trade.

---

86. *Id.*
87. UCC. § 1-103 (2001).

(1) Unless excluded or modified (section 2-316), a warranty that the goods shall be merchantable is implied in a contract for their sale if the seller is a merchant with respect to goods of that kind.
(2) Goods to be merchantable must be at least such as
  (a) pass without objection in the trade under the contract description; and
  (b) in the case of fungible goods, are of fair average quality within the description; and
  (c) are fit for the ordinary purposes for which such goods are used; and
  (d) run, within the variations permitted by the agreement, of even kind, quality, and quantity within each unit and among all units involved; and
  (e) are adequately contained, packaged, and labeled as the agreement may require; and
  (f) conform to the promise or affirmations of fact made on the container or label if any.[88]

Notably, this implied obligation applies only to goods, not services. As discussed below, U.S. courts are mixed regarding whether the sale of software is the sale of a good or service. If software is deemed a good, this implied warranty, as its name suggests, requires that the software meets the standards of performance expected by merchants in the trade. To some degree, this implied warranty turns on industry standards and practice.

Software sellers often disclaim or attempt to disclaim the implied warranty of merchantability. Software merchants disclaim the warranty because they argue that there is no standardized understanding for basic software functionality or quality. Software eludes a normative industry standard or practice or custom within the software trade. The dynamic nature of the software industry, where software is often customized and unique, make industry comparison difficult and therefore ill-suited to the implied warranty of merchantability. Because the repercussions of such a warranty are uncertain, software merchants increasingly seek to disclaim its application.

C. *Duty to Perform in a Workmanlike Manner*

105. If a software contract is characterized as a service, rather than as a good, U.S. law implies a duty upon contracting parties to use reasonable skill and capability in fulfilling their contractual obligations. It is an implied obligation that each party will fulfill their obligations with skill, due care, and faithfulness. Specifically, there is implied in every contract for work, service, or repair, a duty to perform skillfully, carefully, diligently, and in a workmanlike manner. Moreover, if a party to the contract for a service furnishes its own machinery or tools, the contract carries an implied provision that the tools are fit for the use anticipated by the contract. While the law differs from state to state, most states have ruled that the obligation to perform contracted work in a good and workman like manner cannot be waived. Most

88. UCC. § 2-314 (2001).

courts, however, that have so ruled, have done so in the context of construction work and particularly residential or home construction. It remains unclear whether the implied obligation may be waived in other contexts, like a contract to create and develop customized software.

D. Disclaimer of Implied Warranties

106. As noted above, sellers of software often seek to disclaim warranties that are implied by law. The UCC allows sellers to disclaim some implied warranties. As a result, software sellers increasingly provide a limited express warranty that promises a particular quality of performance for a particular application or in line with an identified industry standard while disclaiming all other warranties. If a software producer or seller seeks to disclaim implied warranties, however, such disclaimers must be specific and conspicuous. Many states sanction particular language as sufficient to adequately disclaim implied warranties. If the UCC applies to a transaction, the disclaimer must say that the goods are sold "as is" or "with all faults:"

(1) Words or conduct relevant to the creation of an express warranty and words or conduct tending to negate or limit warranty shall be construed wherever reasonable as consistent with each other; but subject to the provisions of this Article on parol or extrinsic evidence (section 2-202) negation or limitation is inoperative to the extent that such construction is unreasonable.
(2) Subject to subsection (3), to exclude or modify the implied warranty of merchantability or any part of it the language must mention merchantability and in case of a writing must be conspicuous, and to exclude or modify any implied warranty of fitness the exclusion must be by a writing and conspicuous. Language to exclude all implied warranties of fitness is sufficient if it states, for example, that "There are no warranties which extend beyond the description on the face hereof."
(3) Notwithstanding subsection (2):
    (a) unless the circumstances indicate otherwise, all implied warranties are excluded by expressions like "as is,' "with all faults" or other language which in common understanding calls the buyer's attention to the exclusion of warranties and makes plain that there is no implied warranty; and
    (b) when the buyer before entering into the contract has examined the goods or the sample or model as fully as he desired or has refused to examine the goods there is no implied warranty with regard to defects which an examination ought in the circumstances to have revealed to him; and
    (c) an implied warranty can also be excluded or modified by course of dealing or course of performance or usage of trade.[89]

---

89. UCC § 2-316. Exclusion of Modification of Warranties.

IV. Interpreting Software Contracts

107. Emerging technology has generated novel disputes that fall outside traditional judicial precedent. The law, as a result, is unsettled. More and more physical products are valuable for sale in the market because of the software that animates them. Without the software, the physical products themselves lack distinction. “Smart” lightbulbs, doorbells, ovens, and kettles, for example, are distinctive because of the embedded software that enables ordinary objects to communicate digitally through the Internet, apps or other media.

Indeed, software drives an array of products, including products that have the capacity to cause physical injury to users and third parties. Self-driving vehicles, for example, are proliferating, as are robotic mechanisms in the workplace. Software design is often an integral component of both ordinary household objects and more specialized technologies, like artificial intelligence.

The lack of clarity in the UCC on whether and how the UCC applies to software sales undermines the UCC objective of providing uniformity and consistency to the commercial sale of goods. Not only is software resistant to classification as either a good or a service, it is often embedded within a larger good or service. The case law reflects this uncertainty. The threshold question, whether the UCC applies at all, turns on whether software sales are sales of goods.

Some U.S. courts address this issue by asking what the “predominant purpose” of the sale is? Even within those states and jurisdictions that have adopted the predominant purpose test, courts often employ different factors to assess whether the predominant purpose of the transaction is for the provision of goods or services. While some states have concluded that software transactions are a sale of goods, others have reached the opposite conclusion. In 2016, a district court in North Carolina addressed this issue and summarized the fragmented status of the law:

> The applicability of the Uniform Commercial Code to software is a question that has confounded courts in the digital age. For every court that finds that the weight of authority favors application of common law and not the UCC with regard to software licenses, another finds that courts nationally have consistently classified the sale of a software package as the sale of a good for UCC purposes.[90]

Even so, some trends are emerging. For example, U.S. courts tend to characterize software as a “good” when a contractual transaction involves prepackaged software. This is the case even if there are service modifications or implementation services facilitating the transaction. Conversely, courts tend to characterize software-as-a-service when the contractual transaction calls for the design of software for a particularized purpose or when the software is designed from top to bottom for the transaction. As the gravamen of such transactions is service-oriented, the transaction will typically not be characterized as a good.

---

90. SAS Inst., Inc. v. World Programming Ltd., No. 5:10-25-FL, 2016 WL 3435196, at *10 (E.D.N.C. June 17, 2016).

Even if a software transaction is characterized as a good rather than a service, the transaction may also include ancillary obligations, like software implementation, support services, and maintenance services. The UCC, somewhat surprisingly, foments rather than allays this legal ambiguity. The lack of clarity in determining whether a contractual transaction is one for goods or services affects both consumer and nonconsumers alike. Rather than achieving uniformity and simplicity, the UCC has amplified risk and inefficiency in complex software contracting.

V. Software Contracts and the Internet of Things

108. The impact of this ambiguity under the UCC increases with the proliferation of the Internet of Things (IoT). The IoT imbues formerly static and ordinary objects with enhanced digital capabilities that are often facilitated by connection to the Internet. A garage door, teapot, doorbell, and sprinkler system, while formerly inert, are more and more outfitted with software that communicates to the user through the Internet. These products also collect and report usage information to the manufacturers and sellers of the products, including location, consumption, and usage data.

As a result, manufacturers or sellers of such IoT devices engage in contracts that involve goods, services, and software at one time. A Google Nest transaction, for example, includes hardware, software, services that allow the user to record and collect video in the cloud, applications to smartphones, and the company's own recordation and analyzation of the data collected from within the user's home. Indeed, almost any home-based object or good can be retrofitted with software that connects use of that object to cloud computing services and/or the Internet and user applications. Internet of Things devices typically license their software in a way that attempts to disclaim all liability. To avoid the application of UCC Article 2, sellers of Internet of Things devices separate the services and software from the sale of the device by providing different agreements that govern the device's hardware, software, and services.

Again, Google's Nest software provides a salient example. The Nest software license includes a restrictive End-User License Agreement (EULA) that purports to disclaim all liabilities for any Nest failures. Purchasers and users must acknowledge that they will not rely on the product for "life-safety and critical uses," even though the smart smoke detector and smart security camera are designed for those very purposes. More often than not the EULAs that attend Internet of Things devices are nonnegotiable. More and more commonly, EULAs disclaim any liability and warranties, give the user no option to negotiate the contracts' terms, and will essentially nullify devices if the user does not agree to them.

§3. Turnkey Contracts

109. Generally speaking, a turnkey contract is an agreement wherein the supplier assumes final responsibility to the user for the product performing as agreed upon by a certain time. The legal responsibility for the design, installation, and performance of the product after completion rests with the supplier. A turnkey contract for purchase and installation of a computer system, for example, might include hardware, operating systems, and applications designed to perform discrete pre-identified tasks for the user. The word refers to the proposition that the user needs only turnkey in order to properly use the product.

Turnkey contracts are not uncommon in the U.S. Traditional contract law for the supply of hardware and software, as articulated above, applies equally to turnkey contracts. Often small businesses will pay for a turnkey contract, which may include a personal computer with accompanying operating system, traditional applications programs, a monitor, a printer of some ilk, and appropriate cables. A more sophisticated turnkey contract may include a minicomputer, color monitors, graphics board, intelligent terminals, several printers, and modified applications programs.

Under the terms of the contract, the supplier maintains liability for the proper functioning of the product. Determining when an inadequacy or breach occurs can be problematic under such contracts. Often, it takes time to determine whether the product or system functions according to the contractual specifications. That determination requires the product or system to be in use for a period of time using actual data. As a result, parties to such contracts should include terms regarding timelines for testing and use.

Of note, buyers in a turnkey contract may have little legal recourse against third-party providers of components included within the product or system. In *Johnson v. Microsoft Corp.*, the plaintiff purchased a personal computer with a preinstalled operating system. That preinstalled operating system was previously sold by a software manufacturer to the computer manufacturer. Because the plaintiff was only an indirect purchaser of the operating system, the court held that the plaintiff did not directly confer an economic benefit on the software manufacturer, and thus, the plaintiff could not bring common law claims against the software manufacturer for restitution or unjust enrichment.[91]

Finally, because turnkey products in the ICT sector often combine hardware, software, and service maintenance, the question remains whether Article 2 of the UCC applies. While trend may be toward finding turnkey and software systems to be "goods" under UCC, they are still considered intangible by some authorities, particularly when the contract calls for installation and continued maintenance post installation. Attempts to exclude software and maintenance in a turnkey contract from UCC coverage will be strictly construed by the courts.[92]

§4. Distribution Agreements

110. A distribution agreement is a legal contract between a supplier or manufacturer of goods and a distributor of goods. The contract or legal agreement usually includes the effective time period for performance, terms and conditions of supply, terms and conditions of the distributor's sales territory, and whether the agreement

91. 834 N.E.2d 791 (Ohio 2005).
92. *See* U.S.M Corp. v. First State Ins. Co., 641 NE2d 115 (Mass. 1994).

is exclusive or nonexclusive. In an exclusive agreement, the distributor named in the contract will be the only distributor with the right to sell the supplier's product within a particular geographic region or within multiple regions. A nonexclusive agreement, by contrast, allows the supplier to supply other distributors, sometimes competing in the same market. Distribution agreements often incorporate terms and conditions of supply, including the delivery of goods, the transfer of risk in and title to the goods, returns, inspection requirements, and related processes.

Distribution contracts are not uncommon in the U.S. Traditional contract law for the supply of hardware and software, as articulated above, applies equally to distribution contracts. Distribution agreements, especially exclusive distribution agreements, can implicate anti-competition law, and parties must be aware of antitrust restrictions.[93] Topics to address when drafting a distribution contract include:

- exclusivity or non-exclusivity (with an eye on competition law);
- applicable terms and conditions of sale;
- minimum performance obligations;
- the territorial scope of the agreement;
- distributor reporting obligations;
- trademark licensing (especially with software distribution);
- noncompete obligations (with an eye on competition law);
- circumstances in which the agreement may be terminated.

Discrete legal issues may arise with regard to distribution contracts that include dissemination of software, particularly when the software is sold to end users by electronic or digital means. Due to the ease of software duplication and transmission, and due to the difficulty of enforcing copyright law stemming from the fluid and transnational Internet architecture, a distribution agreement might require distributors to incorporate licensing requirements in sales agreements of software to end users. Likewise, distribution contracts dealing with software that is sold digitally or electronically may struggle with the territorial scope of the agreement in light of fluid and transnational nature of Internet transactions. The largest electronics and IT distributors have robust international sales, and include, Ingram Micro, Arrow Electronics, Avnet and Tech Data. These companies, among others, operate subsidiaries in several countries over a wide geographical span.

§5. Maintenance Contracts

111. Maintenance contracts are governed by traditional U.S. contract law, which is largely governed by state common law, as discussed above. The UCC serves to harmonize much of the law from state to state, as most states have adopted many of the most influential portions of the UCC. The UCC and each state begin with the fundamental recognition that individuals and entities may enter into binding contracts that will be enforced by the courts according to the contract's terms. Maintenance contracts are no different. Discrete issues that attend the ICT sector and

93. *Supra*, Part I, Ch. 2, s. 1.

maintenance contracts include copyright concerns regarding software, performance criteria, and warranties. With regard to ICT hardware, the contract should specify the items purchased and the scope of maintenance expected by the purchaser, including preventative and routine maintenance, if applicable. There will often be a need to replace defective parts or components that have worn down with use.

With regard to software maintenance contracts, additional provisions merit inclusion in the maintenance contract. Software maintenance agreements diverge from more traditional maintenance of hardware and machines. Internal bugs frequently emerge after software sale and implementation. Similarly security updates require continuous monitoring. Finally, some software is custom-made and requires ongoing modification to fit the buyer's needs.

The maintenance contract should define the types of problems covered by the agreement. The contract should specify the seller's obligations, if any, to identify and address defects that emerge from other user's applications of the program. Often maintenance contracts include such services even absent an explicit demand for such services from the contracting purchaser. Some U.S. courts have concluded that such an obligation may be included within a contract to provide upgrades, as opposed to strict maintenance. Because upgrade agreements are often limited to each transaction, no body of law determines the scope of coverage. Even so, there are several factors that courts consider, including customs and practices that distinguish between vendor problems in multivendor systems, how to identify user-caused problems, the effect of user modifications, and copyright ownership. A fairly typical provision protecting the supplier's copyright might resemble the following:

> All error corrections, enhancements, new releases, and any other work product created by the SUPPLIER creator(s) in connection with the support services provided under this Maintenance Agreement are and shall remain the exclusive property of the SUPPLIER or the SUPPLIER creator(s), regardless of whether the PURCHASER, its employees, or agents may have contributed to the conception, joined in its development, or paid the SUPPLIER for the development or use of the Work Product. Such Work Product shall be considered SOFTWARE, and subject to the terms and conditions contained herein and in the License Agreement.[94]

Another issue increasingly common to software maintenance contracts deals with the buyer's obligation to pay for maintenance services when the overall software implementation project has failed or underperformed. What are the relative legal obligations when a technological project fails, and a critical part of the transaction includes maintenance services relating to the underlying software? Is the buyer's payment obligation contingent on a successful launch of the larger project? To a large degree, the unambiguous terms of the contract will control, and careful contract construction will address such possibilities. For example, multi-phased projects

94. *See* e.g., Richard Grefé, *Standard Form of Agreement for Design Services*, AIGA (2013), https://www.aiga.org/globalassets/aiga/content/tools-and-resources/46874510-standard-form-of-agreement-for-design-services.pdf.

often include a maintenance obligation that begins on a fixed date. If the project itself is delayed, the maintenance term begins when there is no software to maintain.

Perhaps counterintuitively, IT maintenance contracts regularly include unequivocal payment obligations. Under such contracts, the buyer is contractually obligated to pay even though material changes in circumstances render the service irrelevant. U.S. courts typically enforce these payment obligations, and the common practice in the IT industry acknowledges this risk with regard to maintenance contracts. This perhaps reflects the fast-paced evolution of IT products and services.[95] Again, this practice is arguably justified based on business practicalities. Providers often dedicate staff and other resources to technology projects in advance, incurring opportunity costs and other costs. Of course, courts will not always enforce such unequivocal payment obligations regardless of rationale. In *Integrated Title Data Sys. v. Delanney*, a Texas Court of Appeals held that the original delivered product was so defective that it could not be used. As a result, the obligation to upgrade software or enhancement services had no value or benefit and was therefore not enforceable.[96]

Uncertainty regarding enforceability of maintenance contracts has resulted in clear organizational inefficiencies. A 2018 study conducted by Campaign for Clear Licensing that found that the most commercial entities contacted by the study demonstrated a tendency to automatically renew software maintenance contracts without critically examining the utility therefore. The Campaign for Clear Licensing study suggested that such entities renewed software maintenance contracts regardless of evidence to suggest that the contract provided any value. "Software maintenance renewals are being renewed without sufficient information to make an informed decision."[97] On average, buyers of technology software pay around 20% of the license fee per year in support and maintenance, which effectively means organizations will have paid for their software twice after a five-year term.[98] Indeed, the research seems to suggest that the software maintenance contracts effectively operate as an insurance contract, when in reality it is a completely different entity.

Uncertainty regarding access to the legality of business entities' access to security patches and updates drove demand to retain software maintenance contracts unnecessarily. Termination of ongoing service contracts also carries risk, especially if the underlying contract is not specific with regard to termination. Penalties and backdating maintenance also drive businesses to retain maintenance contracts.

The Campaign for Clear Licensing study showed there was also confusion among businesses over whether they could terminate a software maintenance contract, and if it was possible to then continue support at a later date. The fear of penalties and so-called back maintenance is also a concern for organizations renewing support maintenance agreements, according to Campaign for Clear Licensing. For example,

---

95. *See* ABA, *The Tech Contracts Handbook: Cloud Computing Agreements, Software Licenses, and Other IT Contracts for Lawyers and Businesspeople* (2nd ed. 2015).
96. Integrated Title Data Sys. v. Dulaney, 800 S.W.2d 336 (Tex. App. 1990).
97. Martin Thompson, *$250BN Annual Software Maintenance Market Needs More Scrutiny, a Strategic Opportunity for ITAM*, Software & Maintenance Survey (Sept. 2018), http://clearlicensing.org/wp-content/uploads/2018/09/CCL-Software-and-Maintenance-Report-FINAL-10.09.2018.pdf.
98. *Id.*

"Oracle will charge 150% of the support contract, backdated to the original support lapse or product purchase date. A genuine financial alternative is to drop support and maintenance and buy the product again later when new updates are available, or support is actually needed, but lack of legal clarity often prevents this route."[99]

Again, contracting inefficiencies and liability can usually be avoided by careful and explicit contract drafting. U.S. courts have been largely faithful to the proposition that clear and unambiguous terms will be enforced according to their plain meaning.[100]

§6. Facilities Management

112. A facility management contract typically involves a client, often a company or government agency and a facilities management company, often a company specializing in technology installation, customization, and operation. A client's principal business may be marketing, manufacturing, transportation, or some government operation. The facilities management company will almost always be a company whose dominant purpose is development, implementation and operation of computer or other technology systems.

Facilities management transactions seek to operate and house technology and computer operations on behalf of a client. This service can occur off campus of the client or be integrated into the client's organization structurally. Long-term facilities management transactions frequently entail the facilities management company assuming ownership of the client organization's computing hardware, data processing employees, and other IT components.

Facilities management transactions shift responsibility from the client to a third party for computer operations, implementing new software programs, and the maintenance of those operations and programs. Often, multinational companies will leverage such contracts for work conducted in another country. Similarly, outsourcing agreements are a subset of facilities management contracts. The Internet makes it more efficient for companies to leverage workers and services from a diverse geographic spectrum. Software support personnel in India and Eastern European block countries, for example, perform cost-effective services for projects located in the U.S. and all over the world. Outsourcing, while economically beneficial to the parent company, is legally complex.

Companies that deal in IT face particular obstacles if outsourcing suppliers fail to meet domestic and/or international standards. For example, Apple, Inc. now audits their suppliers to ensure compliance with security, data, and environmental standards.

Facilities management contracts are not uncommon in the U.S., particularly with government agencies that contract with private entities for technical services. Traditional contract law for the supply of hardware and software, as articulated above,

99. *See* e.g., Cliff Saran, *Software Maintenance Contracts Lack Scrutiny*, ComputerWeekly (Sept. 10, 2018, 1:56 AM), https://www.computerweekly.com/news/252448375/Software-maintenance-contracts-lack-scrutiny.

100. *See e.g.*, Wiser v. Enervest Operating, L.L.C., 803 F.Supp.2d 109 N.D.N.Y. (2011).

applies equally to facilities management contracts. Facility management providers that contract with federal agencies for services that include sensitive IT must comply with cybersecurity regulations. Federal Regulation 39.101(d) states:

(a) In acquiring information technology, agencies shall identify their requirements pursuant to:

  (i) OMB Circular A-130, including consideration of security of resources, protection of privacy, national security and emergency preparedness, accommodations for individuals with disabilities, and energy efficiency;

  ***

(c) In acquiring information technology, agencies shall include the appropriate information technology security policies and requirements, including use of common security configurations available from the National Institute of Standards and Technology's website at http://checklists.nist.gov. Agency contracting officers should consult with the requiring official to ensure the appropriate standards are incorporated.

(d) When acquiring information technology using Internet Protocol, agencies must include the appropriate Internet Protocol compliance requirements in accordance with 11.002(g).[101]

These regulations require appropriate IT security policies when government agencies contract with third parties for IT. In particular, security policies must conform to the common security configurations promulgated by NIST. The CFR, includes the NIST checklist from the NIST website at http://checklists.nist.gov.[102] The NIST National Checklist Program Repository for IT Products is a "security configuration checklist ... [that identifies] a series of instructions for configuring a product to a particular operational environment."[103] The central goal of the checklist is to reduce exposure through software and increase product security through a regimented and uniform vetting process. Although the checklist generates some consistency and uniformity across many governmental agencies, each governmental agency can customize its checklist in conformity with its particular IT needs.

The checklist requirements are not without detractors, however. Many mid-level government managers lack the requisite expertise to identify, design, and comply with the proper security protocols that the checklist is meant to facilitate. In fact the NIST, itself, acknowledges that compliance with the checklist requires a high degree of expertise. "It is a complicated, arduous, and time-consuming task even for experienced system administrators to know what a reasonable set of security settings is for many different IT products."[104] Nevertheless, the checklist is considered critical, particularly as larger and integrated systems generate increased exposure and vulnerability to hacking and related threats.

---

101. 48 CFR § 39.101.
102. 48 CFR § 39.101(c).
103. *Id.*
104. *See* FAQ for General Users: National Checklist Program, NIST, https://nvd.nist.gov/ncp/faq (last visited Feb. 10, 2020).

When security protocols are intertwined in a larger software facilities management transaction with the U.S. government, federal regulations require specific contracting formalities. For integrated IT purchases, federal regulations require federal contracting agent to "insert a clause substantially the same as the clause at 52.239-1, Privacy or Security Safeguards, in [IT] solicitations and contracts ... which require security of IT, and/or are for the design, development, or operation of a system of records using commercial IT services or support services."[105] Oddly, the U.S. government promulgated the relevant privacy and security safeguards in 1996, before the U.S. government, itself, relied on IT services and acquisitions. As amended in 1997, and 2014, the pertinent regulation provides:

(a) The contractor shall not publish or disclose in any manner, without the contracting officer's written consent, the details of any safeguards either designed or developed by the contractor under this contract or otherwise provided by the government.
(b) To the extent required to carry out a program of inspection to safeguard against threats and hazards to the security, integrity, and confidentiality of government data, the contractor shall afford the government access to the contractor's facilities, installations, technical capabilities, operations, documentation, records, and databases.
(c) If new or unanticipated threats or hazards are discovered by either the government or the contractor, or if existing safeguards have ceased to function, the discoverer shall immediately bring the situation to the attention of the other party.[106]

In light of increasing threats stemming from malware, Trojan horses, and other such vulnerabilities, government purchases of IT products include a reporting requirement. In other words, subsection (c) above, requires parties to notify each other upon discovery of unanticipated threats or hazards. Although there are not yet reported cases in this context, private providers of IT services and facilities management services to the U.S. government may face liability under this section for failing to report security breaches.

For private and public facilities management contracts, the question of whether the contract provides a "good" or "service," remains important with regard to whether Article 2 of the UCC will govern the transaction. Facilities management contracts often include both goods (hardware) and services (installation, maintenance, and operation). Courts must decide whether the preponderant part of the obligations consists of labor or other services. Often severance provisions in facilities management contracts allow courts to make this distinction while honoring the contract's central purpose. Without severance clauses, the "preponderant part" test has engendered much criticism because it often undermines the primary purpose of the agreement. In other words, the buyer in a facilities management process is typically reliant not only on the new hardware and software, but particularly in the services and expertise required to implement, modify, and apply the IT system generally. In

105. Privacy or Security Safeguards, 48 CFR § 52.239-1 (amended 2014).
106. *Id.*

such instances, the contract sounds in "services" rather than "goods," and a court's articulation otherwise undermines the contracting parties' primary purpose.

§7. NETWORK SERVICES

I. General

113. Facilities management contracts are common in the U.S., and traditional contract law for the supply of hardware and software, as articulated above, applies equally to network services contracts. Network services contracts, or continuous access contracts, give the licensee a contractual right to access IT or network services on a subscription or membership basis. Such network services agreements often limit access by time period or discrete project. Online services agreements, in particular, operate on a subscription or membership basis.

Network services agreements can be viewed as a contemporary application of a more traditional license to use resources. A buyer or transferee not only gains access or data, but also purchases accessibility to the resource on a continuing, contractual basis. Notably, Article 2 of the UCC distinguishes transactions that involve installment contracts. Installment contract law under the UCC and the cases interpreting UCC provisions are materially different from network services access agreements. Installment contracts are typically segmented agreements that amount to multiple offer and acceptance sequences. By contrast, continuing access contracts, requires a licensor to make a system available for the licensee when it chooses within the agreed times for access. Perhaps a closer legal analogue to network access service agreements is represented as an "interactive service provider" under the Communications Decency Act:

> [A]ny information service, system, or access software provider that provides or enables computer access by multiple users to a computer server, including specifically a service or system that provides access to the Internet and such systems operated or services offered by libraries or educational institutions.[107]

As opposed to more generalized installment contracts, definitions like the one above from the Communications Decency Act turns on access to information or information processing systems. The core of the transaction focuses on such access. Of course, some transactions offer more than mere access. In those instances, however, the additional components – like hardware and selected software – are ancillary to the predominant purpose, which is access. As a result, most courts in the U.S. characterize an access contract as a service contract, even if the arrangement leads to the purchase of goods from the licensor.

The Uniform Computer Information Transactions Act (UCITA) is a "model law" and attempts to unify state law, operating as a guideline to state law makers. Notably, UCITA specifically applies to "access contracts."[108] UCITA is a proposed law

107. Communications Decency Act, 47U.S.C.A. § 230(f)(2).
108. *See UCITA Online Homepage*, http://www.ucitaonline.com/ (last visited Feb. 10, 2020).

to create a clear and uniform set of rules to govern such areas as software licensing, online access, and other transactions in computer information. It is intended to bring the same uniformity and certainty to the rules that apply to IT transactions that the UCC does for the sale of goods. As a model law, it is up to individual states to either adopt in whole or part the law itself. In states that have not adopted relevant UCITA provisions, state common law applies. The relevant portions of UCITA follow:

> (a) If an access contract provides for access over time, the licensee's rights of access are to the information as modified and made commercially available by the licensor from time to time during that period. In addition, the following rules apply:
> (1) A change in the content of the information is a breach of contract only if the change conflicts with an express term of the agreement.
> (2) Unless it is subject to a contractual use restriction, information obtained by the licensee is free of any use restriction other than a restriction resulting from the informational rights of another person or other applicable law.
> (3) Access must be available at times and in a manner:
> (A) conforming to the express terms of the agreement; and
> (B) to the extent not expressly stated in the agreement, at times and in a manner that is reasonable for the particular type of contract in light of the ordinary standards of the business, trade, or industry.
>
> (b) In an access contract that gives the licensee a right of access at times substantially of its own choosing during agreed periods, an occasional failure to have access available during those times is not a breach of contract if it is:
> (1) consistent with ordinary standards of the business, trade, or industry for the particular type of contract; or
> (2) caused by: (A) scheduled downtime; (B) reasonable needs for maintenance; 256 1 (C) reasonable periods of equipment, software, or communications failure; or (D) events reasonably beyond the licensor's control, and the licensor exercises such commercially reasonable efforts as the circumstances require.

In a handful of cases courts have held that outsourcing contracts were governed by Article 2 of the UCC when the provider also developed software and/or hardware for the particular contract. But the vast majority of network services contracts regarding use of or access to an online site or service do not implicate Article 2 of the UCC.

By way of illustration, eBay offers access to online auction services, but is itself not a seller of the goods offered at its online auction platform. In *In re Sony Gaming Network and Customer Security Breach Litigation*, the court determined that a contractual agreement between a user and a network provider amounted to a service, rather than a goods transaction. The agreement allowed the user to access and play games – as well as purchase products – through the network console. Even though the network provider transferred the consoles themselves, the predominant purpose was access and the consoles were merely incident to such access. In that case, the court declined to apply Article 2 merchantability warranties to the network services. The principle objective of the transaction was to provide the network services, not the consoles.[109] At its core, the licensor controls the system and information, and the critical obligation requires access to the same.

II. Access

114. Of course, the starting point in determining the scope of the legal obligations owed under a network services contract begins with the contract itself. Terms may vary from the type of access, the duration of access, and the fees associated with access, to say nothing of the expressed products or information the licensee anticipates accessing. Because U.S. courts routinely interpret such transactions as service contracts, perfect performance is not required. Reasonable efforts to make the information available will typically insulate temporary obstacles to access, particularly when those obstacles are not the result of the licensing party's making or negligence.

As noted above, UCITA section 611 provides that in the absence of terms, the proper reference is to the times and manner of availability "reasonable for the particular type of contract in light of the ordinary standards of the business, trade, or industry." As a result, occasional failures to obtain access are likely not breaches, and contracts that identify times and places for discrete access are not breaches. The UCITA proposed uniform law identifies excusable outages:

(A) scheduled downtime;
(B) reasonable needs for maintenance;
(C) reasonable periods of failure of equipment, computer programs, or communications; or
(D) events reasonably beyond the licensor's control, and the licensor exercises such commercially reasonable efforts as the circumstances require.[110]

Although UCITA has not enjoyed widespread adoption through the U.S., these standards are consistent with the industry practice. In other words, the measurement of performance under a network services agreement are often qualitative and therefore require a set of standards that are deemed reasonable by the industry. As with any contractual relationship, the parties are free to expressly identify standards for qualitative evaluation, as with almost any other contract term. Indeed, practitioners should be cognizant of the default contractual provisions as well as the implied contractual obligations discussed in the previous chapters. Default contractual provisions occur when the contract is silent on an important aspect of a transaction. For example, many states require that the obligations burdening an access provider are transferable absent contractual provisions stating otherwise or unless the access provided is uniquely relevant to the original contracting parties.

---

109. In re Sony Gaming Networks and Customer Data Security Breach Litigation, 996 F. Supp. 2d 942, 82 UCC Rep. Serv. 2d 493 (S.D. Cal. 2014), order corrected, 2014 WL 12603117 (S.D. Cal. 2014).
110. Uniform Computer Information Transactions Act § 611.

Another important default rule attends the use of the accessed content. Again, the parties to the agreement traditionally identify and limit the uses a licensee may employ with the accessed content, but if the agreement is silent, the UCITA includes a default rule that benefits the licensee. Content downloaded pursuant to a network agreement is free of any restrictions other than those imposed by other sources of law, like intellectual property law. Although the law remains unsettled on this issue, the U.S. Copyright Office has signaled that mere downloading does not qualify as a first sale of a copy. As a result, a licensee's rights in downloaded content that is itself copyrighted, limits the licensee's use of the material significantly.

In short, parties to the contract can be explicit with regard to any and all of these issues. But in the absence of express contractual terms, U.S. law attempts to balance the provider's interest in installing and operating a system that is ultimately imperfect against the user's investment in a network services product that materially achieves the user's contractual needs. By way of example, occasional blockages or unavailability of content does not typically constitute a material breach of contract.

Again by default, a network services or access contract does not require the licensor to maintain explicit or particular digital information. By default, access is construed to mean the information or other data as it exists at the time of each access attempt. Of course, the central contractual objectives cannot be undermined by a licensor's deletion of critical data or programs, but data may be modified, added, and even deleted without breaching the licensor's obligations. Again, contracting parties can ensure that particular data or programs remain available to the licensee by expressly providing as much in the contract.

III. Network Access and Security

115. Network security has long been and continues to be a critical concern to owners of computer networks as well as users. Unauthorized access to proprietary computer systems often leads to legal liability and economic harm to network operators and owners. Controlling access to such systems is also a principal concern for data security purposes. Access contracts not only apply to public access of the Internet, but also private intranets, which are internal communication networks structured similarly to the public Internet. Intranet networks leverage similar protocols to the Internet and allow company employees to access company data privately while using search engines and applications common to the Internet. Intranets, however, are separate from public access by firewalls and other security mechanisms. Suffice it to say that network access contracts vary and are increasingly cognizant of security threats.

Network services contracts increasingly include provisions that attempt to assign risk and/or liability for security obligations and breaches. A sample security clause included in a network services contract might resemble the following:

> Buyer and its customers are responsible for the security of their own programs and equipment. Neither Buyer nor Seller assumes liability or responsibility for failures or breach of protective measures on the other Party's network, whether

> implied or actual, even in the event that the security measures have been installed or configured by the Party whose network fails or is breached. The Parties are solely responsible for their respective networks, although both Parties must notify the other Party when a security breach involves compromise of the other Party's security.

Breaches in corporate network security resulted in the loss of hundreds of millions of dollars. A study conducted by an IBM affiliate entitled "The annual Cost of a Data Breach Report," analyzed data breach costs reported by 507 organizations and concluded that in 2019, affected U.S. entities on average lost approximately USD 8.19 million.[111] A significant majority of mid to large-sized business organizations report significant attempts and often successful data breaches each year. Access contracts and network services agreements increase vulnerability to hackers and malware.

Increased access also magnifies vulnerability to data theft and eventual intellectual property violations. Although early security breaches stemmed largely from email access, security threats increasingly come from Web browsers and other access points. More and more, companies are restricting access to the Internet by employees when using company computers and other devices. External file sharing and instant-messaging often expose such entities to security threats.

Some particularized security clauses are used in services agreements that involves the use, storage or other processing of personal information, including highly sensitive personal information, by a service provider on behalf of a customer. When drafting or negotiating data security clauses, it is important to consult with an information security or privacy lawyer and tailor the security clause to the particular transaction. Specific areas of consideration include identification and definition of the sensitive data requiring supplemental security, the effect of incorporating the data security clause into the broader services agreement, and the legal ramifications of the security clause as it relates to statutory law, including the Gramm-Leach-Bliley Act, the Health Insurance Portability and Accountability Act, the Health Information Technology for Economic and Clinical Health Act, the Fair Credit Reporting Act and the Children's Online Privacy Protection Act. Of course, if the transaction involves the cross-border sharing of personal information, the laws of the relevant foreign jurisdictions must be reviewed for compliance. For example, the transfer of personal data from the EU to the U.S. and other countries may require the inclusion of standard contractual clauses that further specify how the processing of personal data will be treated.

The National Information Infrastructure Protection Act of 1996 (NIIPA) was enacted by U.S. Congress, in part to extend the scope of existing security statutes that had previously focused on protecting financial organizations and their computer systems. The NIIPA has been broadened beyond financial databases to include

---

111. *See 2019 Cost of a Data Breach Report*, IBM, https://www.ibm.com/security/data-breach?p1=Search&p4=p50370571056&p5=e&cm_mmc=Search_Google-_-1S_1S-_-WW_NA-_-cost%20of%20data%20breach%202019_e&cm_mmca7=71700000061027915&cm_mmca8=kwd-800436491412&cm_mmca9=EAIaIQobChMIo8fcxcyV5wIVEf5kCh2a9QE3EAAYASAAEgKgV_D_BwE&cm_mmca10=405839889777&cm_mmca11=e&gclid=EAIaIQobChMIo8fcxcyV5wIVEf5kCh2a9QE3EAAYASAAEgKgV_D_BwE&gclsrc=aw.ds (last visited Feb. 10, 2020).

protection for all computerized data used in interstate and foreign commerce or communications. In addition, the U.S. Department of Commerce released a broad plan to enhance the security of U.S. data networks, a plan that includes increased funding and network security training. Network security will continue to dampen the market for access transactions, while U.S. Congress and the international community seek to implement strategies that better protect against ongoing and increasingly significant security risks.

§8. Government Contracts

I. General

116. Contracts for federal government procurement usually involve funding appropriated by U.S. Congress or a federal agency for services, goods, real property purchases and leases, and program development. Government contracting and procurement is highly regulated in the U.S. and includes various and diverse legal requirements found throughout much of Titles 10 and 41 of the United States Code for military and civilian procuring agencies, respectively. Title 15 of the United States Code includes numerous provisions regulating federal procurement related to small business contracts, and Titles 31 and 40 include ancillary requirements.

Generally speaking, government contracting shares the basic legal parameters that govern private contracting. The agreement must be lawfully created and include an offer, acceptance, mutuality of understanding, consideration, and legal purpose. From there, however, federal contracting diverges dramatically due to the heavy volume of regulations that restrict the process, manner, and content of procurement contracts. The Fifth Circuit Court of appeals has characterized federal procurement law accordingly: "Government contracting law is complex, technical, esoteric, important, and monumental."[112]

Some commentators liken the federal regulations that apply to federal procurement contracts to the density and complexity of the Internal Revenue Code and the Social Security Act.

In summary, the governing law begins with federal statutes found in the titles identified above. These statutes are further explicated by federal regulation, primarily Title 48 of the CFR s. And finally federal common law applies to fill the gaps. The U.S. federal government is the largest buyer of goods and services in the world, and procurements with federal agencies and the executive branch, particularly the Department of Defense (DOD), make most of these purchases. The Federal Acquisition Regulation (FAR) is the most important legal authority when addressing federal procurement and the executive branch.

Specific statutes also affect the legality of government procurement contracts. The primary statutes governing federal procurement are the Armed Services Procurement Act and the Federal Property and Administrative Services Act, which, respectively, govern the procurements of defense and civilian agencies. The Armed Services Procurement Act (ASPA), as amended, applies to DOD, National Space

112. In re Gary Aircraft Corp., 698 F.2d 775, 779 (5th Cir. 1983).

and Aeronautics Administration and Coast Guard procurements where the agency enters the agreement with funds appropriated by Congress. The Federal Property and Administrative Services Act governs most civilian executive branch agencies, including but not limited to, the GSA, DOJ, and State and Health and Human Services.

A number of even more particularized statutes may also apply, including the Buy American Act, the Contract Work Hours and Safety Standards Act, the Davis-Bacon Act, the Defense Production Act, the Economy Act, the Federal Activities Inventory Reform Act, the Small Business Act, and the Truth in Negotiations Act.

In many instances specific statutes, like those identified above, interact with FAR terms and provisions. In other words, the FAR implements statutory provisions in some cases. Frustratingly, in other cases specific statutory provisions trump contrary FAR regulations, like those found in the Small Business Act. Other such examples include statutory grounds for debarment, authorization to enter noncompetitive contracts related to hazardous fuels reduction activities, and certain restrictions upon the purchase of incandescent lamps. In 2005, the federal government implemented a plan to source 23% of all subcontracts from small businesses. The government eventually met this goal in 2013 when it subcontracted over USD 83 billion from small businesses.

More specifically, ICT procurement is a challenging endeavor. It is difficult for a number of reasons, including the following: (1) technical content is often diverse and difficult to define; (2) ICT contracts usually call for a varied range of professional services as well as hardware and software; (3) ICT and associated technologies evolve and change quickly; (4) ICT components are specific to an entity's business or governing processes; (5) ICT costs are not typically finite, but include software, Internet access, training, and other support.

When a U.S. government agency or department seeks ICT services from a private sector provider, it will issue a request for tender (RFT), which is an organized invitation to vendors to bid to supply the ICT products or services. The RFT will describe the results of the agency's needs analysis, identify what is requested for the procurement, stipulate contractual requirements, and describe how bidders should respond. An RFT is released in a public forum rather than sent to potential suppliers. That said, a request for information may be sent to potential vendors before the RFT is published asking vendors to describe the suitability of their product or service for the upcoming tender. There are many types of tender processes. For example, tenders may be open or restricted. Restricted tendering means the government agency seeks in a nondiscriminatory manner bids from at least three suppliers from which the goods or services are known to be available. Frequently, such suppliers are selected from an approved list maintained by the government. Restricted tenders may also have other conditions such as being open only to companies in the U.S.

Two-stage tendering is usually used to identify a supplier or vendor more expeditiously. In the first stage, bidders submit tenders without a price, and a preferred vendor or contractor is competitively selected for further negotiation on the basis of limited information. Tenders may cover the goods' technical aspects, quality, or other characteristics; services; contractual terms and conditions of supply; and the bidder's professional and technical competence and qualifications. The government agency may then negotiate in the second stage with any potential supplier whose tender has not been rejected.

To ensure fairness and competition, U.S. agencies often require the RFT or supporting documents to demonstrate several capacities up front. For example, the RFT often defines all ready-made equipment and materials (e.g., servers, desktop computers, printers), with preinstalled software packages and consumables only (e.g., paper print cartridges), so there is no unusual pre-bid uncertainty. The government agency will also often identify with specificity all services and work elements that are incidental to the ICT purchase, such as installation (including wiring of local area networks) and standard training on hardware and software. The RFT will define mandatory and preferred qualifications for key personnel, particularly project manager and lead trainer. For a major project, bidding documents may stipulate the qualifications of the project management, including experience, and university degrees or certifications. Government ICT contracts routinely require hardware upgrades or replacement during the contract life cycle.

After the government agency has issued the RFT and evaluated bids, the agency issues a letter of intent to the winning bidder, notifying it of award and requesting acknowledgement and willingness to negotiate a contract. After the bidder acknowledges award, the agency's evaluation of the bidding process and the bids themselves can be made public. Bidders that did not win may request a proposal evaluation and may lodge a complaint if they are not satisfied with the explanation. At the time of contract signing or shortly thereafter, the winning bidder usually furnishes a performance bond or bank guarantee if required by the bidding documents.

Because several layers of bureaucracy often attend governmental procurement contracts, an important tool allows work to begin pending final approval. A government agency's "letter of intent" confirms the basic understanding of the parties that intend to enter into contract and authorizes the winning bidder to begin work pending conclusion of contract negotiations. It is useful when either the vendor or the government agency, or both, is awaiting internal approvals or when immediate action by the vendor is required. The letter of intent often includes a narrow scope of work and schedule and a not-to-exceed price.

An important legal backdrop exists behind all of these statutes and regulations. Federal common law, a body of law developed from court decisions, informs contemporary contracting law. The UCC is the most important statement of the common law. The UCC applies to the purchase and sale of goods and to security interest in personal property. Most states have adopted all or significant portions of the UCC to be the positive law in those states, which has harmonized previously disparate contract law among the fifty states. This distinction is important because contracts between the federal government and private contractors are typically controlled by the statutes, regulations, above as well as federal common law. But related contracts between the general contractor and its subcontractors are controlled by the contract law of the respective states.

This legal imbalance can be confusing, as private contractual transactions enjoy more latitude in devising contract terms than a party contracting with the federal government. In a private transaction each private party represents its own interests and can obligate itself in any lawful manner. Federal government contracts, however, foreclose open negotiation in several areas, areas that would be open to negotiation in a private transaction. Such areas in federal contracting legally require the use of prescribed provisions and clauses. Moreover, in U.S. government contracting, the government agent's bargaining authority is limited by statutes and regulations reflecting national policy choices and restrictions on the capacity of such agent's ability to obligate federal funds. Conversely, only mutually agreeable terms and lack of fraud limit private contracting parties.

II. Federal Acquisition Regulation

117. The FAR is the most important legal authority when addressing federal procurement and the executive branch and is codified at Chapter 1 of Title 48 of the CFRs.[113] As noted by the U.S. Congressional Research Service, "prior to the establishment of the FAR system and the initial publication of the FAR, two primary procurement regulations existed: the Federal Procurement Regulations and the Defense Acquisition Regulation."[114] The FPR applied to civilian agencies and the DAR applied to the DOD and its components. The FAR was published initially in 1983, and took effect on October 1, 1984. It has been periodically amended since then.

Title 48 of the CFRs governs the purchase of services and goods by federal agencies. That title includes provisions that regulate contract formation, contract management, contract security, breach and enforcement.[115] The policies or principles that motivate discrete regulations are also included in the FAR. Those policies focus on fair contracting and customer satisfaction as it relates to quality, timeliness of performance, minimization of unnecessary costs, transparency and integrity. Additional public policy objectives sometimes attend discrete procurement areas.

More specifically, the FAR often restricts government officers in charge of procurement contracts. For example, several regulations require that government officers must first demonstrate full and open competition in the bidding process for the government contract before the government contract will be awarded. Other regulations mandate when and how agencies may waive a contractor's exclusion, when and how a contract may be terminated, and specific security and privacy provisions that must be included in a contract. With regard to the "acquisition process," FAR outlines a process that consists of three phases:

(1) Need recognition and acquisition planning.
(2) Contract formation.
(3) Contract administration.

The FAR governs the activities of government agents as they facilitate this process. Almost all federal agencies must comply with FAR procurement processes,

113. 48 C.F.R. 1, et. seq.
114. *See Federal Acquisition Regulation (FAR): Answers to Frequently Asked Questions*, CRS Report (Nov. 16, 2012), https://www.secnav.navy.mil/rda/Documents/FARfaq.pdf.
115. 48 C.F.R. 1, Parts 1 through 53.

although a handful are exempt. For example, the U.S. Mint and the Federal Aviation Administration draft and follow their own individualized procurement protocols. Despite these exceptions, an animating purpose of the FAR is to provide "uniform policies and procedures for acquisition."[116]

> (b) The Federal Acquisition System will-
> (1) Satisfy the customer in terms of cost, quality, and timeliness of the delivered product or service by, for example-
> (i) Maximizing the use of commercial products and services;
> (ii) Using contractors who have a track record of successful past performance or who demonstrate a current superior ability to perform; and
> (iii) Promoting competition;
> (2) Minimize administrative operating costs;
> (3) Conduct business with integrity, fairness, and openness; and
> (4) Fulfill public policy objectives.[117]

The statutory authority to issue new regulations and to and maintain the current FAR identifies the Secretary of Defense, the Administrator of General Services, and the Administrator of the National Aeronautics and Space Administration. These department heads also confer with and seek approval from the Administrator of Federal Procurement Policy.

Notable contract provisions and restrictions include several provisions that focus on eliminating graft and favoritism in federal contracting. These restrictions prohibit disclosing proposal information regarding contracting bids before the award of a federal procurement contract, and include provisions that disqualify an award if the contract was improperly acquired by an agent or intermediary.[118]

The FAR requires both the government agent and the private contractor to sign the procurement contract in a specific manner. Only the government's "contracting officer" may sign on behalf of the United States, along with the officer's official title. The FAR requires specified private party signatures depending upon whether the private party is an individual, partnership, corporation, agent or joint venturer.[119]

For government contracts that involve sensitive or confidential matters, specific contractual clauses must appear in the contract. A program instituted by the U.S. President in 1993 established procedures to safeguard sensitive federal government information that is released to contractors, through these transactions. The program has since been incorporated into the FAR, culminating in mandatory contract language for security reasons when the contract includes classified information:

> Security Requirements.
>
> (a) This clause applies to the extent that this contract involves access to information classified "Confidential," "Secret," or "Top Secret."

116. 48 C.F.R. 1.101 (2012).
117. 48 C.F.R. 1.102.
118. 48 C.F.R. 3.104–3, 3.104–5.
119. 48 C.F.R. 4.101–4.102.

(b) The Contractor shall comply with-
   (1) The Security Agreement (DDForm441), including the National Industrial Security Program Operating Manual (DoD 5220.22-M); and
   (2) Any revisions to that manual, notice of which has been furnished to the Contractor.

(c) If, subsequent to the date of this contract, the security classification or security requirements under this contract are changed by the Government and if the changes cause an increase or decrease in security costs or otherwise affect any other term or condition of this contract, the contract shall be subject to an equitable adjustment as if the changes were directed under the Changes clause of this contract.

(d) The Contractor agrees to insert terms that conform substantially to the language of this clause, including this paragraph (d) but excluding any reference to the Changes clause of this contract, in all subcontracts under this contract that involve access to classified information.[120]

As the most prolific purveyor of goods and services in the U.S. and possibly the world, government contracting is a critical aspect of the Cyber Law landscape. In 2016 alone, the U.S. federal government spent USD 461 billion on contracts. The vast majority of those funds were dedicated to the DOD with the Department of Energy and Health and Human Services in a distant second. It is also a very complex field, with a myriad of federal statutes, an overlay of federal regulations, including the FAR, as well as federal common law and state common law principles.

§9. Smart Contracts and Blockchain

118. Although blockchain-based cryptocurrency has received significant public attention in the last several years, the increased attention at the governmental level has not resulted in significant legislation or new regulations. The primary areas of interest from a regulatory perspective are with respect to securities, money transmission, and taxation. In each of these cases, the relevant regulatory authorities (at the federal level) have attempted to treat cryptocurrencies within the existing regulatory regimes and thus have only issued guidance documents, rather than engaging in new rulemaking. However, as cryptocurrency values and valuations have increased significantly in the last several years, and corresponding accusations of fraud and/or theft have increased, it is likely that regulators and/or legislators will be under increasing pressure to do something substantive to address the blockchain-based technologies. Accordingly, it would be reasonable to expect new rulemaking and/or legislation on blockchain technologies in the U.S. in the next few years.

120. 48 CFR § 52.204–2.

Chapter 2. Electronic Signatures

§1. General

119. As demonstrated above, legal contracts in the U.S. constitute a binding promise, the breach of which renders a legal remedy. Contract law has evolved from a formalistic to a more flexible legal standard, most commonly embodied by the UCC. Legal standards developed under the UCC regarding offer, acceptance, consideration, the mailbox rule, and breach, however, do not readily translate to electronic transactions. While it may seem to translate traditional contracting concepts to an electronic offer, acceptance, and consideration, a raft of legal uncertainties plagues electronic transfers. The UCC requires that the writing be signed by the party against whom enforcement is sought.

> Except as otherwise provided in this section a contract for the sale of goods for the price of $500 or more is not enforceable by way of action or defense unless there is some writing sufficient to indicate that a contract for sale has been made between the parties and signed by the party against whom enforcement is sought or by his authorized agent or broker. A writing is not insufficient because it omits or incorrectly states a term agreed upon but the contract is not enforceable under this paragraph beyond the quantity of goods shown in such writing.[121]

This provision does not determine contract formation but seeks to ensure that the parties truly intended their actions by observing these formalities. The lynchpin of the Statute of Frauds is the requirement that the agreement be in writing. What constitutes a writing has not historically been problematic. It was interpreted flexibly to include several writings or pieces of paper taken together. A famous case held that a scribbled agreement on a bar napkin was sufficient. The piece of paper serves as tangible evidence of a contract. However flawed, the paper is more reliable than oral testimony.

In like fashion, what actually constitutes a signature has generated a great deal of litigation. One early case involved a sales contract that was relayed by telex. The parties litigated whether the messages were "signed." In holding that the telex was "signed," the court relied on a liberal definition of "signature" derived from prior case law. Moreover, each party was not deceived by the communication and each party acknowledged the authenticity of the other. Today, electronic commerce leverages varying technologies such as Internet marketing, online transaction processing, mobile commerce, electronic funds transfer, and electronic data interchange (EDI), to say nothing of automated data collection systems. Many of these methods rely on the Internet for at least one component of the transaction.

The UCC ultimately reflected the liberalized signature precedent developed by case law. Comment 1 to section 2-201(1) defines "signed" to include any authentication that identifies the party to be charged. That provision goes on to aver that

121. UCC § 2-201(1).

a signature "includes any symbol executed or adopted by a party with present intention to authenticate a writing." Authentication can be printed, stamped, or written, or a thumbprint. In fact, it is not possible to list a complete catalogue of possible means of authenticating a document.

More and more, cases do not require that something actually be written but courts have instead accepted faxes, telegrams, computer disk recordings, and emails as writings. Similarly, the essence of the "signature" requirement has morphed into an analysis of the intent of the party to authenticate the writing. If a court determines that a party intended to adopt or authenticate a writing, a formal signature is not required. This means that a signature may be a thumbprint, initials, a stamp, and in some instances the subject line in an email.

In *Cloud Corp. v. Hasbro*, the Seventh Circuit held that adding one's name to the bottom of an email satisfied the signature requirement for the Statute of Frauds. In that case Hasbro manufactured a toy that required packets that simulated water. Cloud Corp. prepared and supplied the packets for Hasbro. Hasbro's purchase orders contained the standard contract terms and were used each time Hasbro placed an order. After Hasbro placed its last order, Cloud Corp. sent an acknowledgement for additional packets. Hasbro did not respond directly to the acknowledgement, but it continued to communicate by email. The emails referenced a larger number of packets to be delivered on specific dates. The court held that the emails were amendments to the forgoing purchase orders and that Hasbro signed the amendments by affixing the sender's name to the emails.[122]

By way of contrast, in *Singer v. Adamson*, a court held that email messages between the seller's broker and the buyer in a real estate negotiation did not form a contract because the emails did not constitute an offer and acceptance. In the at case, the putative buyer went to an open house and quickly emailed the real estate agent, asking whether the house could be bought for USD 240,000. The real estate agent rejected the USD 240,000 offer the same day, stating in the email that the seller would not accept "an offer" of USD 240,000. Several email exchanges followed. The realtor later emailed, stating that seller would sell for USD 253,000. Thereafter, the buyer gave the realtor a form agreement with the USD 253,000 purchase price, requiring seller's signature within a specified time. The seller never signed, and the buyer sued to enforce the contract. The court, however, ruled that the realtor's email promising to sell for USD 250,000 was not a firm offer, but only ongoing negotiation. The court ruled that the realtor's email lacked indicia that the parties were memorializing anything of legal significance.[123]

§2. The Uniform Electronic Transaction Act

120. In 1999, the National Conference of Commissioners on Uniform State Laws adopted two uniform acts meant to bring legal clarity to the explosion of electronic commerce in the information-based economy. The Uniform Electronic Transactions Act (UETA) drafters admitted that technological advances were disturbing

122. 314 F. 3d 389 (7th Cir. 2002).
123. 65 Mass. App. Ct. 1103 (2005).

traditional business models and that existing laws governing these business transactions were slowing the speed, blocking efficiencies of modern day transactions. The primary purpose of UETA was "to remove barriers to electronic commerce by validating and effectuating electronic records and signatures."[124] The Act was not intended to be a general contracting or electronic signature statute; instead it was purposely intended to complement existing state laws and to only apply to specific transactions and not to all writings or signatures. Forty-seven states, the District of Columbia, and the U.S. Virgin Islands have adopted the UETA, largely achieving its purpose of harmonizing state laws concerning electronic signatures. Washington, Illinois, and New York have not adopted the UETA, however similar legislation that governs how electronic transactions are handled has been enacted in each of these three states.

UETA basically gives legal recognition to electronic agreements for a wide range of commercial transactions. However, it does not govern wills, trusts, and a number of other transactions that are managed by the courts. Instead, the UETA focuses primarily on electronic transactions related to "business, commercial and governmental matters." In the U.S., the UETA is the most effective statute governing procedures for entering into contracts online. Notably, the UETA applies to parties who have agreed to conduct transactions between themselves by electronic means.

The section entitled Legal Recognition of Electronic Records, Signatures, and Contracts, contains the Act's fundamental principles, namely that the specific fashion in which a record, signature, or contract is created, presented, or retained does not affect its legal significance. The Act's other provisions serve these principles:

(a) A record or signature may not be denied legal effect or enforceability solely because it is in electronic form.
(b) A contract may not be denied legal effect or enforceability solely because an electronic record was used in its formation.
(c) If a law requires a record to be in writing, an electronic record satisfies the law.
(d) If a law requires a signature, an electronic signature satisfies the law.[125]

Because UETA is procedural in nature, whether an electronic signature or record has any legal significance and creates rights and obligations is determined by other, substantive law.

§3. The Electronic Signatures in Global and National Commerce Act

121. The Electronic Signatures in Global and National Commerce Act (the E-Sign Act), became effective October 1, 2000, and allows electronic documents and signatures to have the same validity as paper documents and handwritten signatures.[126] Although every U.S. state has a law addressing electronic signatures, the E-Sign Act likely carries outside influence because it applies to transactions relating

124. Unif. Elec. Transactions Act prefatory note (1999).
125. *Id.* at § 7.
126. 15 U.S.C 7001 et seq.

to interstate commerce. The overarching purpose of the E-Sign Act is identified in the first provision, and states that a contract or signature "may not be denied legal effect, validity, or enforceability solely because it is in electronic form."[127] The law signals that electronic signatures and records are just as good as their paper equivalents, and therefore subject to the same legal scrutiny of authenticity that applies to paper.

The E-Sign Act treats commercial and consumer transactions differently, however. For commercial transactions, the parties' agreement to conduct the transaction will be implied from the facts and circumstances surrounding the transaction or by an express statement of intent. For consumer transactions, the E-Sign Act requires that companies provide consumers with a specific set of disclosures before being able to provide required disclosures electronically. Like the E-Sign Act, UETA adopts the simple principle that electronic signatures and records should be accorded the same legal status as ink signature and paper records. UETA, however, differs from the E-Sign Act in a few areas. For example, UETA does not contain any requirement that consumers be provided with specified disclosures before agreeing to proceed electronically. Further, UETA addresses when an electronic record has been sent and received while the E-Sign Act does not. Finally, the E-Sign Act is a federal law and therefore preempts any inconsistent state law. That said, if a state adopts UETA without amendment, The E-Sign Act will not preempt that enactment.

Disclosures in consumer transactions provided in electronic form satisfy the E-Sign Act only if the financial institution received proper consent from the consumer first as specified under the E-Sign Act. If a financial institution provides disclosures in both paper and electronic form, the paper form can be used to meet the disclosure requirements, rendering E-Sign consent unnecessary. Section 106 of the ESIGN Act includes these definitions:

> (2) ELECTRONIC – The term 'electronic' means relating to technology having electrical, digital, magnetic, wireless, optical, electromagnetic, or similar capabilities.
> (4) ELECTRONIC RECORD – The term 'electronic record' means a contract or other record created, generated, sent, communicated, received, or stored by electronic means.
> (5) ELECTRONIC SIGNATURE – The term 'electronic signature' means an electronic sound, symbol, or process, attached to or logically associated with a contract or other record and executed or adopted by a person with the intent to sign the record.[128]

127. *Id.*
128. *Id.*

Chapter 3. Trust Services

122. The U.S. does not have a significant regulatory environment for so-called trust services, or services that provide electronic certificates, electronic mail services, or the like. Instead, these types of functions are handled by the private sector under traditional contracts law and principles. There are private certification authorities which companies, such as online retailers, can use to provide certification services. However, these private certification authorities are not subject to a specific overarching regulator regime and instead depend on cooperation and confidence among the private companies for operation and success.

Chapter 4. Online Financial Services

§1. General

123. The banking industry is one of the most highly regulated industries in the U.S. In light of the critical role banks play in allocating credit and affecting the nation's entire economy, the federal regulatory system includes an increasingly complex array of laws that require strict compliance. Due to the dual sovereignty that states enjoy with the federal government, a bank in the U.S. can gain formal recognition through a charter by doing so through any one of the fifty states or at the federal level. Regardless of whether a bank is chartered at the state level, it will have at last one federal supervisor.

At some level, electronic banking has been part of the market in the U.S. for many years. Commercial deals used Electronic Data Exchange well before the online banking systems that are now commonplace throughout the U.S. EDI transactions are a type of electronic commerce that companies use for transactions such as when one company wants to electronically send a purchase order to another. Even so, by 2000, only 26% of national banks in the U.S. were offering Internet banking services. Those electronic banking services were themselves limited, and included opening an account for deposits, accessing account history, and limited transferring of funds among accounts.

What is noteworthy about so much of Cyber Law in the U.S. is the relative rapidity with which technology disrupted traditional markets. As of May 1995, approximately fifty financial institutions worldwide even had websites. Seven years later 14,000 financial businesses had websites. Likewise, consumer use of online banking grew from 5 million in 1995 to 100 million in 2002. In the next ten years, online banking grew by orders of magnitude, including the diversity of digital services provided to customers. Electronic stock trading and statements, mutual fund transactions, real-time digital analysis from financial experts, and individualized customer reports now supplement the basic online account services.

Electronic financial and banking transactions from business to business are valued in the billions of dollars, and the ease and rapidity of those transactions continues to increase. Enhanced efficiencies allow individuals and businesses to buy goods and services, identify new markets, and expand business reach without the overhead costs historically associated with such efforts. As of 2017, about two-thirds of Americans use digital banking tools in their day-to-day lives. Four in ten Americans manage their bank accounts online, the survey found, while 26% of consumers use their mobile devices most often. Consumers are drawn to the convenience of banking through their computers or mobile devices, while financial institutions appreciate the cost savings from e-banking.

§2. Legal Compliance

124. As noted above, the legal framework in the U.S. for electronic banking is highly complex and highly varied. Not only are there two sovereigns, the federal government and state governments, but within each sovereign there are a number of entities imbued with the authority to generate binding law. Many of these entities share an overlapping scope of authority, which further complicates the legal landscape. Because banks play a critical role in lending credit and thereby affecting the national economy, banking policy as primarily dictated by federal Congress is perhaps the most important legal guide. The following federal statutes are commonly cited as affecting U.S. banking policy and practice:

- The National Bank Act of 1863: established a National Banking System.
- The Federal Reserve Act: established the Federal Reserve System as the central bank of the U.S. in order to provide the nation with a more stable monetary and financial system.
- The Banking Act of 1933: regulated interbank control, to prevent the undue diversion of funds into speculative operations; separated commercial banks from investment banks.
- The Federal Deposit Insurance Act: authorized the Federal Deposit Insurance Corporation (FDIC) to be the receiver of failed banks.
- The Bank Holding Company Act: regulates bank holding companies that own both banking and nonbanking businesses. Requires approval of Federal Reserve before acquiring additional banks.
- The International Banking Act: establishes legal system for regulating international banks that operate in the U.S.

While the above laws are central to banking compliance in the U.S., they do not directly address electronic banking. The more recent legislative acts, however, include more relevant provisions:

I. The Gramm-Leach-Bliley Act

125. Enacted in 1999, this law requires financial institutions, identified as companies that offer consumers financial products or services, to explain their information-sharing practices to their customers and to safeguard sensitive data.[129] In the age of digital information and electronic banking, this law has become increasingly important. Unlike the EU, the U.S. does not have an overarching data privacy law. Instead, data privacy regulation is sectoral, or industry-specific. The personal data and security provisions for consumer finance transactions (the banking industry) is best captured in this law.

If the law applies, compliance is mandatory and includes publication of the organizations' privacy policy, demonstrating a commitment to protect the consumer financial information from foreseeable threats in security and assurance of data integrity. The Act also includes provisions governing a financial institution's collection, disclosure, and protection of consumers' nonpublic personal information. Financial institutions must give their customers a conspicuous notice that explains what information the institution gathers about the customer, where and with whom

129. 15U.S.C. § 6801 et seq.

this information is shared, and how the company secures that information. The law requires that such notice be given to the client before any formal business transaction takes place.

There have been several important cases in which the FTC has prosecuted U.S. financial institutions for violating the Gramm-Leach-Bliley Act. Most of them involve some aspect of electronic banking. By way of example, in 2018 prosecuted PayPal, alleging that its Venmo service violated the privacy provisions of the Gramm-Leach-Bliley Act in three ways. First, Venmo failed to provide a conspicuous privacy notice. Instead, Venmo's notice in the Venmo App was in light grey text on a light grey background. Second, Venmo's notice was inaccurate. It did not accurately relay how Venmo shares the user's personal information. Instead of only sharing with a "social web," as represented by Venmo's notice, Venmo in fact shared user date with everyone online, even those who did not have a Venmo account. Finally, Venmo did not make the privacy notice available in a way that each customer could reasonably encounter the notice and react according to the user's wishes. The privacy notice was included as a hyperlink, and no user acknowledgement was required before using Venmo's service.

In light of these alleged infractions, the FTC and PayPal announced a settlement in 2018. This was the second significant FTC prosecution and settlement in a three-month period addressing similar issues arising under the Gramm-Leach-Bliley Act's privacy and safeguards rules.

II. The Dodd-Frank Act

126. One of the most important and critical laws affecting contemporary banking stems from the Dodd-Frank Wall Street Reform and Consumer Protection Act (Dodd-Frank Act). It is a comprehensive attempt at financial reform legislation passed in 2010 as a response to the financial crisis of 2008. The law overhauled financial regulation and made changes affecting all federal financial regulatory agencies and almost every part of the financial services industry in the U.S. Dodd-Frank established a number of new government agencies tasked with overseeing the various components of the Act and the financial system in general.

The Consumer Financial Protection Bureau (CFPB) was charged with protecting consumers against abuses related to credit cards, mortgages, and other financial products. More specifically, the CFPB seeks to prevent predatory mortgage lending, which many viewed as the underlying cause of the 2008 worldwide economic recession. The CFPB seeks to make it easier for consumers to understand the terms of a mortgage before agreeing to them. The Act also created the Financial Stability Oversight Council and the Office of Financial Research. These entities are tasked under Dodd-Frank with monitoring the financial sector and identifying threats to the financial stability. Dodd-Frank also granted the Federal Reserve new powers to regulate systemically important institutions.

Another key aspect of Dodd-Frank is commonly termed, the Volcker Rule. This provision restricts the ways banks can invest, limiting speculative trading, and eliminating proprietary trading. In short, the Volcker Rule restricts banks from making certain kinds of speculative investments. Banks are prohibited from running or closely associating with hedge funds or private equity firms due to the inherent risk associated with those financial services. In an effort to minimize possible conflicts of interest, financial firms are not allowed to trade proprietarily without sufficient investment of their own, or "skin in the game."

Because credit rating agencies facilitated the 2008 financial crises by publishing misleading investment ratings, Dodd-Frank established the SEC Office of Credit Ratings. The office is charged with ensuring that agencies provide meaningful and reliable credit ratings of the businesses, municipalities, and other entities they evaluate.

More recently, President Trump sought to repeal or at least amend Dodd-Frank to allow financial institutions greater freedoms in their varied business transactions. Through the Economic Growth, Regulatory Relief and Consumer Protection Act, signed in 2018, U.S. Congress relaxed regulations imposed by Dodd-Frank. The 2018 Act raised the threshold to USD 250 billion from USD 50 billion under which banks are deemed too important to the financial system to fail and withdrew application of the Volcker Rule for small banks with less than USD 10 billion in assets. Although many of these legal obligations and restrictions are not directly tailored to electronic banking, they clearly affect the legal background in which banking transactions occur in the U.S.

III. Regulating Entities

127. The number and variation of federal agencies with authority over the U.S. financial industry adds to the complexity of the legal landscape:

- The *Federal Reserve System*, as the central bank of the U.S., performs several general functions to promote the effective operation of the U.S. economy and, more generally, the public interest. The Federal Reserve determines the nation's monetary policy to promote maximum employment, stable prices, and moderate long-term interest rates in the U.S. economy. It also seeks to minimize and contain systemic risks through active monitoring and engagement in the U.S. and abroad.
- The *Federal Deposit Insurance Corporation* (FDIC) is an independent federal agency insuring deposits in U.S. banks and thrifts in the event of bank failures. The FDIC insures deposits up to USD 250,000 per depositor as long as the institution is a member firm.
- The *Office of the Comptroller of the Currency* (OCC) is an independent bureau of the U.S. Department of the Treasury. The OCC charters, regulates, and supervises all national banks, federal savings associations, and federal branches and agencies of foreign banks.
- The *Consumer Financial Protection Bureau* protects consumers from unfair, deceptive, or abusive financial practices and prosecutes entities that violate financial laws that protect consumers.
- The *Financial Stability Oversight Council*, established under the Dodd-Frank Wall Street Reform and Consumer Protection Act, provides comprehensive monitoring of the stability of the nation's financial system.

§3. Online Banking Transactions

128. In addition to the banking transactions that large financial institutions engage in with one another, electronic banking capabilities as they affect consumers is increasingly relevant. These electronic customer banking services range from a simple opening of an account to electronic payment of bills, to more complex transactions like virtual banks that provide only electronic banking services.

Several large banks in the U.S. currently provide pure electronic payment services to customers. Bank One, for example, requires no paper check as precedent to automated bill payment. There are still many institutions that require a paper check, even though the resulting automatic payment programs utilize electronic media like apps and automatic transfer etc. Although the transactions appear electronic to users, the bank or financial institution still converts the actual payment using a paper transaction.

Electronic bill payment processes continue to proliferate. Many banks now prefer and sometimes require electronic payment services. There is some data to suggest that banks retain customers who set up automatic or electronic payment systems because consumers invested time in setting up the process. New electronic banking products are seemingly endless. For example, Microsoft established a program to offer online bill-paying capabilities for consumers in which a Microsoft subsidiary acts a clearinghouse through which a wide range of customers and banking services transmit payments and other banking transactions. The program targets both customers and financial institutions that bill consumers. Electronic banking has extended to mortgages, as well, with many lending institutions offering mortgage services online. The merger of E*Trade Group, Inc. and Telebanc Financial Corporation provides another illustration of seemingly disparate businesses can associate or merge to provide a wider array of financial services facilitated by electronic transactions.

In addition to the sources of legal authority outlined above, the U.S. Office of the Comptroller of the Currency provides generalized legal authorization for U.S. banks to use electronic systems to facilitate banking services. That general authorization is supplemented by the Electronic Fund Transfers Act (EFTA).[130] The EFTA is a federal law that protects consumers when they transfer funds electronically. Specifically it protects consumers in their use of debit cards, automated teller machines (ATMs), and automatic withdrawals from bank accounts. Electronic fund transfers are defined as transactions that use computers, phones or magnetic strips to authorize a financial institution to credit or debit a customer's account. Consumers typically use a card or pin number to initiate transfers from one account to another.

The EFTA allows users to challenge errors and have them corrected within a forty-five-day period with limited financial penalties. The Electronic Fund Transfer Act (EFTA) outlines requirements for banking institutions and consumers to follow when errors occur. When errors occur, EFTA outlines requirements for banking institutions and consumers to follow. It also requires banks to provide certain information to consumers and defines how consumers can limit liability in the case of a lost or stolen card.

130. 15U.S.C. § 1693 et seq.

The law has been clarified to apply to new technological advances, like digital wallets. Beginning in spring 2019, the Consumer Financial Protection Bureau will enforce its Prepaid Accounts Rule, which will ensure that consumers receive full credit card protection, while making it easier to link those accounts to digital wallets that can store funds. Such updates are seen as increasingly important as analysts value the prepaid card and reloadable card industry to have grown from just over USD 1 billion in 2003 to USD 65 billion in 2012 and is expected to reach USD 116 billion by 2020.

As the capacity, frequency, and diversity of online banking modalities proliferates, the legal questions attending such activities will also. By way of illustration, the OCC was recently asked to determine which banking law and/or regulation applied to Internet-based auctions for the sale of certificates of deposit. Questions such as these will only increase in the near term.

Interestingly, a crosscurrent of self-regulation also marks U.S. privacy regulation. A number of specialized financial trades self-regulate by adopting non-legally binding guidelines and promoting privacy "best practices." The Direct Marketing Association, for example, drafts and promotes online privacy guides that call for its members to post a prominent notice on their websites alerting consumers to information-collection practices. The credit card industry self-imposes encryption obligations and requires reporting on lost data. Such self-regulation is not accidental. The Clinton Administration promoted self-regulation as a preferable method of protecting consumer privacy without saddling businesses with bureaucratic interference, stating, "We believe that private efforts of industry working in cooperation with consumer groups are preferable to government regulation . . . ."[131]

Policy makers continue to review the effectiveness of private self-regulation and public laws that address the burgeoning industry of electronic banking. For example, new banking regulations envision online marketplaces or malls that facilitate digital certification for electronic transactions. Such regulation adds legitimacy and encourages continued efficiencies through technological innovations for the banking industry.

---

131. *See* William J. Clinton & Albert Gore, Jr., *A Framework for Global Electronic Commerce*, White House (July 1, 1997), http://clinton4.nara.gov/WH/New/Commerce/read.html [https://perma.cc/ZFH4-ZWJZ].

Chapter 5. Law of Evidence in the Digital Environment

129. In the United States, parties in federal litigation are granted broad powers of discovery under the Federal Rules of Civil Procedure (FRCP). In particular, FRCP 26 allows parties to take discovery on "any nonprivileged matter that is relevant to any party's claim or defense and proportional to the needs of the case." This rule essentially gives parties the ability to seek discovery of any evidence that would be relevant and admissible under the Federal Rules of Evidence, which includes most electronic data that a company possesses. Many states have similar procedural and evidentiary rule systems that permit broad discovery of relevant evidence.

In order to facilitate the broad discovery contemplated by the discovery rules, courts can impose sanctions or other adverse consequences on parties in litigation if they destroy evidence or otherwise fail to properly safeguard evidence for use at trial. Accordingly, it is important for companies operating in the U.S. to have, and abide by, document retention policies that preserve evidence that may be relevant in later litigation. Additionally, once litigation becomes likely, companies may need to take additional steps to ensure that relevant evidence is not destroyed either inadvertently or through a preestablished data culling mechanism. It is typical for companies in the U.S. to issue a mandate, often called a "litigation hold," to all relevant employees regarding the retention of evidence once litigation is initiated or becomes likely.

Of particular importance to companies operating in the digital environment, is evidence of security measures taken or security vulnerabilities discovered either internally or through expert analysis. Companies may engage in routine self-evaluations or hire outside experts to evaluate their digital infrastructure security. The reports generated by these experts or evaluations can be extremely relevant in a lawsuit following, for example, a data breach incident where a plaintiff is asserting that the company used inadequate security measures in protecting the plaintiff's data. The ability of plaintiffs to access these reports through discovery, places companies in a difficult dilemma. On the one hand, companies want to test and validate their security measures and identify any gaps, if present. On the other hand, doing so is likely to lead to reports detailing inadequacies. These reports can then be compelling evidence against the company in the later suit. Accordingly, some companies will hire attorneys to manage their infrastructure analysis in the hopes of having the generated reports protected from discovery through attorney-client privilege or the work product doctrine. These exceptions to the broad discovery rules are fairly narrow, however, and so the companies may not be successful in shielding this information from discovery.

Chapter 6. Consumer Protection

§1. General

130. Consumer protection laws in the U.S. are several and varied. On the national level, the U.S. Congress has enacted several statutes affecting consumer protection and several federal agencies both enforce and promulgate their own set of regulations that have the force and effect of law. On the state level, each of the fifty states have consumer protection laws and some states have agencies that also draft regulations protecting consumers. Many of these statutes and regulations were in place prior to the dramatic increase in electronic services and the Internet age. Even so, many of these laws contain language broad enough to capture electronic transactions.

Some of the most notable federal statutes include the Food, Drug, and Cosmetic Act, the Fair Debt Collection Practices Act, the Fair Credit Reporting Act, the Gramm-Leach-Bliley Act, the Children's Online Privacy Protection Rule, Truth in Lending Act, and the Fair Credit Billing Act. The most prominent enforcers of consumer protection laws at the federal level are the FTC, the Food and Drug Administration, the DOJ, and the Consumer Financial Protection Bureau. Although state consumer protection laws vary from state to state, most states have adopted some form of a proposed uniform law, the Uniform Deceptive Trade Practices act. The Uniform Deceptive Trade Practices Act attempts to outlaw and police two activities: (1) unfair or fraudulent business practices, and (2) misleading or untrue advertising.

With regard to protecting consumers of electronic services, the federal agencies charged with enforcing consumer protection laws are increasingly focusing on violations that turn on electronic and online transactions. The FTC has emerged as the leading enforcer of consumer law violations that occur almost entirely online. Because interstate trade and international trade were early technology adopters, the FTC also had early experience in the application of laws to digital and electronic transactions. It is not surprising, then, that the FTC has taken a central role in customer complaints and consumer protection stemming from alleged online infractions.

As a result of the fluid nature of online transactions and services, the FTC has partnered or worked with a spate of regulatory authorities both among the many states and internationally. One international business was prosecuted for leveraging sexual content to then overcharge consumer for long-distance calls. From bogus pyramid schemes, to fraudulent advertisement of bandwidth sales, to tax-filing scammers, the FTC continues to prosecute fraudulent and unfair businesses practices that are facilitated online. According to the FTC, "[i]n 2017, the FTC filed more than 70 law enforcement actions, obtained more than 145 orders against defendants, and refunded more than $269 million to consumers."[132]

In February 2019, the FTC announced it first prosecution of a marketer's fake paid reviews that were placed on an independent retail website. According to the

---

132. *See* FTC Aids Criminal Prosecutions, https://www.consumer.ftc.gov/blog/2018/06/ftc-aids-criminal-prosecutions.

FTC, Cure Encapsulations, Inc. made false claims on behalf of their weight-loss supplement and then paid a third-party website to write and post fake reviews on Amazon.com. "The FTC alleges that the defendants paid a website, amazonverifiedreviews.com, to create and post Amazon reviews of their product. The FTC contends that Jacobowitz told the website's operator that his product needed to have an average rating of 4.3 out of 5 stars."[133] The laudatory reviews the defendants bought were posted on Amazon.com and gave the product a five-star rating. The FTC charged the defendants with "representing that the purchased Amazon reviews were truthful reviews written by actual purchasers, when in reality they were fabricated."[134] The settlement included prohibitions from engaging in similar false advertising and included a judgment of USD 12.8 million, however, the judgment allowed suspension of the monetary payment upon payment of USD 50,000 to the FTC and the payment of certain unpaid income tax obligations.

The broad authority to protect consumers against unfair and deceptive practices in the marketplace, coupled with its previous experience in digital commerce has made the FTC the lead regulator of consumer protection in the area of electronic commerce. The FTC's prosecutions, while beginning with basic business transactions online, has extended to information privacy protection, consumer data protection, as well as other areas. Data aggregators are largely unregulated, and the FTC's role in protecting personal data after its extraction remains uncertain, especially as more and more data is gathered by ordinary objects that are increasingly connected to the web, often known as the "Internet of Things."

§2. Federal Statues

131. As noted above, several federal statues address consumer protection, with increasing enforcement in the context of electronic services. Examples include the Food, Drug, and Cosmetic Act, the Fair Debt Collection Practices Act, the Fair Credit Reporting Act, the Gramm-Leach-Bliley Act, Truth in Lending Act, the Children's Online Privacy Protection Rule, and the Fair Credit Billing Act.

I. The Fair Credit Billing Act

132. The Fair Credit Billing Act is law enacted in 1974 that was originally designed to protect consumers from unfair credit billing practices. Today, the Act protects consumers that use a charge card online or otherwise pay by credit online.[135] The statute specifically focuses on consumer protection, as noted in the statute's declaration of purpose:

(a) Informed use of credit

---

133. *See* FTC Brings First Case Challenging Fake Paid Reviews on an Independent Retail Website (February 26, 2019), https://www.ftc.gov/news-events/press-releases/2019/02/ftc-brings-first-case-challenging-fake-paid-reviews-independent.

134. *Id.*

135. The Fair Credit Billing Act, 15U.S.C. § 1601.

> The Congress finds that economic stabilization would be enhanced and the competition among the various financial institutions and other firms engaged in the extension of consumer credit would be strengthened by the informed use of credit. The informed use of credit results from an awareness of the cost thereof by consumers. It is the purpose of this subchapter to assure a meaningful disclosure of credit terms so that the consumer will be able to compare more readily the various credit terms available to him and avoid the uninformed use of credit, and to protect the consumer against inaccurate and unfair credit billing and credit card practices.[136]

Under this statute, consumers may dispute charges in some instances and even withhold payment to a creditor during the pendency of the dispute. Consumers have sixty days from the time they receive their credit card bill to dispute a charge with a card issuer. If an unauthorized user makes charges to the consumer's account or credit card, the consumer may be protected under the Act from having to pay for the charges. However, the consumer is liable for the first USD 50 in charges. Of course, several credit card companies extend warranties to protect their consumers beyond what is provided in statue.

II. The Children's Online Privacy Protection Act

133. The Children's Online Privacy and Protection Act (COPPA) is a federal law dealing with how websites, apps, and other online operators collect data and personal information from kids under the age of 13.[137] Congress enacted COPPA in 1998, and required the FTC to draft regulations comporting with COPPA and to then enforce those regulations concerning children's online privacy. The FTC's original COPPA Rule became effective on April 21, 2000, and the FTC amended Rule in 2012, which took effect in July 2013.

Perhaps obviously, the central goal of the statue is to give parents and caregivers control over information collected about young children online. According to the FTC, "[t]he Rule applies to operators of commercial websites and online services (including mobile apps) directed to children under 13 that collect, use, or disclose personal information from children, and operators of general audience websites or online services with actual knowledge that they are collecting, using, or disclosing personal information from children under 13."[138] COPPA mandates that those covered under the statute comply with several provisions:

- post a clear and comprehensive online privacy policy describing their information practices for personal information collected online from children;
- provide direct notice to parents and obtain verifiable parental consent, with limited exceptions, before collecting personal information online from children;

---

136. *Id.* at § 1601(a).
137. 15U.S.C. § 6501–6505.
138. *See* Complying with COPPA: Frequently Asked Questions, https://www.ftc.gov/tips-advice/business-center/guidance/complying-coppa-frequently-asked-questions.

- give parents the choice of consenting to the operator's collection and internal use of a child's information, but prohibiting the operator from disclosing that information to third parties (unless disclosure is integral to the site or service, in which case, this must be made clear to parents);
- provide parents access to their child's personal information to review and/or have the information deleted;
- give parents the opportunity to prevent further use or online collection of a child's personal information;
- maintain the confidentiality, security, and integrity of information they collect from children, including by taking reasonable steps to release such information only to parties capable of maintaining its confidentiality and security; and
- retain personal information collected online from a child for only as long as is necessary to fulfill the purpose for which it was collected and delete the information using reasonable measures to protect against its unauthorized access or use.[139]

The effect of COPPA has been widespread and particularly important for providers of video content. For example, YouTube paid USD 179 million to settle a lawsuit brought by the New York Attorney General for allegedly violating COPPA. After the prosecution, YouTube attempted to put the obligation of complying with COPPA on those who create videos and upload them to YouTube's platform. YouTube now warns its users with the following: "If you fail to set your audience accurately, you may face compliance issues with the FTC or other authorities, and we may take action on your YouTube account."

Under the settlement, YouTube made several other concessions that may weaken the company's market share in the long run. For example, YouTube videos designated for kids will not be able to include targeted advertising, and other features that depend on user data will be disabled, like the "donate" button, cards and end screens, live chat and live chat donations, and assorted notifications. COPPA has been enforced against other web purveyors, of course, and will continue to be an important piece of legislation that protects the private data of young children.

III. The Gramm-Leach-Bliley Act

134. For discussion of the Gramm-Leach-Bliley Act, *see* Chapter 4, Online Financial Services, section 2, "Legal Compliance."

IV. The Electronic Fund Transfer Act

135. For discussion of the EFTA, *see* Chapter 4, Online Financial Services, section 3 "Online Banking Transactions."

---

139. *Id.*

§3. PRODUCT LIABILITY

I. General

136. In the absence of contractual liability, U.S. common law extends liability in certain instances through the law of torts in the U.S. Tort law is civil in nature and typically allows private parties to bring a lawsuit against one another for breaches of obligations that have been developed under the common law. Generally speaking, tort law in the U.S. consists of three categories: negligence, intentional torts, and strict liability torts.

Strict liability torts allow for a claimant to recover against a defendant even though the defendant did not have any bad intent or motivation to harm the claimant. In fact, strict liability torts allow the claimant to recover against the defendant irrespective of whether the defendant intentionally caused the harm or negligently caused the harm. Because there is no intent requirement, strict liability torts are limited to abnormally dangerous activities, like dynamite blasting. A subset of strict liability torts is called "strict products liability." This form of strict liability applies when a defective product for which certain defendants maintain responsibility causes injury to an appropriate plaintiff. Strict liability also applies to copyright infringement and some trademark cases.

While tort law certainly developed well before the cyber technologies at the heart of this manuscript, tort law has nevertheless been applied in the digital era. Most specifically, software designed to ensure personal safety and software that controls or manages larger systems can cause serious injuries giving rise to tort liability. For example, software is critical in the safe use of cars, medical devices, aircraft, automated teller machines, medical diagnostic systems, and much more. In 2009, the electronic throttle control systems in several Toyota cars malfunctioned. Software errors in those systems caused multiple incidents of sudden acceleration, ultimately killing eighty-nine people. In light of the Internet of Things, more and more ordinary objects are brought to life by connection to the Internet while simultaneously creating potential tort liability should the software malfunction and cause injury.

II. Product Liability, IT and Software

137. Not only is software critical to a rising number and diversity of objects that can cause serious injury if it malfunctions, concerns over information gathering, emergence and sophistication of hacking, the open-source movement, the Internet of Things and increased computer crime tend to complicate the legal landscape. Moreover, each technological advance increases reliance, exposure, and complexity to any given system.

Tort law, however, is often ill-suited to address injuries that stem from software failure. First, warranty law and End-User License Agreements often preempt tort liability and limit damages to recovery of product cost. That said, some product liability theories are not superseded by such unilateral warranties. Product liability in most U.S. states arises (1) when a defect in a product causes the product to fail and not operate in a safe and reasonably expected manner, and (2) when personal injury, death, or property damage directly results from the product defect.

The Restatement (Third) of Intentional Torts is an aggregation of the majority law among U.S. states. With regard to products liability, the Restatement provides: "A product is defective in design when the foreseeable risks of harm posed by the product could have been reduced or avoided by the adoption of a reasonable alternative design ... and the omission of the alternative design renders the product not reasonably safe."[140]

As applied to software, proof that the defect was in the software and that the software defect caused the plaintiff's alleged injury or property damage is the principal consideration. Proving that the software is defective is often cost prohibitive due to the non-standardized design of software and technological sophistication required to identify and characterize both how the software should technically operate as compared to the defective software leading to claimant's injury.

Moreover, the software must be implemented in an item for recovery under products liability law. A claimant cannot recover if the software is characterized as a service. Several software offerings are service-oriented in nature, making this distinction an important one. For example, in *James v. Meow Media, Inc.*, a federal court of appeals ruled that video games and websites were not products and therefore not susceptible to liability under product liability jurisprudence.[141]

Finally, the claimant must have used the software in its intended manner when the defect arose causing injury. If the software and product into which the software was embedded causes injury when used outside of its intended purpose, the claimant cannot recover. Some products and software require the user to modify the software or product before using or operating it. In such cases, the software designer or product manufacturer will not be liable under product liability law in the U.S.

Through the economic loss rule, most courts conform that tort liability generally does not permit recovery of damages arising from the loss or destruction of the defective product itself. This limitation on recoverable damages, however, can be circumvented when defective software is a component part of a large product which is damaged as a result of the software defect.

In summary, most U.S. courts have rejected the application of strict liability for defective software. As noted above, strict liability is disfavored because strict liability does not require any showing of intentional or negligent mindset. Courts are loath to impose tort liability, absent a showing of fault. Ultra-dangerous activities arguably support imposition of strict liability due to the hazardous nature of the activity. But because strict liability and other tort lawsuits against software vendors are so expensive for plaintiffs to pursue, they have only proven practical when a class action lawsuit can be initiated. Software design is often mysterious and unique. It is not standardized and it requires a claimant to invest significant resources to hire specialty lawyers, expert witnesses, and software researchers at the front end of the lawsuit.

---

140. Restatement (Third) of Intentional Torts: Products Liability.
141. 300 F.3d 683 (6th Cir 2002).

§4. NONCONTRACTUAL LIABILITY

I. General

138. In the absence of contractual liability, the historical basis for liability stems from the law of torts in the U.S. Of course, the delineation between tort and contract liability is not absolute. There are many instances in which a plaintiff may receive a recovery in tort law despite the existence of a contractual relationship just as there are circumstances in which a plaintiff asserts a contract claim but the defendant successfully argues that the critical legal issue sounds in tort. For example, a plaintiff may argue that a defendant breached their contract by failure to perform under the contract. A potential defense, if the evidence supports it, is fraudulent inducement, a cause of action that is noncontractual in nature.

Most U.S. courts, if a contract exists and if the dispute can reasonably be said to derive from the scope of the contractual agreement, will apply contract liability stemming from the four corners of the contract itself. The primary policies that U.S. courts seek to honor when determining whether to apply contract law or tort law when determining liability are the protection of parties' expectations, the interests of justice, and the reinforcement of larger public policy interest. As a result, if the dispute arises from the contract itself, U.S. courts will ordinarily apply contract law. Context is of critical importance, however. For example, in the insurance context, U.S. courts have recognized tort liability for bad faith breach of contract. This liability exceeds contractual liability for economic loss, but is typically limited to wrongful withholding of insurance proceeds stemming from an insurance contract.

Tort law is civil in nature and typically allows private parties to bring a lawsuit against one another for breaches of obligations that have been developed under the common law. Generally speaking, tort law in the U.S. consists of three categories: negligence, intentional torts, and strict liability torts.

139. Strict liability torts allow for a claimant to recover against a defendant even though the defendant did not have any bad intent or motivation to harm the claimant. In fact, strict liability torts allow the claimant to recover against the defendant irrespective of whether the defendant intentionally caused the harm or negligently caused the harm. Because there is no intent requirement, strict liability torts are limited to abnormally dangerous activities, like dynamite blasting. A subset of strict liability torts is called "strict products liability."' This form of strict liability applies when a defective product for which certain defendants maintain responsibility causes injury to an appropriate plaintiff. Strict liability also applies to copyright infringement and some trademark cases.

140. Intentional torts, by contrast, require the claimant to prove that the defendant intentionally caused the complained of harm, or knew to a substantial certainty that his/her act would cause the complained of harm. Intentional torts include battery, assault, false imprisonment, intentional infliction of emotional distress, trespass to chattel and conversion.

141. Finally, negligence is the most common unintentional tort in U.S. common law. Negligence is contrasted to contractual liability, in that the obligation springs from a common law obligation to act with reasonable prudence in certain circumstances unrelated to contractual obligation. In order to state a claim for negligence, a claimant must typically produce evidence of four factors. First, the plaintiff must show that the defendant owed a duty or obligation to the plaintiff under the circumstances giving rise to the case. Second, the plaintiff must show that the defendant breached that obligation owed to the plaintiff. Part of this inquiry asks whether the defendant acted as a reasonably prudent person would act under similar circumstances. If the defendant is an expert or specialist or holds himself out as an expert, the standard of care is that of a reasonably prudent expert in that field. Unlike other professionals such as lawyers, doctors, and engineers, etc., no educational or other credentialing body provides a standard by which to identify experts in IT or software design. As a result, professional negligence claims against computer industry personnel is very difficult. Third, the plaintiff must prove that the defendant's negligent behavior caused plaintiff's injury. Fourth, the plaintiff must prove that she was, in fact, damaged or harmed in such a way that the law provides a remedy.

142. While tort law certainly developed well before the cyber technologies at the heart of this manuscript, tort law has nevertheless been applied in the digital era. Most specifically, software designed to ensure personal safety and software that controls or manages larger systems can cause serious injuries giving rise to tort liability. For example, software is critical in the safe use of cars, medical devices, aircraft, automated teller machines, medical diagnostic systems, and much more. In light of the Internet of Things, more and more ordinary objects are brought to life by connection to the Internet while simultaneously creating potential tort liability should the software malfunction and cause injury.

II. Tort Law, IT and Software

143. Not only is software critical to a rising number and diversity of objects that can cause serious injury if it malfunctions, concerns over information gathering, emergence and sophistication of hacking, the open-source movement, the Internet of Things and increased computer crime tend to complicate the legal landscape. Moreover, each technological advance increases reliance, exposure, and complexity to any given system. Theoretically, tort negligence permits recovery if a software defect can be proven to result from the service provider's failure to apply due care when designing or implementing ('manufacturing') the software.

144. Tort law, however, is often ill-suited to address injuries that stem from software failure. First, courts have rejected the application of strict liability for defective software. As noted above, strict liability is disfavored because strict liability does not require any showing of intentional or negligent mindset. Courts are loath to impose tort liability, absent a showing of fault. Ultra-dangerous activities arguably support imposition of strict liability due to the hazardous nature of the activity.

145. Likewise, liability for negligently creating or testing software has proven to be a difficult avenue for harmed plaintiffs to cross. First, it is often difficult to prove that a program was negligently created or written. Most lay people are not experts, and there is no uniform standard for proper software design. Expert testimony would be required, which can be cost prohibitive. Responsibility is limited to only harmful defects that could have been detected and corrected through "reasonable"' software practices. Finally, a standard of care for software creators is illusive because the industry assumes that mistakes are inevitable and that it is nearly impossible to design flaw-free software.

146. For example, the court rejected tort claims arising out of an airplane crash in Illinois. In *Thornton v. Hamilton Sundstrand Corp.*, the court rejected claims that the ground proximity warning system computer was defectively designed or dangerous. The deceased passengers' estates argued that the producer of the ground proximity warning system negligently failed to warn the plaintiffs of the systems defects, but the court found no evidence of the same.[142]

147. In another case, a dentist office alleged that software company was grossly negligent in the design and installation of dental practice management software. When the dentist office lost much of its patient information due to alleged software malfunction, the court held that the dentist office had an obligation to backup data routinely, which the dentist office had failed to do.[143]

148. Of course, it is not impossible for a claimant to successfully bring a tort cause of action against a provider of IT or software services. In *In re Sony Gaming Networks and Customer Data Security Breach Litigation*, a court determined liability from Sony's 2011 discovery that hackers had broken into its network and obtained user data for as many as 31 million users, including credit and debit card information. A week after the security breach, Sony informed the public that the personal information had been stolen and admitted that its own failures "may have had a financial impact on our loyal customers," the complaint said. The plaintiffs alleged that Sony failed to follow "basic industry-standard protocols"' to keep personal and financial information secure. The plaintiffs maintained that the company should have known its security measures were inadequate and that its network was vulnerable to an attack. Under negligence law, the court held that Sony had a legal duty to provide reasonable data security protocols. Moreover, by not taking reasonable steps consistent with the industry, Sony breached the standard of care.

149. To date, U.S. tort law has failed to adapt and therefore apply to an increasingly software dependent and computer-reliant system. Contract liability has not fared as poorly as tort law in addressing harms caused by IT failures. But End-User License Agreements and other contractual waivers of liability often emasculate any

142. 54 F. Supp. 3d 929 (N.D. Ill. 2014).
143. *Blaisdell v. Dentrix Dental Systems, Inc.*, 284 P.3d 616 (Utah 2012).

chance of recovery brought by a user based in contract law. For a claimant to successfully prosecute a software company for negligence, an uphill battle awaits. Software design is often mysterious and unique. It is not standardized and it requires a claimant to invest significant resources to hire specialty lawyers, expert witnesses, and software researchers at the front end of the lawsuit.

§5. Ongoing Challenges

150. Given the fluidity and often anonymous nature of electronic transactions and services, protecting consumers is often very difficult. Unwanted commercial email, also known as "spam" email, for example, is frequently used to deliver unwanted material. That material may be merely annoying, but often times the material includes malware or other programs designed to gather private information or inflict serious harm.

151. SPAM is typically advertising in nature, and includes messages promoting dating, gambling, pharmaceuticals, fake charities, and get-rich schemes. The Controlling the Assault of Non-Solicited Pornography And Marketing Act (CAN-SPAM Act) of 2003 attempted to forestall some of these harms by identifying requirements for commercial messages, and giving recipients the right to demand that SPAM emails stop.[144] Perhaps frustratingly, the Act does not require emailers to get permission before they send marketing messages. Although the FTC has authority to enforce the Act's permission, it has been largely ineffectual. Critics of the Act maintain that it appeared to give federal approval to the practice, and spam increased as a result of the law.

152. Even so, some criminal enforcement measures exist under the law. In 2004, for example, the FTC prosecuted the first criminal and civil charges under the Act. The defendants were charged with sending hundreds of thousands of spam emails advertising a diet and hormone products. The FTC stated that these products were effectively worthless and the defendants face up to five years in prison under the anti-spam law. The challenge of controlling spam evolves as technology and market forces change. From email advertisements embedded in blogs to cloaking the identity of the entity responsible for the commercial advertisements, consumers in the U.S. will continue to struggle with this issue.

153. Like SPAM, the emergence of online auctions raises novel legal issues from the standpoint of providing protection to consumers of online auctions. Initially providers of online auctions attempted self-regulation to ensure that buyers and sellers used the auction fairly. But providers have not efficiently policed transactions, instead relying on informal feedback and after-the-fact complaint reporting. If a buyer or seller continuously behaves unfairly, that person will gain a bad reputation. So far, it appears the courts have sanctioned a hands-off approach. For

144. 15U.S.C. § 7701-7713.

example, one opinion held that eBay was not responsible for critical possibly defamatory comments made by buyer sand sellers under the Communications Decency Act. The court thus reinforced an online auction system in which auction providers are inoculated from alleged misdeeds of the true parties to the transaction.

154. Protecting consumers online remains difficult, at best. Customers often have little recourse when bringing complaints to organizations that facilitated the harm but did not directly cause it. Moreover, identifying the parties responsible for directly causing the harm can prove difficult, costly, and ultimately meaningless if such a party is outside the jurisdiction of the court or federal agency.

Chapter 7. Liability of Online Service Providers

§1. Liability of Network Operators

I. General

155. Noncontractual liabilities for network operators either arise from services that the network providers offer or content that third parties post, or transmit through, the network. Liability for content posted by users is similar to liability incurred by service providers, which is examined in the following chapter. To the extent that there is redundancy in services provided by a network operator and ISP in terms of providing a platform for users to post their own content and review content posted by other users, liability for the activities of such customers is typically based on the Network Operator's overt awareness or knowledge of the user's activity. Like ISPs, if the Network Operator is unaware of the behavior of its user, most courts in the U.S. are reluctant to hold the Network Operator liable for that behavior.

156. As to services offered by network operators, the terms of the contracts and terms of services will determine liability typically. As noted above, U.S. law engrafts obligations of fair dealing, good faith, and that services are provided with reasonable skill and care in many instances, which potentially creates added liability above and beyond the textual provisions of contracts and their terms of service. In particular circumstances, like periodic outages of service, most U.S. courts refuse to hold providers liable for such outages, as outages are customary and often impossible to completely forestall.

157. Liability of Network Operators in the U.S. sometimes arises from claims of fraud and/or fraudulent misrepresentation, largely stemming from advertisements or promises made by Network Operators. Several legal definitions attend "fraud," which can lead to confusion. Generally speaking however, fraud stems from a purposeful attempt to deceive or mislead. It includes both commission and omission. It often attends a legal duty that the defendant owes to the claimant. Liability for fraudulent behavior extends beyond civil liability to criminal liability in some instances. As noted above, U.S. law interjects an obligation to act in good faith in contractual transactions, the opposite of purposeful misrepresentation that leads to fraud. Courts have sometimes expressed the legal understanding of fraud-based claims in terms of elements:

- a false representation;
- in reference to a material fact;
- made with knowledge of its falsity;
- with the intent to deceive; and
- justifiable reliance on the representation.

158. Most state laws prohibit fraud in a generic sense with regard to business transactions, such that the relevant inquiry is whether the state law forbidding fraud is preempted by a more specific federal statute. For example, an Indiana court held that federal law did not preempt state law regarding the practice of "cramming," or billing telecommunications customers for services that customers did not consent to or authorize, under provision of the Telecommunications Act of 1996. The decision, although not binding across U.S. jurisdictions, maintained Indiana's right to protect its citizens against similar fraudulent actions.[145]

159. Network Operators may also face liability in tort for the tort of unlawful interference with contract rights. Liability under such a cause of action cuts both ways. In a Florida case, it was the customer who tortiously interfered with a prepaid wireless service provider's contractual rights. There, the customer launched a scheme to sell the provider's prepaid airtime minutes without the consent or authorization of the provider. This interfered with provider's business, because the provider sold subsidized telephones in order to then sell additional airtime minutes. Because the offending customer was aware that the provider had business relationships and contracts with other customers for this purpose, the court held that the offending customer intentionally interfered with the provider's contracts with its other customers. In other words, the provider lost airtime sales it would have obtained but for the interference. The provider also claimed a loss of business goodwill.[146]

160. Noncontractual liabilities for network operators either arise from services that the network providers offer or content that third parties post to, or transmit through, the network. Liability for content posted by users is similar to liability incurred by service providers, which is examined in the following chapter. Generally speaking, U.S. legal systems protect online intermediaries, like ISPs and Network Operators, when third parties seek to hold them liable for the conduct of ISP or Network Operator users. This protective regime is not absolute, of course, and is largely driven by the Digital Millennium Copyright Act safe harbor provision, section 512 of the U.S. Copyright Act, and section 230(c) of the Communications Decency Act. Network operators often house enormous data regarding users. Liability for privacy infractions is discussed in Part VI. Similarly, liability for antitrust or anticompetitive behavior is examined above.

§2. Liability of Service Providers

I. General

161. Noncontractual liabilities for ISPs either arise from services that the ISP offers or content that third parties post to, or transmit through, the ISP. Generally speaking, U.S. legal systems protect online intermediaries, like ISPs, when third parties seek to hold ISPs liable for the conduct of their users. This protective regime

145. *Micronet, Inc. v. Indiana Utility Regulatory Com'n*, 866 N.E.2d 278 (Ind. Ct. App. 2007).
146. *TracFone Wireless, Inc. v. Adams*, 98 F. Supp. 3d 1243 (S.D. Fla. 2015).

is not absolute, of course, and is largely driven by the Digital Millennium Copyright Act safe harbor provision, section 512 of the U.S. Copyright Act, and section 230(c) of the Communications Decency Act. ISPs often house enormous data regarding users. Liability for privacy infractions is discussed in Part VI. Similarly, liability for antitrust or anticompetitive behavior is examined above.

162. As the putative creator of the Internet and major Internet platforms that host data and content, U.S. law, perhaps unsurprisingly, protects ISPs as integral to the system itself. However, a disproportionate body of content hosted and transmitted by ISPs generates from within the U.S. as well, creating a confrontation between ISPs and users who experience violations with regard to content those users own or control. Copyright, of course, provides a prime example, with ISPs facilitating infringement possibilities. Privacy and data security issues, however, are also significant.

163. But other third-party liability claims derive from defamation, false light, fraudulent misrepresentation, false advertising, and child pornography. Longstanding protections for free speech and expression differentiate the U.S. from similar trading partners, like the EU. The First Amendment to the U.S. Constitution codifies an individual's freedom of speech and volumes of legal precedent both institutionalizes that right and limits it. Notably, courts scrutinize and strike government restriction of speech much more readily than private speech restrictions. Even a court order seeking to limit digital content can amount to government regulation that is highly disfavored. As a result, the rights of the speaker in the U.S. frequently conflicts with efforts to curtail content on the Internet and content hosted by ISPs.

164. The manner in which U.S. law allocates liability among these varied interests, of course, reflects policy priorities. Minimizing liability stemming from third-party complaints over content hosted or transferred by ISPs, encourages economic growth in the technology and services sector while reducing consumer protection and copyright protection.

II. Digital Millennium Copyright Act

165. The Digital Millennium Copyright Act (DMCA), which, generally speaking, statutorily limited liability relating to material online, was specifically designed to reduce the liability of ISPs for acts of copyright infringement.[147] This exemption for ISPs shields them from infringement actions brought by their subscribers and from infringement actions based on linking to sites that contain infringement information. To qualify for one of the exemptions under the Act, the service provider's activities at issue must involve functions described in one of four specified categories: (1) Transitory Digital Network Communications, (2) System Caching, (3)

147. 17U.S.C. 512.

Information Residing on Systems or Networks At Direction of Users, and (4) Information Location Tools.[148] Those four categories are distinct, and a service provider's ability to qualify for the exemption associated with any one of the categories must be based solely on the criteria in the applicable category. The liability exemption is arguably justified due to the automatic nature of an ISP's servers. Providing universal access through automated means, dissipates allegations of intentional or volitional wrongdoing.[149]

166. To qualify for immunity for alleged infringement due to content on an ISP's system or network, the following must occur:

(i) does not have actual knowledge that the material or an activity using the material on the system or network is infringing;
(ii) in the absence of such actual knowledge, is not aware of facts or circumstances from which infringing activity is apparent; or
(iii) upon obtaining such knowledge or awareness, acts expeditiously to remove, or disable access to the material;
  (B) does not receive a financial benefit directly attributable to the infringing activity, in a case in which the service provider has the right and ability to control such activity; and
  (C) upon notification of claimed infringement as described in paragraph (3), responds expeditiously to remove, or disable access to, the material that is claimed to be infringing or to be the subject of infringing activity.

167. As evident, the exemption from liability is not unlimited. The exemption applies as long as the service provider is not aware of the "facts and circumstances from which infringing activity is apparent," gets no financial benefit from the infringing activity, and does not itself take part in editing the material or selecting its audience. In other words, an ISP or other computer system operator is contributorily liable for copyright infringement if it has actual knowledge about discrete infringing material on its system and could have exercised reasonable means to prevent further infringement, but nevertheless continues to provide access to infringing works.[150] For example, in a 2009 California case, the fact that a video-sharing website hosted an entire category of content—music—that was subject to copyright protection did not establish that the operator had actual knowledge of infringement, as required to prove that it was not entitled to coverage under the safe harbor provision.[151]

168. In *Arista Records LLC v. Usenet.com, Inc.*, operators of a file distribution service were not protected under this provision because they actively engaged in conduct that facilitated direct infringement of recording companies' copyrights. The plaintiffs in that case were able to prove that the operators were aware that digital

148. 17U.S.C.A. § 1201(a)(b)(c)(d).
149. *Rosen v. Hosting Services, Inc.*, 771 F. Supp. 2d 1219 (C.D. Cal. 2010).
150. 17U.S.C.A. § 512(c)(1).
151. *UMG Recordings, Inc. v. Veoh Networks Inc.*, 665 F. Supp. 2d 1099 (C.D. Cal. 2009).

music files were among the most popular items on the service, and took active measures to create servers dedicated to music files. The operators also purposely increased retention times of particular groups containing those files, and engaged in several overt efforts that demonstrated their control over the groups that could access their servers.[152]

III. Communications Decency Act

169. As stated above, liability for ISPs and similar hosts generally stems from the ISP's knowledge of tortious content. In the nascent years following this approach, ISPs were essentially incentivized to look the other way, or assure their own ignorance of content they hosted. While many hosts and intermediaries had the capability to filter out offending content, such filtering invited liability. This tension prompted Congress to draft section 230 of the Communications Decency Act.[153] Congress hoped to both maintain and encourage interactive content sharing while also protecting third parties and their rights to protect their own content.

170. Section 230 states that "No provider or user of an interactive computer service shall be treated as the publisher or speaker of any information provided by another information content provider," effectively shielding intermediaries like ISPs from being liable to users as a publisher of content. Online intermediaries that host or republish content are protected against an array of laws that might otherwise be used to hold them legally responsible for what other users say and do. The law defines an "interactive computer service"' as "any information service, system, or access software provider that provides or enables computer access by multiple users to a computer server . . ."' As a result, protected intermediaries are broad and apply beyond large ISPs. They include most services that publish third-party content like social media websites, message boards, search engines, and blogging platforms.

171. Although section 230 does not protect against certain criminal and intellectual property claims, it does protect against claims of tortious interference, defamation, invasion of privacy, and general negligence claims stemming from third-party content. The law does not protect statements of the ISP or intermediary itself. U.S. courts have also indicated that section 230 does not protect an intermediary when an intermediary materially edits the content of a third party and substantially alters its meaning in a way to engender liability—for example, defamation. Similarly, if an intermediary mandates that users submit unlawful content, or if the intermediary promises to remove material and then fails to do so, section 230 will likely not protect the intermediary.

172. Overall, this important protection has facilitated great expansion in content across a variety of platforms. Vimeo and YouTube use continues to grow. Yelp reviews, Facebook sharing, and Twitter networking and transmission of content

---

152. *Arista Records LLC v. Usenet.com, Inc.*, 633 F. Supp. 2d 124 (S.D. N.Y. 2009).
153. 47U.S.C. § 230.

have all increased in frequency and volume. Liability that traditionally would have been shared by online intermediaries is now relegated for the most part to users. U.S. courts, although not always, tend to decide ambiguous claims in favor of service providers.

173. The most prominent decision covering the scope and effect of section 230 of the CDA is *Zeran v. America Online, Inc.*[154] After the Oklahoma City bombing in 1995, an individual posed advertisement for offensive t-shirts that made fun of those who died in the bombing. The advertisements were posted on AOL's message boards. The individual who posted the advertisement gave a false telephone number for t-shirt purchases—to one Zeran. Zeran was not an AOL subscriber but received death threats from several who were offended. Zeran asked AOL to remove the advertisement, claiming it was a hoax. AOL agreed and truncated the account, but the offending individual set up new AOL accounts. AOL could not identify the individual or effectively block the AOL accounts. Zeran sued AOL and argued that AOL negligently failed to take down the advertisements or block ensuing messages that were tied to Zeran's phone number.

174. In response, AOL argued that CDA § 230(c) immunized it from the false and offensive statements posted on AOL's system. Zeran claimed that AOL should be liable because it negligently distributed offensive materials after AOL had been advised on their defamatory nature. The court granted judgment for AOL with the Fourth Circuit Court of Appeals relying on section 230 of the CDA and Congress' intent to encourage service providers to self-regulate with regard to transmission of offensive material on their platforms. The court interpreted section 230 of the CDA broadly. It extended immunity to ISPs for the otherwise defamatory materials disseminated over their systems even if the ISPs are aware that the materials are defamatory:

> By its plain language, § 230 creates a federal immunity to any cause of action that would make service providers liable for information originating with a third-party user of the service. Specifically, § 230 precludes courts from entertaining claims that would place a computer service provider in a publisher's role. Thus, lawsuits seeking to hold a service provider liable for its exercise of a publisher's traditional editorial functions—such as deciding whether to publish, withdraw, postpone or alter content—are barred.[155]

175. Subsequent cases have largely conformed to the broad protection identified in *Zeran v. America Online, Inc.*

154. 129 F.3d 327, 330 (4th Cir. 1997), *cert denied*, 538 524U.S. 937 (1998).
155. *Ibid.*

IV. Common Law

176. The statutory constructs outlined above go a long way in modifying traditional common law precepts regarding the publication of defamatory material, reputational harms, and other common law remedies available against the publisher. Under U.S. common law, publishing false statements about a person that results in reputational harm can generate liability. Defamation, however, is more difficult to successfully prove in the U.S. as opposed to most nations in the EU because of First Amendment protections in the U.S. Constitution for free speech, free assembly, and free press.

177. Moreover, common law tort liability stemming from publication of false or misleading statements varies from state to state. Generally speaking, however, a claimant must demonstrate three elements: (1) that the defendant published the offending statement; (2) that the statement was false and that it was not an opinion or puffery; and (3) that the defendant acted negligently at the time it was published. Some gradations apply. With element three, a public figure enjoys less protection. For a public figure to successfully bring a defamation claim, he must show that the defendant acted maliciously—or with knowledge of the statement's falsity.

178. Prior to online intermediaries and ISPs, newspapers, magazines, and the like were liable for defamatory content if these elements were met, even when the content itself clearly originated with a third party. Such liability was not typically extended to wholesalers or mass distributors like libraries and bookstores, even if those entities had reason to know of a magazine's or book's defamatory nature. Many commentators analogize the library, or bookstore to modern day online intermediaries, and the protections afforded by the CDA appear to support that analogy.

Part IV. Intellectual Rights

Chapter 1. Patent Law

§1. General

179. Historically, intellectual property protections have evolved into four main categories: copyrights, trademarks, trade secrets, and patents. These protections guard a wide range of ideas, inventions, and creations, but each honors an underlying principle to protect a product of human creation from the unauthorized use by others. As detailed above, copyrights give exclusive rights to authors and creators of copyrightable works, such as books, songs, or works of art, by granting the ability to exclude others from reproducing or publicly performing or displaying the work for a limited amount of time. As detailed below, trademark protections aim to prevent fraud and deception in the marketplace by attaching protections to words, symbols, or devices that are used to identify and distinguish a unique product from one sold or manufactured by others. Trade secret protections aim to protect against anyone acquiring or disclosing confidential information through improper actions, such as corporate espionage. Finally, patent law seeks to promote innovation by giving inventors a limited right to exclude others from using their new inventions or methods without permission. Generally speaking, IP law attempts to satisfy the twin objectives of rewarding innovators and creators for their valuable creations while simultaneously promoting further innovation throughout society. Thus, IP law in the U.S. is a primarily utilitarian-justified scheme.

180. Like many legal constructs in U.S. law, the U.S. patent system derived from western European practices, particularly those in the UK. While the guild system worked in England for a time, around the sixteenth and seventeenth centuries the system began to fail. A system that was intended to protect innovations instead turned into a system of the government taking payments in return for the conferment of a monopoly. In order to combat this faltering system, England passed the Statute of Monopolies in 1623, which provided a limited monopoly of fourteen years of exclusivity to a "true and first inventor" of a patent.[156]

---

156. *Statute of Monopolies 1623*, c. 3. available at: http://www.legislation.gov.uk/aep/Ja1/21/3/section/VI (last accessed Jan. 29, 2020).

181. Intellectual property law in the U.S. originally developed in the thirteen colonies, with each colony passing its own laws. This led to issues with enforceability and conflicts among the colonies. To remedy this problem, the Patent Act was passed shortly after independence in 1790 to codify and align patent laws across the U.S. The Patent Act allowed for exclusive rights to the invention for fourteen years and described the requirements for application for a patent:

> [A] specification in writing, containing a description, accompanied with drafts or models, and explanations and models (if the nature of the invention or discovery will admit of a model) of the thing or things, by him or them invented or discovered, and described as aforesaid, in the said patents; which specification shall be so particular, and said models so exact, as not only to distinguish the invention or discovery from other things before known and used, but also to enable a workman or other person skilled in the art or manufacture, whereof it is a branch, or wherewith it may be nearest connected, to make, construct, or use the same, to the end that the public may have the full benefit thereof, after the expiration of the patent term.[157]

182. Since 1790, the U federal patent laws have undergone several changes, most notably in a major overhaul through the Patent Act in 1952[158] and the America Invents Act of 2011.[159] Even so, many key terms and concepts from the 1790 Act are still present in contemporary U.S. patent law.

183. The federal patent laws that govern the U.S. today derive their authority from the U.S. Constitution. Under Article I of the Constitution, Congress has the power "[t]o promote the Progress of Science and useful Arts, by securing for limited Times to Authors and Inventors the exclusive Right to their respective Writings and Discoveries."[160] As noted above, until 1790, patent protections were offered by state legislatures until the Patent Act of 1790 codified the basis of the federal patent laws that currently exist in the U.S. Shortly thereafter, a second patent statute was enacted in 1793 which established four enumerated categories of patentable subject matter—art, machine, manufacture, and composition of matter. Both the 1790 and the 1793 Acts established a fourteen-year patent length and included a requirement for the inventor to file a written specification that described her invention.

184. Throughout the years, U.S. patent law had many small changes and amendments, but it was not until 1952 that major deviations occurred. The Patent Act of 1952 made two major changes to patent law. First, a statutory requirement was added that an invention had to be nonobvious in order to be patentable. Second, the patentable subject matter category of "art" was replaced with "process." Both these changes helped to codify years of case law that had already identified these guidelines.

157. Patent Act of 1790, Ch. 7, 1 Stat. 109–12 (amended 1793).
158. Patent Act of 1952, Pub. L. No. 82-593, 66 Stat. 792 (1952).
159. Leahy-Smith America Invents Act, Pub. L. No. 112-29, 125 Stat. 284 (2011).
160. U.S. Const. Art. I.

185. There have been numerous alterations to U.S. patent law since 1952, both through statutes and case law. In 1966, the Supreme Court set out the test for deciding whether or not a claimed invention is obvious in Graham v. John Deere:

> Under § 103, the scope and content of the prior art are to be determined; differences between the prior art and the claims at issue are to be ascertained; and the level of ordinary skill in the pertinent art resolved. Against this background, the obviousness or nonobviousness of the subject matter is determined.[161]

186. The test announced in Graham came to be called the Graham Factual Inquiries and these factors are still used to analyze obviousness today.

187. In 1980, the Supreme Court held that a genetically engineered bacterium was patentable by quoting a Congressional report that stated that Congress intended the 1952 Act to "include anything under the sun that is made by man."[162] In 1998, the Court of Appeals for the Federal Circuit held that U.S. patent law does not prohibit patents for business methods as long as they are new, useful, and nonobvious in *State Street Bank v. Signature Financial.*[163]

188. A significant change also occurred in 1996 when the U.S. Congress enacted the Uruguay Round Agreements Act to implement the Marrakesh Agreement of 1994. The biggest change to patent law from the Act was the change of the patent term from seventeen years from the grant date to twenty years from the filing date. In addition to harmonizing U.S. patent law with the patent laws of other countries, this change put an end to a practice that had been used by some inventors to extend the patent monopoly on their inventions far beyond twenty years.

189. More recently, in 2011, the America Invents Act was enacted by the U.S. Congress. The law changed the U.S. patent system from a "first to invent" to "first inventor to file" system.[164] These changes went into effect in March of 2013. Also in 2013, the Supreme Court limited some potentially patentable subject matter in *Molecular Pathology v. Myriad Genetics* by "hold[ing] that a naturally occurring DNA segment is a product of nature and not patent eligible merely because it has been isolated."[165] While U.S. patent law has evolved since its creation, the principal objectives have remained constant.

---

161. *Graham v. John Deere*, 383U.S. 1, 18 (1966).
162. *Diamond v. Chakrabarty*, 447U.S. 303, 309 (1980).
163. *State Street Bank v. Signature Financial*, 149 F.3d. 1368 (Fed. Cir. 1998).
164. Leahy-Smith America Invents Act, Pub. L. No. 112-29, 125 Stat. 284 (2011).
165. *Association for Molecular Pathology v. Myriad Genetics, Inc.*, 569U.S. 576 (2013).

§2. Requirements of Patentability

190. As U.S. patents can only be granted by the United States Patent and Trademark Office (USPTO), there are a series of formal administrative processes that must be completed before an inventor can gain patent protection. The patent process begins when an inventor files an application for her patent which describes the invention and enables a hypothetical "person skilled in the art" to make and use the invention. This application will also specify claims in the description. These claims describe the subject matter that the inventor regards as her invention, as well as stating the legal boundaries of the products or processes that the patent owner can legally protect.

191. From a practical standpoint, patent law defines the patentee's invention not by what the inventor actually built or described but by the parameters of the patent claims. Claims are the legal definition of the invention. Because the words of the claim, not what the patentee actually built, determines whether the patent is valid, claim language has come to have outsized importance in patent law. Some scholars maintain that almost every patent case involves argument and assessment of the meaning of the words written by lawyers to try to capture the outer boundaries of the patentee's legal right.

192. In addition to the application, the patented product or process must meet the substantive requirements of U.S. patent law. Section 101 of Title 35 describes the functional requirements of a patent: "Whoever invents or discovers any new and useful process, machine, manufacture, or composition of matter, or any new and useful improvement thereof, may obtain a patent therefor, subject to the conditions and requirements of this title."[166] These requirements are broken down into four different areas: utility, novelty, nonobviousness, and patentable subject matter.

I. Utility

193. The utility requirement of patentability refers to the usefulness of the invention. To be considered useful today, an invention must be capable of providing some identifiable benefit. The qualifying use does not need to be commercial or industrial in its benefit. Additionally, immoral or harmful uses are not prohibited. However, in the early days of U.S. patent law, this was not the case. In 1817, Justice Story created the doctrine of "moral utility," which required that a new invention be moral and not mischievous in nature:

> All that the law requires is, that the invention should not be frivolous or injurious to the well-being, good policy, or sound morals of society. The word 'useful,' therefore, is incorporated into the Act in contradistinction to mischievous

166. 35U.S.C. Section 101 (2015).

or immoral. For instance, a new invention to poison people, or to promote debauchery, or to facilitate private assassination, is not a patentable invention.[167]

194. This "moral utility" requirement impacted patent cases in the U.S. until it was terminated in 1999, via a case before the Federal Circuit. This case, *Juicy Whip, Inc. v. Orange Bang, Inc.*, dismissed the "moral utility" requirement and once again set the standard to be whether an invention or process provided some identifiable benefit. The usefulness requirement is a very low bar, and it is uncommon for a patent application to be rejected, or a patent to be later invalidated, for not meeting the usefulness requirement.

II. Novelty

195. As directed by section 102 of Title 35, an invention must be new in order to be eligible for a patent. To be new, an invention must not be anticipated by prior art. Generally speaking, prior art includes all published information and publicly available information as of the filing date of the application. If a single prior art reference contains each and every limitation of a patent claim, the prior art is held to "anticipate" the claim and preclude patentability of that claim. Unlike obviousness, the prior art for anticipation purposes does not need to be from the same technical field as the claimed invention. Anticipation by a single prior art reference can be established by both the express teachings and the inherent teachings in the prior art reference.

196. Prior to the America Invents Act, an inventor could satisfy the novelty requirement for patentability by showing that her invention was new at the time she invented it, even if her invention would not have been new on the date of her application filing. This is due to the U.S. "first to invent" system. As of 2013 though, the U.S. patent system is using a "first inventor to file" system. Under this system, an invention will be blocked from patent protection if it was patented, described in a printed publication, or in public use, on sale or otherwise available to the public before the filing date of the application in which the claimed invention is presented.[168] The revised statute still provides an approximately one-year grace period for an inventor to file their patent application, but exercising the grace period may impact the inventor's ability to obtain patent rights in other international jurisdictions.

III. Nonobviousness

197. In addition to satisfying the novelty requirement under 35 U.S.C. § 102, an invention must satisfy the requirement for nonobviousness under 35 U.S.C. § 103.

167. *Lowell v. Lewis*, 15 F. Cas. 1018, 1019 (C.C.D. Mass. 1817).
168. 35U.S.C. s. 102(a) (2015).

In other words, even if the claimed invention is new, it may not be patented if the invention would have been obvious to one of ordinary skill in the art to which the claimed invention relates (also known as the phosita) based on the prior art. This prior art must be viewed as a whole and must be in existence before the effective filing date of the patent application. As mentioned above, the Graham Factual Inquiries provide the method by which courts and the USPTO determine whether a particular patent or patent application claim is obvious in view of the prior art.

198. The final step of the Graham analysis is to determine whether the invention is obvious in view of the teachings of the prior art and the level of ordinary skill in the art. Following the lead of the Federal Circuit, for many years courts (and patent examiners) used the Teaching, Suggestion, or Motivation (TSM) test to make this determination. The TSM test asked whether there were some TSM in the prior art that would have led a person of ordinary skill in the art (phosita) to combine the relevant prior art teachings in the manner claimed in the invention. However, in *KSR International Co. v. Teleflex, Inc.*, the Supreme Court substantially revamped obviousness analysis in the U.S. In rejecting the TSM test as the sole test for obviousness, the court stated: "A person of ordinary skill is also a person of ordinary creativity, not an automaton."[169] The court went on to announce a host of different rationales under which a claimed invention could be found obvious, one of which was the TSM test. The *KSR* decision by the Supreme Court caused the USPTO to publish new guidelines to help examiners recognize when a patent application may be obvious. These new guidelines detail seven rationales that can be used to properly reject a claim for obviousness:

(1) combining prior art elements according to known methods to yield predictable results;
(2) simple substitution of one known element for another to obtain predictable results;
(3) use of known technique to improve similar devices (methods, or products) in the same way;
(4) applying a known technique to a known device (method, or product) ready for improvement to yield predictable results;
(5) "Obvious to try" – —choosing from a finite number of identified, predictable solutions, with a reasonable expectation of success;
(6) known work in one field of endeavor may prompt variations of it for use in either the same field or a different one based on design incentives or other market forces if the variations are predictable to one of the ordinary skills in the art;
(7) some TSM in the prior art that would have led one of the ordinary skills to modify the prior art reference or to combine prior art reference teachings to arrive at the claimed invention.[170]

169. *KSR International Co. v. Teleflex, Inc.*, 550U.S. 398, 421 (2007).
170. MPEP § 2141, at 2100-143–2100-144 (9th ed. Mar. 2014).

199. Due to the fact-intensive and somewhat subjective nature of the obviousness analysis, this requirement is often the most difficult one to overcome in either getting a patent granted by the USPTO or maintaining the validity of an issued patent during litigation. Especially in a patent infringement case, where a jury member may be asked to step into the shoes of a scientist or engineer at the time when the patent application was filed, obviousness can become a difficult requirement.

§3. Patentable Subject Matter

200. Although the U.S. Supreme Court once opined that patent-eligible subject matter is virtually "anything under the sun that is made by man,"[171] several important restrictions, in fact, apply. Due to long-standing common law precedent, laws of nature, physical phenomena, and abstract ideas are not patent eligible. Additionally, until 1981, the USPTO held that computer programs were generally unpatentable. In 1981, the Supreme Court analyzed a patent on a method that utilized a computer program as part of a rubber curing process in *Diamond v. Diehr*. The court upheld the patent because the *Diehr* inventors did "not seek to patent a mathematical formula. Instead they s[ought] patent protection for a process of curing synthetic rubber."[172] The court also reasoned that while "[t]heir process admittedly employ[ed] a well-known mathematical equation . . . they d[id] not seek to preempt the use of that equation."[173] The court differentiated this case from previous cases they deemed unpatentable on the grounds that the patent in *Diehr* involved a physical transformation. The court stated that physical transformation is "the clue to the patentability of a process claim that does not include particular machines."[174]

201. Following *Diehr*, the Federal Circuit court of appeals continued to expand software patentability by holding that a patent on a processing system implementing an investment structure was valid as a statutory machine claim in *State Street Bank & Trust Co. v. Signature Financial Group*. These cases, as well as many other cases, used a multitude of tests to determine the patentability of software innovations. These tests included the Mental Steps Exception, found in *CyberSource Corp. v. Retail Decisions, Inc.*;[175] the Inventive Concepts test, found in *Parker v. Flook*;[176] and the Machine-or-Transformation Test, first found in *Gottschalk v. Benson*.[177] Despite these multitude of different tests, uncertainty remained as to the full scope of patentability for software innovations.

202. The Supreme Court addressed the issue of software patents most recently in *Alice Corp. v. CLS Bank International*.[178] In that case, the court invalidated patent

171. *Diamond v. Chakrabarty*, 447U.S. 303, 309 (1980).
172. *Diamond v. Diehr*, 450U.S. 175, 187 (1981).
173. *Id.* at 187–88.
174. *Id.* at 184.
175. *CyberSource Corp. v. Retail Decisions, Inc.*, 654 F.3d 1366 (Fed. Cir. 2011).
176. *Parker v. Flook*, 437U.S. 584 (1978).
177. *Gottschalk v. Benson*, 409U.S. 63 (1972).
178. *Alice Corp. Pty. Ltd. v. CLS Bank Int'l*, 134 S. Ct. 2347 (2014).

claims for a method of performing hedging because the claims were "directed to an abstract idea."[179] Additionally, there was no inventive step transforming that idea into a patent-eligible invention. More specifically, the court held that "the mere recitation of a generic computer cannot transform a patent-ineligible abstract idea into a patent-eligible invention."[180] The court determined that Alice Corp. was attempting to patent the abstract idea of a "fundamental economic practice" by having a computer perform the practice. Unfortunately, the court in *Alice* did not articulate a bright line test for software patentability, so questions still abound on what software is eligible for patents and which test should be used to determine said eligibility. Nevertheless, the court did set forth a two-step analysis to determine whether a particular claimed invention is directed to patent-eligible subject matter. The two-step Alice Test proceeds as follows: first, the court determines whether the claims at issue are directed to one of the patent-ineligible concepts (abstract ideas, laws of nature, or physical phenomena), and then the court considers the elements of each claim both individually and as an ordered combination to determine whether the additional elements transform the nature of the claim into a patent-eligible application. The latter part of the test is often referred to as the search for an "inventive concept," in other words, an element or combination of elements that is sufficient to ensure that the patent in practice amounts to significantly more than a patent upon the ineligible concept itself.

203. Following *Alice*, both the USPTO and the courts have struggled to precisely define what inventions meet the inventive concept requirement of the Alice Test. Both the courts and the USPTO have been active in using different tests (either through court decisions or through internal USPTO guidance) to try and address this issue. Several of these tests are addressed below, but none of them have been thus far approved by the Supreme Court.

I. The Mental Steps Exception

204. This test involves ascertaining whether an invention encompasses only methods that may be carried out in the human mind. Such a method "is merely an abstract idea and is not patent-eligible under § 101." The motivating sentiment behind this test is the unease felt toward a scheme that effectively makes a thought process legally protected. In early cases, the U.S. Supreme Court applied this test rather narrowly, and allowed patents unless an invention as conceived by the inventor *necessarily* required steps performed in the human mind.

205. In *In re Bernhart*, for example, the software enabled a two-dimensional portrayal of a three-dimensional object from any desired angle and distance and on any desired plane of projection. The patent disclosed the use of a general purpose computer and the specific equations used to generate the projections. The patent

179. Id.
180. *Id.* at 2358.

claim recited steps of programming the computer to perform equations and generate the plots. In holding that these claims were eligible for patentability, the court stated:

> Moreover, all machines function according to laws of physics which can be mathematically set forth if known. We cannot deny patents on machines merely because their novelty may be explained in terms of such laws if we are to obey the mandate of Congress that a machine is subject matter for a patent. We should not penalize the inventor who makes his invention by discovering new and unobvious mathematical relationships which he then utilizes in a machine, as against the inventor who makes the same machine by trial and error and does not disclose the laws by which it operates.[181]

206. But more recently, U.S. courts have broadened the "mental steps" doctrine in way that narrows patentability of software. In *CyberSource Corp. v. Retail Decisions, Inc.*, the U.S. Court of Appeals for the Federal Circuit addressed disputed patent eligibility for a patent that described a method and system for detecting fraud of credit card transactions through the Internet. More specifically, the patent articulated a method and system for detecting fraud of credit card transactions through the Internet by using IP addresses, MAC addresses, email addresses, and other similar data in order to determine if an address was associated with the credit card. The court likened the claim to something which can be performed mentally by a human, ruling that it is not patent-eligible. The court held that the innovations were not patent-eligible because they attempted to capture "unpatentable mental processes." No algorithms of any kind attended the innovation and each of the steps were conceivably doable in the human mind. As a result, the court ruled that the innovations were akin to "basic tools of scientific and technological work."[182]

II. Preemption and Meaningful Limitations

207. This two-step test involves evaluating whether the patent too broadly preempts any further use of a natural law, natural phenomena, or abstract idea due to a lack of meaningful limitations. First, a court determines whether the patent is drawn to one of the previously mentioned exceptions; second, a court asks if there are meaningful limitations that would prevent wholesale preemption. Some preemption is a natural result of giving a monopoly on the practice of an invention. The purpose of this analysis, however, is to ensure that the preemption does not restrict future innovation too expansively.[183]

181. 417 F.2d 1395 (C.C.P.A. 1969).
182. 654 F.3d 1366 (Fed. Cir. 2011).
183. Shane D. Anderson, *Software, Abstractness, and Soft Physicality Requirements*, 29 Harv. J.L. & Tech., 567, 572–73 (2016).

III. Flook-like Inventive Concepts ("point of novelty")

208. This analysis is similar to that done when looking for meaningful limitations to a possibly preemptory invention. There is, however, a subtle difference in formulation. Under this test, non-inventive concepts are first eliminated from the scope of the invention. The remaining components are assumed to be the invention for which protection is sought and they are what is analyzed under § 101. This test has been chastised for bringing an inherent § 103 nonobviousness analysis into the § 101 patentability analysis.

209. *In re Abrams* involved claims "for Petroleum Prospecting Method." In this case, a portion of the claimed patent was objected to as "purely mental in character." The patent claim recited "a method of prospecting for petroliferous deposits" with six steps; the court determined the last three were "mental steps." The three mental steps involved "measuring the rate of pressure rise," "determining the rate . . . at a standard reference," and "comparing the rates . . . to detect anomalies." The court adopted a different approach to patentability by sorting claims into one of the three categories. The first category is where all method steps "are purely mental in character," which would clearly not be patentable. The second and third are more challenging. The second category is where "a method claim embodies both positive and physical steps as well as so-called mental steps," but the novelty is in the mental steps; "then the claim is considered unpatentable for the same reason that it would be if all the steps were purely mental in character." The last category is where the novelty "resides in one or more of the positive and physical steps," and contains patentable subject matter.[184]

210. The court found that the patent claim fell within the second category of claims. The court found steps "involving therein such purely mental terms as "determining," "registering," "counting," "observing," "measuring," "comparing," "recording," and "computing"" to be non-statutory. The point-of-novelty test articulated in In re Abrams was prominent in the U.S. Patent and Trademark Office for about two decades before it began to fall out of favor from the courts in the 1970s. Even so, the court has not formally rejected the test. It was applied to a computer program in 1978 in *Parker v. Flook*. Flook applied for a patent for a method of updating alarm limits during catalytic conversion. According to the majority opinion, "[t]he only novel feature of the method is a mathematical formula," which is used to calculate the alarm limit that signals the "presence of an abnormal condition indicating either inefficiency or perhaps danger." The examiner rejected Flook's application because "a patent on this method "would in practical effect be a patent on the formula or mathematics itself."[185]

---

184. 188 F.2d 165 (C.C.P.A. 1951).
185. 437U.S. 584 (1978).

IV. The Machine-or-Transformation Test

211. As noted above, this test addresses processes that qualify for consideration if they (1) are implemented by a particular machine in a nonconventional and non-trivial manner or (2) transform an article from one state to another. Transformation of an article from one thing or state to another is said to be a clue to patent eligibility. In *Gottschalk v. Benson*, the court analyzed the machine-or-transformation test and partially embraced the test, stating that "transformation and reduction of an article to a different state or thing is the clue to the patentability of a process claim … ."[186]

212. Although the Supreme Court relegated this test to a lesser status – more like a factor in determining patentability, it remains a useful indicator. The Supreme Court's opinion in *Bilski v. Kappos*, rejected machine-or-transformation as the sole test of patent eligibility, and confirmed that it is only a "useful clue." In a case mentioned above, *CyberSource Corp. v. Retail Decisions, Inc.*, the court also considered a patent claim under the machine-or-transformation text. The patent described a method and system for detecting fraud of credit card transactions through the Internet. The court held that limitation of a process to implementation "over the Internet" does not satisfy the machine-or-transformation test. The court found that the Internet is not a "particular machine," but more akin to an intangible abstraction. The court also noted that the limitation to a particular technological environment is a mere field-of-use limitation, which does not suffice under § 101. Finally, the court held that the use of the Internet does not impose meaningful limits on the preemptive scope of the claims.[187]

213. The decision in *Alice* may be seen as a call for an altered machine-or-transformation test, where the computer that operationalizes the software is the machine and the software must meet the transformation requirement of the test. However, even using the machine-or-transformation test, software patents may run into issues where only the software remains to be patented. Many difficulties exist in the software patent realm, partly due to the vague tests of patent eligibility and partly to the complexity of software. This can lead to innovators avoiding the patent system altogether when it comes to new software.

§4. Infringement

I. Literal Infringement and the Doctrine of Equivalents

214. Under U.S. law, anyone who, without permission of the patentee, makes, uses, sells, offers for sale, or imports a patented invention is liable for patent infringement. Because of the focus on claims as defining the patent right in U.S. patent practice, infringement litigation proceeds in two steps. First, the claims are

186. 409U.S. 63 (1972).
187. 654 F.3d 1366 (Fed. Cir. 2011).

construed in what is termed a "Markman Hearing." The purpose of the Markman Hearing is to determine the precise meaning of all of the claim terms so that infringement can be determined. Once the claims are construed, the case will proceed to the next step, which is the infringement determination. In order to infringe a patent claim, each and every element of the asserted claim(s) must be present in the accused product, process, etc. must include each and every element of the asserted claim, either literally or equivalently.

215. Because of the imprecision of language, over a century ago, the Supreme Court created the Doctrine of Equivalents to account for the situation where an accused device does not literally include every element of the asserted claim, but the differences between the claim and the accused device are so slight, that they could essentially be considered equivalents. To determine whether an equivalent is sufficient to establish infringement, courts use the Function/Way/Result Test. This test asks whether the alleged equivalent performs substantially the same function, in substantially the same way, to achieve substantially the same result, as the claim limitation. If this test is met, a device can be found infringing if it includes the equivalent in place of a literal claim element.

II. Damages

216. By statute, patent infringers are required to pay damage sufficient to compensate the patent holder, but not less than a reasonable royalty. Practically speaking, this means that patent plaintiffs can obtain either lost profits damages or a reasonable royalty. Lost profits is the less common measure of damages for a couple of reasons. First, in order to prove lost profits, the plaintiff actually needs to be in the market in competition with the infringer. Many patent plaintiffs are not actually practicing their patents in the market and so the lost profits damages measure would result in no damages award. Second, determining the actual amount of lost profits with the precision required for a court damages award can be quite difficult. This can be a very fact-intensive analysis, typically including expert testimony, and the ultimate amount determined may not be significant. Finally, building off of the last point, using a lost profits damages measure may lead to a comparatively small damages award, which may not be sufficient to deter future infringement.

217. Because of the issues with lost profits calculations, many, if not most, plaintiffs elect to proceed on a reasonable royalty damages basis. The mechanism for determining the reasonable royalty is termed the "hypothetical negotiation."' In this approach, the court will attempt to determine the amount of royalty a willing licensee and willing licensor would settle on in an arms-length negotiation taking place before the infringement commenced. The Georgia Pacific Factors are typically used to guide the hypothetical negotiation analysis. The factors are too numerous to list here,[188] but they include all of the considerations that a would-be licensee and licensor are likely to take into account in determining a royalty. One factor is particularly relevant, which is the amount of any established royalty related to the patents at issue. This evidence is not available in every case, but when it is available it can be strong evidence that a comparable royalty is reasonable.

218. Each side will typically provide expert testimony as to the correct royalty amount and in most cases, the estimates proffered by the respective experts will differ significantly. Nevertheless, after all of the testimony has been provided, the fact finder will be required to make a damages determination. In certain exceptional cases, damages may be tripled and the plaintiff may also obtain an award of attorney's fees.[189]

219. In addition to money damages, an infringement plaintiff may also be able to obtain an injunction against continuing or future infringement. Plaintiffs will often attempt to obtain a preliminary injunction at the beginning of the proceeding as such an injunction can provide a powerful incentive to defendants to settle the case. After establishing liability for infringement, plaintiffs will also often try to obtain a permanent injunction to prevent future infringement. Irrespective of whether the injunction is sought at the beginning or end of a case, the standard for granting an injunction is essentially the same. Previously, patent plaintiffs enjoyed a presumption that injunctive relief was appropriate, but now, following Supreme Court precedent, plaintiffs have to show that an injunction is appropriate based on four factors.[190] In particular, a party seeking an injunction must show: "(1) that it has suffered an irreparable injury; (2) that remedies available at law, such as monetary damages, are inadequate to compensate for that injury; (3) that, considering the balance of hardships between the plaintiff and defendant, a remedy in equity is warranted; and (4) that the public interest would not be disserved by a permanent injunction."[191] Accordingly, obtaining an injunction can be more difficult, but if obtained, it can be an important part of the plaintiff's overall remedy for patent infringement.

III. Defenses

220. There are a variety of defenses available in patent infringement cases, including obviously, no infringement. Because establishing infringement requires an element-by-element analysis of the accused device in view of the claims, the alleged infringer only needs to show that a single element is not present in the accused

188. There are fifteen Georgia Pacific Factors. *See Georgia-Pac. Corp. v.U.S. Plywood Corp.*, 318 F. Supp. 1116, 1120 (S.D.N.Y. 1970), modified sub nom. *Georgia-Pac. Corp. v.U.S. Plywood-Champion Papers, Inc.*, 446 F.2d 295 (2d Cir. 1971).
189. *See Octane Fitness, LLC v. ICON Health & Fitness, Inc.*, 572U.S. 545, 134 S. Ct. 1749 (2014).
190. *See eBay Inc. v. MercExchange, L.L.C.*, 547U.S. 388, 391, 126 S. Ct. 1837, 1839 (2006).
191. *Id.*

device to avoid infringement. Because the claim construction adopted by the court at the Markman Hearing (discussed above) can be outcome determinative with respect to infringement, defendants have a strong incentive to argue claim construction positions that are likely to preclude a finding of infringement.

221. In addition to noninfringement, patent defendants can also argue invalidity. Issued patents have a presumption of validity, but defendants can still mount a substantial challenge to the validity of an issued patent based upon prior art or subject matter ineligibility. With respect to prior art invalidity, defendants may uncover prior art that was not considered by the USPTO when originally issuing the patent and thus, such prior art may provide strong evidence of invalidity due to either anticipation or obviousness. With respect to subject matter eligibility, as discussed above, particularly as it relates to software and business method patents, the law for subject matter eligibility is currently very muddled, and thus defendants have a strong incentive to bring invalidity claims based on subject matter eligibility of these types of patents.

222. In the past, defendants would often try to establish that the plaintiff had engaged in inequitable conduct in obtaining the patent. The effect of establishing inequitable conduct is that the associated patent is rendered unenforceable. A typical argument to establish inequitable conduct is that the patentee knew of relevant prior art and did not disclose it to the USPTO during prosecution, which would be a violation of the applicant's duty of candor. However, recently, the Federal Circuit tightened the standards for establishing inequitable conduct in Therasense v. Becton.[192] In particular, in order to establish inequitable conduct, "the accused infringer must prove that the patentee acted with the specific intent to deceive the PTO."[193] Accordingly, assertions of inequitable conduct are now less common, but it can be raised as a defense if the facts warrant.

192. *Therasense, Inc. v. Becton, Dickinson & Co.*, 649 F.3d 1276 (Fed. Cir. 2011).
193. *Id.* at 1290.

Chapter 2. Trademarks

§1. General

223. Protection for business trademarks has existed in the U.S. in some form for over 100 years. Trademark law has its roots in the law of unfair competition and eventually emerged into its own, first in the common law and eventually in statutes. The goal of trademark law is to protect consumers from confusion in the marketplace as to the source of goods and services. By protecting the goodwill established in trademarks through use in commerce, trademark law lowers the search costs for consumers in obtaining the goods or services from sources they have come to trust. Trademark law also provides a benefit to producers in being able to protect the investments they make in their brand identity and the resulting goodwill consumers attach to their products or services. This protection may also incentivize brand owners to invest in improving the quality of their products or services. Trademarks can be a very valuable business asset for a going concern, and in some cases, the value of a business' trademarks may be in the millions of dollars or more.

224. Trademark law in the U.S. consists of both federal and state statutory schemes, as well as common law trademark rights. Trademark rights generally arise through use of the trademark in commerce, and thus actual use of the trademark (or a bona fide intent to use within a relatively short period of time) is required to obtain registration of a trademark. At the federal level, the Lanham Act, codified at 15 U.S.C. §§ 1051 et seq., is the statute addressing trademark[194] and trade dress protection. The Lanham Act provides for federal registration of trademarks meeting the registration requirements in the statute. Federal registration provides the trademark owner with particular benefits, particularly with respect to protection and enforcement of the mark, but registration is not strictly required to initiate litigation against infringers. The United State Patent and Trademark Office is the agency responsible for maintaining the federal trademark registry and examining new trademark applications. Many states also have state-specific trademark statutes with varying requirements for registration and/or protection.

I. Process and Requirements for Registration

225. The USPTO maintains two federal trademark registries: the Principal Register and the Supplemental Register. The Principal Register is the registry for trademarks that have met all of the requirements for full federal registration and protection and is the most desirable registry for trademark applicants. The Supplemental Register is the registry for trademarks that have not yet met all of the

194. For the most part, service marks are treated identically under the Lanham Act as other trademarks and so they will not be addressed separately here. See 15U.S. Code § 1053 ("Subject to the provisions relating to the registration of trademarks, so far as they are applicable, service marks shall be registrable, in the same manner and with the same effect as are trademarks, and when registered they shall be entitled to the protection provided in this chapter in the case of trademarks.")

requirements for full registration but may do so over the passage of time. A common issue that will cause a trademark to end up on the Supplemental Register is the USPTO's view that the trademark is descriptive of the goods and services with which the trademark is used. Descriptive trademarks can be registered in the U.S. if the trademark owner can establish that the trademark has acquired secondary meaning through continuous and exclusive use. Accordingly, a trademark owner may choose to register their trademark on the Supplemental Register for five years and then apply to move the trademark to the Principal Register based on acquired secondary meaning.

226. In order to register a trademark the owner must submit an application to the USPTO, along with the required fee. In addition to various demographic information, the applicant is required to identify the first use of the trademark (and the first use in commerce), the goods and services with which the mark is being used, and a drawing of the mark. In the case of a mark that is not yet in use, the applicant must submit a verified statement attesting to their bona fide intention to use the trademark in commerce. For purposes of federal trademark registration, the use in commerce requirement generally refers to use in any commerce that the U.S. Congress has the power to regulate under the U.S. Constitution.

227. Once a proper application is submitted, the application will be reviewed by an examining attorney at the USPTO to ensure that the application meets the requirements of registration. In particular, the examining attorney will be looking to the requirements in 15 U.S. Code § 1052, which requires, among other things, that the applicant's mark not be likely to cause confusion with an existing trademark or be merely descriptive of the associated goods and services. If the examining attorney determines that the applicant's mark meets all of the requirements of registration, they will approve the mark and it will become registered on the Principal Register.

II. Benefits of Registration

228. Because U.S. trademark rights are based upon use in commerce, rather than simply an assertion or claim of rights, registration with the USPTO is not required to establish rights in a trademark. However, obtaining a federal registration does provide certain benefits to a trademark owner. In particular, registration on the Principal Register provides nationwide constructive notice of the trademark and nationwide constructive use as of the application date, both of which can be relevant in a trademark infringement action. In addition to the constructive notice, federal registration allows the trademark owner to use the "®" symbol as notice of their federal registration and the associated trademark rights. Moreover, federal registration can give the trademark owner the right to sue in federal courts and obtain enhanced damages against certain infringers. Finally, maintaining a federal registration for five years (along with continuous use during that time) can enable the trademark owner to establish "incontestability"' of the trademark, which may also provide additional benefits in protecting the mark from infringement and enforcing the owner's rights in the mark.

§2. Types of Trademarks

229. The Lanham Act defines a trademark as including "any word, name, symbol, or device, or any combination thereof." In practice, trademarks in the U.S. are generally categorized as either word marks, design marks, or nontraditional marks. Word marks consist of any combination of letters, whether pronounceable or not, that can be used to distinguish a company's products or services from those of other market participants. Design marks consist of some unique design that may be very simple or could be quite intricate. Design marks can include word components, but the owner's rights in a design mark do not protect word elements separately from the design as a whole. Nontraditional trademarks include any other type of unique source identifier, such as colors, shapes, smells, and sounds.

230. One high-profile case addressing nontraditional remarks is Qualitex.[195] In that case, the purported trademark owner attempted to acquire rights in a particular color of green used in association with dry cleaning pads. The court held that the color of a product could have a source-identifying function and therefore could serve as a trademark.

231. Following Qualitex, the ability to obtain trademark rights in, and register, nontraditional trademarks is well-established. Although nontraditional trademarks are far less common than word and design marks, there are many nontraditional trademarks currently registered with the USPTO and potentially many more in use for which an owner may be able to claim common law rights. Accordingly, just about any type of source identifier is registrable in the U.S. if the other requirements for registration can be met.

§3. Limitations on Trademarks

232. As discussed above, the primary limitation on a trademark owner's ability to acquire trademark rights is the use in commerce requirement. However, there are multiple other requirements and/or limits on an owner's trademark rights. In particular, trademark rights cannot be acquired in so-called generic words or symbols. Generic symbols are incapable of acting as a source identifier because the symbol indicates the name of the goods or services themselves, rather than indicating the source of the goods or services. It is important to note that, even if a symbol initially acts as a source identifier, its source-identifying ability may abate over time due to widespread use as a generic term and the trademark may thus be considered abandoned.

195. *Qualitex Co. v. Jacobson Prod. Co.*, 514 U.S. 159, 115 S. Ct. 1300 (1995).

233. Similar to generic symbols, there are also limitations on obtaining rights in descriptive marks. Descriptive symbols are those that describe the goods and services, rather than identifying the source of those goods and services. However, it is possible to eventually acquire rights in descriptive symbols if the trademark owner can establish that, through a period of exclusive use, the symbol has acquired secondary meaning. In other words, the owner will need to show that the mark has acquired a source-identifying function among consumers, which is typically considered established by five years or more of continuous and exclusive use. Once secondary meaning is established, descriptive marks can be registered on the Principal Register.

234. The other major limitation on trademark rights is that a trademark owner cannot establish rights in a symbol that is likely to cause confusion with another trademark for which an owner has established rights. The senior mark does not have to actually be registered to prevent later use or registration of a confusingly similar mark. The test for confusing similarity for the purposes of acquiring trademark rights is the same as that for establishing trademark infringement described below. If the USPTO determines that an applicant's applied-for symbol is confusingly similar to an existing registered trademark, the USPTO will deny registration of the applied-for symbol.

235. The Lanham Act includes a host of other special categories of symbols that cannot be registered, including names of living individuals (without permission), flags or coats of arms, names of deceased presidents, and various types of geographic indicators. The specifics of these categories can be found at 15 U.S. Code § 1052.

236. One final basis of registration has been the subject of several recent court cases. That is the prohibition on "immoral, deceptive, or scandalous matter" and "matter which may disparage" groups or individuals.[196] The disparaging limitation had been the subject of controversy for many years as representatives of some indigenous peoples had attempted unsuccessfully to cancel the registration for the Washington football team's name, which many considered disparaging of indigenous peoples in this country. The matter was finally brought before the U.S. Supreme Court in the case of Matal v. Tam.[197] Simon Tam was the head of a music group called The Slants that consisted of several Asian-American individuals. The trademark for The Slants had been rejected by the USPTO based on the prohibition against registering disparaging marks. Tam argued successfully to the Supreme Court that the prohibition against disparaging marks was unconstitutional. Shortly thereafter, the court reviewed the prohibition on scandalous marks and similarly struck down that portion of the statute.[198] Accordingly, the prohibitions on immoral, scandalous, and disparaging marks are of limited, if any, continuing validity.

196. 15U.S. Code § 1052.
197. *Matal v. Tam*, 137 S. Ct. 1744, 198 L. Ed. 2d 366 (2017).
198. *Iancu v. Brunetti*, 139 S. Ct. 2294, 204 L. Ed. 2d 714 (2019).

§4. TRADEMARK INFRINGEMENT

I. Likelihood of Confusion

237. In the U.S. liability for trademark infringement is based upon whether the defendant's symbol is likely to cause consumer confusion with the plaintiff's trademark. The likelihood of confusion analysis is very fact-specific and each U.S. Courts of Appeals circuit has their own version of the test. As an example, the D.C. Circuit uses the so-called Du Pont factors. The Du Pont factors are:

1. The similarity or dissimilarity of the marks in their entireties as to appearance, sound, connotation, and commercial impression.
2. The relatedness of the goods and services.
3. The similarity or dissimilarity of established, likely to continue trade channels.
4. The conditions under which and buyers to whom sales are made, i.e., "impulse" vs. careful, sophisticated purchasing.
5. The fame of the senior mark.
6. The number and nature of similar marks in use on similar goods.
7. The nature and extent of any actual confusion.
8. The length of time during and the conditions under which there has been concurrent use without evidence of actual confusion.
9. The variety of goods on which a mark is or is not used.
10. The market interface between the applicant and the owner of a prior mark.
11. The extent to which applicant has a right to exclude others from use of its mark on its goods.
12. The extent of potential confusion.
13. Any other established fact probative of the effect of use.

238. The Du Pont factors are particularly important because this is the test that the USPTO uses to determine whether an applicant's applied-for mark will be approved for registration. The USPTO places particular emphasis on factors 1 and 2, but must also consider factors 3, 4, and 6 if there is pertinent evidence in the application record.

239. A recent case applying the Du Pont Factors is Stratus Networks, Inc. v. UBTA-UBET Commc'ns Inc.[199] Images of the two trademarks at issue are reproduced below. In the Stratus case, the plaintiff had attempted to register the design mark shown below and the defendant filed an opposition proceeding to the applied-for mark based on likelihood of confusion with its previously registered trademark.[200] The Trademark Trial and Appeal Board at the USPTO analyzed the DuPont factors and determined that there was a likelihood of confusion and thus, refused

199. 955 F.3d 994 (Fed. Cir. 2020).
200. *Id.* at 995.

registration of the applied-for mark.[201] In particular, the Board found the first, second, and third DuPont factors to either weigh in favor of, or weigh heavily in favor of, a likelihood of confusion.[202] The Board went on to find that the fourth, sixth, and eighth factors were neutral and thus confusion was likely.[203] On appeal, the appellate court reviewed the Boards findings and affirmed the determination of likelihood of confusion.[204]

The Applied-for Trademark.

The Previously Registered Trademark.

240. Another recent example of courts applying the Du Pont Factors is Quik-Trip W., Inc. v. Weigel Stores, Inc.[205] Images of the two trademarks at issue in this case are reproduced below (from the published decision of the case). In the Quik-Trip case, the defendant attempted to register the design mark shown below and the plaintiff filed an opposition proceeding to the applied-for mark based on likelihood of confusion with its previously registered trademark.[206] The Trademark Trial and Appeal Board at the USPTO analyzed the DuPont factors and determined that there was not a likelihood of confusion and thus, dismissed the plaintiff's opposition proceeding.[207] In this case, the Board found the second, third, fourth, and tenth DuPont factors to weigh in favor of a likelihood of confusion and that the seventh, eighth, ninth, and twelfth factors were neutral.[208] The Board went on to find that the first and thirteenth (bad faith) factors weighed against a likelihood of confusion and that overall, confusion was not likely.[209] On appeal, the appellate court reviewed the Board's findings and affirmed the determination of no likelihood of confusion.[210]

---

201. *Id.* at 996-97.
202. *Id.*
203. *Id.*
204. *Id.* at 1000.
205. 984 F.3d 1031 (Fed. Cir. 2021).
206. *Id.* at 1034.
207. *Id.*
208. *Id.*
209. *Id.*
210. *Id.* at 1037.

The Applied-for Trademark

The Previously Registered Trademark

241. As shown from these cases, the likelihood of confusion analysis is very fact-specific and requires courts (and the USPTO) to balance many factors to make the ultimate determination of infringement or registrability.

II. Dilution

242. Trademark infringement liability can also arise due to trademark dilution. Dilution occurs when a junior user uses a symbol that is likely to cause dilution by either blurring or tarnishment of a famous mark. In order to assert that its mark is famous, a trademark owner must show that the mark is "widely recognized by the general consuming public" of the U.S.[211] Dilution by blurring occurs when a junior user's use of a particular symbol is impairs the distinctiveness of the senior, famous mark. Dilution by tarnishment occurs when use of the junior mark harms the reputation of the famous mark. It is important to recognize however, that the First Amendment right to free speech may serve as a limitation on a trademark owner's ability to pursue claims of trademark dilution.[212]

243. An example of dilution by tarnishment is the case of *V Secret v. Moseley*.[213] In this case, the owner of a famous trademark used in association with lingerie products sued the operator of a small shop selling, among other things, "sexually oriented products."[214] The court concluded that "a new mark used to sell sex related products is likely to tarnish a famous mark if there is a clear semantic association between the two."[215]

---

211. 15U.S. Code § 1125.
212. *See*, e.g., *AM Gen. LLC v. Activision Blizzard, Inc.*, 450 F. Supp. 3d 467, 488 (S.D.N.Y. 2020).
213. *V Secret Catalogue, Inc. v. Moseley*, 605 F.3d 382 (6th Cir. 2010).
214. *Id.* at 384.
215. *Id.* at 385.

244. A recent example of trademark dilution by blurring is *Visa International v. JSL Corp.*[216] In this case, the owner of a famous mark ("Visa") used in connection with financial services sued the operator of a "multilingual education and information business that exists and operates exclusively on the Internet" for use of the mark eVisa.[217] The court affirmed the grant of an injunction in favor of the plaintiff because "[t]he marks here are effectively identical; the only difference is the prefix "e," which is commonly used to refer to the electronic or online version of a brand … [t]hat prefix does no more to distinguish the two marks than would the words "Corp." or "Inc." tacked onto the end."[218]

III. Defenses to Infringement

245. There are several defenses available to a trademark infringement claim, including parody, descriptive fair use, nominative fair use, abandonment, and equitable defenses (laches, estoppel, and unclean hands). The defense of abandonment can be relevant if the trademark owner has ceased using the trademark in commerce. Nonuse for a continuous three-year period raises a presumption of abandonment. Assignments in gross and naked licenses can also lead to a finding of abandonment.

246. Parody, descriptive fair use, and nominative fair use can be grouped together as uses where the alleged infringer is not using the trademark to divert sales from the trademark owner and/or confuse consumers as to the source of goods. To be a valid parody, the parody must be clear from the context in which the mark is used.[219] Descriptive fair use arises when a trademark is used to refer descriptively to goods or services. Nominative fair use is applicable when a trademark is used to refer to actual owner of the trademark. For example, a vehicle mechanic shop might use a car manufacturer's trademark to identify the types of vehicles they work on.

IV. Secondary Liability

247. Secondary liability for trademark infringement, or contributory infringement, is well-established in U.S. law and the Inwood case is often cited on this issue.[220] The Inwood test has two prongs for potential liability: intentional inducement; and continuing to provide a product or service to one who the provider knows

216. *Visa Int'l Serv. Ass'n v. JSL Corp.*, 610 F.3d 1088 (9th Cir. 2010)
217. *Id.* at 1089.
218. *Id.* at 1090.
219. *Louis Vuitton Malletier S.A. v. Haute Diggity Dog, LLC*, 507 F.3d 252, 260 (4th Cir. 2007)
220. *See,* e.g., *Inwood Lab'ys, Inc. v. Ives Lab'ys, Inc.*, 456U.S. 844, 854 (1982) ("[I]f a manufacturer or distributor intentionally induces another to infringe a trademark, or if it continues to supply its product to one whom it knows or has reason to know is engaging in trademark infringement, the manufacturer or distributor is contributorially responsible for any harm done as a result of the deceit.")

or has reason to know is engaging in trademark infringement.[221] In the online context, online marketplaces could face potential liability under the second *Inwood* prong. However, the question arises as to what level of knowledge about counterfeiting occurring on their platform is sufficient to establish contributory infringement. An important case on this issue is Tiffany (NJ) Inc. v. eBay, Inc.[222] In *Tiffany*, the plaintiff attempted to establish contributory trademark infringement based on the defendant's generalized knowledge that some trademark infringement was occurring on its online sales platform.[223] The court held that generalized knowledge that infringement might be occurring on a platform was not sufficient to establish the requisite knowledge necessary for contributory infringement liability.[224] The approach taken in the Tiffany case continues to be the predominant approach in the U.S. for determining whether online platforms can be held liable for contributory trademark infringement.[225] However, due to the prevalence of online misbranding and/or counterfeiting, the U.S. Congress is currently considering legislation that may alter the extent to which online sellers face liability for trademark infringement occurring on their platforms.

221. *Id.*
222. 576 F. Supp. 2d 463 (S.D.N.Y. 2008), affimed in part, revised in part, 600 F.3d 93 (2d Cir. 2010).
223. *Id.* at 507.
224. *Id.* at 510.
225. Note that, as of the time of this writing, legislation is proposed in the U.S. Congress that may impact the continuing validity of the Tiffany approach and make it much more likely that online platforms could be liable for contributory trademark infringement. This proposed legislation is currently called the "SHOP SAFE Act."

Chapter 3. Design Protection

248. In the U.S. product designs are protectable by two distinct regimes: design patents and trade dress protection.

§1. Design Patents

249. Design patents protect the original, ornamental design of articles of manufacture. In the U.S., design patent applications are examined by the USPTO, similar to utility patents. However, the requirements for patentability are somewhat different. To be patentable, designs need to be new and nonobvious, but they also need to be primarily ornamental, rather than primarily functional. Primarily functional designs need to go through the utility patent process in order to be protected. The term of design patents is fifteen years (as opposed to twenty years for utility patents) and the owner of a design patent is not required to pay maintenance fees during the term to keep the design patent from expiring. The owner of a design patent has the right to exclude others from making, using, selling, offering to sell, or importing articles that include the same, or a substantially similar, design. Accordingly, design patents may provide a reasonable approach to protecting ornamental product designs in the U.S.

§2. Trade Dress Protection

250. Trade dress protection is available in the U.S. for both product design trade dress and product packaging trade dress. The rules applicable to trademarks discussed above also apply trade dress. Thus, in order to obtain trade dress protection, the trade dress must be used in commerce in connection with particular goods or services. Moreover, the trade dress must serve a source-identifying function and cannot be functional in a utilitarian sense. The functionality requirement is particularly relevant for product design trade dress claims. It is possible to register trade dress with the USPTO, but most trade dress claims are litigated without being registered. Ownership of valid trade dress gives the owner the right to prevent others from using confusingly similar trade dress in commerce for as long as the trade dress continues to be used, which could be indefinitely. Thus, trade dress protection provides a good option for protecting source-identifying product design for an extended period of time.

Chapter 4. Copyright Protection in the Digital Context

§1. General

251. Although patents and trademarks are relevant forms of intellectual property, copyright law clearly has the most impact in the area of ICT. Digital media and the Internet have expanded copying capabilities by orders of magnitude. The ease with which digital works can be copied, modified, transmitted, and transformed contrasts sharply with the difficulty inherent in copying written texts, which spurred the first copyright laws. Whether digital text, visual, audio, or software, the Internet and digital media provide a near-universal ability to copy original works.

252. The great majority of the content on the Internet is capable of copyright protection. Due to the ease of duplicating that content, the Internet is viewed as a prime locus of copyright infringement. U.S. copyright law, with its origin in written text, imperfectly addresses the digital age and the Internet's fluid architecture. Recent proposed legislation and judicial opinions demonstrate that U.S. copyright law is in a state of flux, as both digital media users and copyright owners confront new vulnerabilities enabled by converging technology.

253. Generally speaking, U.S. copyright law prohibits the making of a copy of a work unless the copyright owner granted consent. While copyright law imperfectly addresses digital media, it has proved flexible enough to extend protection beyond written text and into audio, visual, video and the like. But digital media are consumed differently than analogue media. Traditional works, like books, do not require copying in order to use the work. Conversely, software programs and other digital works require copying as an incident to use. Moreover, digital copies are perfect copies, whereas analogue copying generally generated an imperfect replica. It is far easier to create digital copies, and global transmission of the copies distinguishes our current climate from its analogue predecessor.

254. Users or consumers also face increased vulnerability. Unlike reading a book or watching a television program, where consumers were confident that no copyright violation attended the use, today digital media often requires copying, and the accessibility and variety of potentially copyrighted works saturates the Internet. As a consequence, user agreements and restrictive contractual clauses often attend the purchase of digital media as a tool for the copyright owner's attempt to protect the economic vitality of the work.

255. Copyright law in the U.S. begins—as do so many legal concepts—with the U.S. Constitution. The Constitution's copyright and patent clause empowers Congress "To promote the progress of science and useful arts, by securing for limited times to authors and inventors the exclusive right to their respective writings and discoveries."[226] The constant tension inherent in copyright law pits the rights of the

226. U.S. Const. Art. I, § 8.

creator of the work to benefit from the work against the right of the public to freely use, copy, and benefit from the work. Without copyright protection, creators have little incentive to fabricate useful works. But overprotection reduces the ability of the public to benefit from the work. Therefore, the main thrust of copyright law seeks to balance incentivizing authors to create works by granting them a limited monopoly with the ability of that creation to benefit the public in a competitive market and for others to later build from that creation. As one famous judge framed the issue: "Culture is impossible without a rich public domain […] Culture, like science and technology, grows by accretion, each new creator building on the works of those who came before. Overprotection stifles the very creative forces it's supposed to nurture." He went on to suggest that "overprotecting intellectual property is as harmful as under protecting it."

§2. The Copyright Act of 1976

256. The U.S. Constitution's general and amorphous mandate has spawned a complex body of U.S. copyright law. The most notable legislation in the panoply of U.S. copyright law is the Copyright Act of 1976, which states that the law protects "original works of authorship fixed in any tangible medium of expression, now known or later developed, from which they can be perceived, reproduced, or otherwise communicated, either directly or with the aid of a machine or device."[227] For a piece of work to fit within this purview, it must meet three requirements: fixation, originality, and expression.

257. Fixation refers to the tangible manifestation of the work. A science fiction novel, for example, achieves fixation when the story is reduced to paper or dictated into a voice recorder. Fixation serves the primary purpose of demarking the time copyright protection begins. A science fiction story in the author's mind is not protected until it has been reduced to a fixed and lasting form from which others can experience it. The concept of fixation differs depending on the media, as music, video, and written works are often memorized differently.

258. Although there remain ambiguities with regard to the doctrine of fixation, the originality requirement is significantly more complex. First, originality certainly encompasses novelty. Novelty, however, is itself fraught, as many commentators insist that most everything has been done before. For the most part, in every art form, every innovation comes out of some form of imitation. Federal Court of Appeals Judge Alex Kozinski famously wrote in a copyright decision that "Nothing today, likely nothing since we tamed fire, is genuinely new: Culture, like science and technology, grows by accretion, each new creator building on the works of those who came before."[228]

227. Copyright Act of 1976, Pub. L. 94-553, 90 Stat. 2541.
228. *White v. Samsung Electronics America, Inc.*, 989 F.2d 1512, 1513 (9th Cir. 1993).

259. Perhaps as a result, originality encompasses more than that which is novel. It must be a creative product generated by the individual's own undertaking. As Judge Learned Hand put it, if a person unknowingly and legitimately creates the exact poem that previously existed, copyright protection would exist: "if by some magic a man who had never known it were to compose anew Keats' Ode on a Grecian Urn, he would be an 'author,' and if he copyrighted it, others might not copy that poem, though they might of course copy Keats'."[229]

260. One clarification that helps define originality is that facts may not be the basis of copyright protection. Facts are not considered the original work of any other, including the discovery of a heretofore unknown fact that resulted from the discoverer's expertise, research, and dedication. As a result, facts are part of the public domain, usable by everyone. Creation and discovery demark that which can be copyrighted from that which cannot.[230]

261. But originality is not the most difficult requirement to understand. The last requirement protects expressions of ideas, not the ideas themselves. It is not easy to separate the idea from the expression of it. Again, Judge Learned Hand attempted to better define this concept by reducing it to the "abstractions test," perhaps the most cited legal authority interpreting this third requirement:

> Upon any work, and especially upon a play, a great number of patterns of increasing generality will fit equally well, as more and more of the incident is left out. The last may perhaps be no more than the most general statement of what the play is about, and at times might consist only of its title; but there is a point in this series of abstractions where they are no longer protected, since otherwise the playwright could prevent use of his "ideas," to which, apart from their expression, his property is never extended.[231]

262. Of course, the "abstraction test" is, itself, not easy to apply. But the underlying premise remains good law in the U.S.: a copyright holder has protection for the expression of the idea but no protection for the idea itself. Subsequent users may copy and publish the idea freely. The court's decision in Baker v. Selden provides an oft-cited illustration.[232]

263. The claimant in that case obtained copyright in a book he wrote, which described a new and improved system of accountancy and bookkeeping. The book depicted a ledger used for accounting bookkeeping, containing about twenty pages of primarily bookkeeping forms. In addition, the books contained examples and an introduction. In 1867, the defendant (Baker) produced a book describing a very similar system. Unlike the claimant, Baker was more successful at selling his book. The court ruled in favor of Baker, the subsequent publisher. In so doing, the court

229. *Sheldon v. Metro-Goldwyn Pictures Corp*, 309U.S. 390 (1940).
230. *See*, *Feist Publications v. Rural Tel. Serv.*, 111 S.Ct. 1282, 1288 (1991).
231. *Nichols v. Universal Pictures Corp.*, 45 F.2d 119 (2d Cir. 1930).
232. 101U.S. 99 (1879).

established a precedent that remains meaningful today: a description of an idea will not create a property interest in the idea itself. Only the expression of the idea is protected, which effectuates the differentiation between idea and expression.

264. A subcategory of the idea vs. expression dichotomy is represented by the merger doctrine. The merger doctrine applies when there is only one way or only very few ways of expressing an idea. In such instances, copyright law will not protect the expression of the idea because it has "merged" with the idea itself. In the 1967 case, Morrissey v. Procter & Gamble Co., the court formally recognized the doctrine.[233] When only a few ways exist to express an idea, the expression receives little to no protection. Slogans, metaphors that are naturally restricted to conveying a stereotyped meaning serve as examples. Policy justification for disallowing copyright protection include the little creativity, originality, and labor required to generate the expression and importance of keeping the idea itself in the public domain.

265. A second subcategory further enhances understanding of U.S. copyright law and its protection of expressions rather than ideas. Derivative works are original and new works that include overt aspects of a preexisting and already copyrighted work. Only copyright owners have exclusive rights to produce derivative works, which are based off their original, copyrighted works, so it is critical to understand what constitutes a derivative work. Derivative works are those in which the original, copyrighted work of another person is "recast, transformed, or adapted."[234] Derivative works can include musical arrangements, art reproductions, movies, sound recordings or translations. They can also include dramatizations and fictionalizations, such as a movie based on a play.

266. To be a derivative work, the work must substantially copy from the original, prior work, and include the original expression. In other words, a secondary work that only includes ideas from the prior work will not be a derivative work protected under U.S. copyright law. If the work is a derivative work, copyright protections from the original work will extend to the subsequent work, but only with regard to those elements or components that are original variations or additions. Derivative work protects the copyright holder of the original work and is often referred to as the adaptation right. As a result, the copyright protections for the original and derivative work are legally separate, even while they coexist. Layers of copyright protections often protect the copyright holder in varying contexts. A copyright owner can grant permission to someone else to make a derivative work based on his or her original—if permission is granted (in the form of a license or assignment), then creation of the derivative work is not infringement. If permission to create a derivative work is granted by the copyright holder, a contractual arrangement regarding copyright benefits and identification of the copyright holder for the derivative work often attends the agreement itself. If no specification is made, the creator of the derivative work has the burden of proving that the copyright holder

233. 379 F.2d 675 (1st Cir. Mass. 1967).
234. 17U.S.C. § 101 (1976).

authorized creation of the derivative work before the creator of the derivative work may claim copyright protection for the derivative work.

267. Graphics Interchange Format (GIFs) works provide a relevant and recent inquiry into how far derivative work protections should extend. Internet users commonly convey entertaining, critical, or artistic messages by combining pictures, video segments, art, and other media readily available in the digital era. GIFs enable users to convey more than text alone can convey, with a seemingly endless index of art, movies, television, and music available to communicate a more contextualized message. Most GIFs, however, incorporate part of an original copyrighted work. When published (copied) over the Internet, some argue that such GIFs unfairly reduce the copyright owner's ability to create and control derivative works, including monetary proceeds from those derivative works. As of 2015, no definitive U.S. court decision or legislation demarks whether creating and sharing GIFs that incorporate copyrighted material constitutes infringement.

268. This protection of expression and not the idea itself reflects the balancing act at the heart of U.S. copyright law. Ideas are to be disseminated to the public for public use and accretion, while legal protection for expression incentivizes introduction of new material into the public arena. The Copyright Act – as amended -- identifies several protected categories for "original works of authorship:"

- literary works, including computer programs;
- musical works;
- dramatic works;
- pantomimes and choreographic works;
- pictorial, graphic, and sculptural works;
- motion pictures and other audiovisual works;
- sound recordings; and
- architectural works.

269. Although the Copyright Act of 1976, along with the many judicial decisions interpreting the Act, provide the baseline regulatory approach, U.S. statutory copyright law is largely contained in chapters 1 through 8 and 10 through 12 of Title 17 of the United States Code. In some cases, statutory enactments affecting copyright law are not codified in Title 17.

§3. Scènes à Faire

270. Scène à faire, French for "scene that must be done" refers to a scene or reference from a prior work that is so universal as to almost demand inclusion in a subsequent work. These "scenes" or themes, due to their universality take on the aspects of ideas, unto themselves, and are therefore not protected in U.S. copyright law. Recognized tropes that run throughout literature are often repeated from one work to the next. Examples include the torment of star-crossed lovers, Cinderella-type tales of rags to riches, and other universal narratives that are deemed too embedded and necessary to public expression to allow the originators to curtail use through copyright enforcement.

271. This protection extends to tropes used in settings and to typical stock characters. With regard to settings, the U.S. Court of Appeals for the Second Circuit interpreted the scènes à faire doctrine to hold that a movie about the South Bronx area of the U.S. would necessarily feature rats, drunks, prostitutes, and abandoned cars. This setting was perceived as universally understood, and therefore a later film that replicated these features of an earlier film did not infringe.

272. An example of this doctrine as it relates to computer coding can be found in the U.S. Court of Appeals for the Second Circuit's decision addressing nonliteral elements of computer code in *Computer Associates International, Inc. v. Altai, Inc.*[235] Familiar characters, like the austere judge and the aggressive prosecutor that attend criminal trial dramas do not garner copyright protection.

273. The policy justification for this doctrine reflects the larger policy goals of U.S. copyright law identified above. Granting the originator exclusive rights over scènes à faire would retard others in their expressive attempts within the same genre, diminishing the public's access to new expressions and subsequent expressive works, while the benefit of such a monopoly would inordinately benefit a certain few.

§4. Compilations of Fact

274. As noted above, facts are not protectable under U.S. copyright law. An important differentiation, however, exists with regard to compilations of fact. Originality, as a requirement, does not require a high degree of creativity. As the court has noted, only a slight showing of creativity is needed, "no matter how crude, humble or obvious."

275. As a result, copyright protection may be available for the creative coordination and arrangement of factual information forming a list, database or other compilation. If so, the copyright protection extends only to the original or creative aspect of the work. The facts contained in the database or compilation are not protected. In most cases, a fact compilation is generated by identifying and selecting data that is in the public domain, like telephone numbers, names, and addresses and arranging them in a minimally creative manner. Examples include almanacs, a catalogue of professional experts within a field, and other such databases. Even simple directories that include no explicit written copyrightable expression, only listings of

235. 982 F.2d 693 (2d Cir. 1992).

facts, may be protected if they include an original arrangement. Of course, the individual facts may still be used freely, but the listing itself may not be reproduced and distributed in a way that mimics the organization or combination used by the compiling author.

276. Some compilations are not just facts, but compilations of copyrighted material. In such cases, the copyright in the compilation extends solely to the work of the author, not the underlying pieces that make up the compilation. For example, if an author creates a book of "The 10 Best Love Poems," the author only has a copyright for the compilation. That copyright protects only that author's original selection of the ten poems selected. The compilation copyright does not extend to the poems themselves. Such copyrights are often referred to as "thin"' copyrights because of the minimal protected content.

277. In accord with general copyright goals, the policy with regard to compilations illustrates the value of a useful service in gathering facts and ideas. Accordingly, the originators of such writings deserve some economic incentive for providing this service. The court in *Feist Publications v. Rural Telephone Service*, for example, attempted to distinguish the author's labor in gathering the facts from the originality in selection and arrangement of those facts. The court considered the premise that compilations typically garner flimsy protection based on their minimal expressive content, and that labor and research should be recognized in order to economically incentivize compilers.[236] The Supreme Court ultimately rejected the labor theory, however, holding that protection in compilations extends only to original selection and arrangement of the facts and not the research involved in gathering them.[237] Thus, the court rejected the "sweat of the brow"' doctrine as applied to copyrights in the U.S.

§5. Multiple Authors

278. Generally speaking, the Copyright Act provides for joint authorship when a work is prepared by more than one author "with the intention that their contributions be merged into inseparable or interdependent parts of a unitary whole." If joint authorship exists, the law recognizes the joint authors as co-owners of the copyright in that work. For these purposes, the "author" is the party who in fact creates the work, the person who translates an underlying idea into a fixed, tangible expression. Of course, employment, authorization, and mere implementation qualify the legal understanding of "author." A printer of another's work or a mold-maker of another's design are not "authors" within the meaning of the law.

279. The legal standard for determining whether the parties intended to be coauthors does not solely turn on the subjective attestations of the relevant parties. Indicia of authorship is also objective and includes inquiries over the putative author's

236. 499U.S. 340 (1991).
237. *Id.*

control over the work, and objective evidence indicating a shared intent to be coauthors, as well as other factors. The most common example of a joint work is when a book or article has two or more authors. However, if a book is written primarily by one author, but another author contributes a specific chapter to the book and is given credit for that chapter, then this would not be a joint work because the contributions are not inseparable or interdependent. The question turns on whether a specific finding of mutual intent is present to find co-authorship.

280. As noted below, where one of the contributors to a joint work contributed while working within the scope of employment, the employer may become an owner or co-owner of the copyright. If a copyrighted work was properly cocreated, the law treats the co-owners as tenants in common. A tenancy in common is a specific type of concurrent, or simultaneous, ownership typically applicable to real property owned by two or more parties. In copyright law, each co-owner owns an undivided, independent right to use the work. This means that each party has the right to alienate, or transfer the ownership of, her ownership interest. This can be done by deed, will, or other conveyance. When a co-owner dies, for example, her share goes to her beneficiaries or heirs, not to the other co-owner. Each co-owner has an independent right to use or nonexclusively license the work—provided that he or she accounts to the other co-owners for any profits. In most cases, this means that a party who obtains the permission of any one co-owner, can use the work.

281. The U.S. Copyright Office considers joint copyright owners to have an equal right to register and enforce the copyright. Unless the joint owners make a written agreement to the contrary, each copyright owner has the right to commercially exploit the copyright, provided that the other copyright owners get an equal share of the proceeds.

282. In *Richlin v. Metro-Goldwyn-Mayer Pictures, Inc.*, the court ruled that a motion picture had not been jointly authored with regard to the underlying story treatment. The court ruled that the motion picture adopted the characters and original story from the treatment. Without the story treatment, the motion picture would likely not exist. Because the author of the treatment assigned the treatment to the motion picture producer and wrote the motion picture screen play as a work for hire, the court denied any recovery or ownership in the author's heirs.[238]

§6. Works Created Under Employment

283. Works prepared or created by an employee who is acting within the course and scope of his or her employment are deemed "works for hire" and are owned by the employer for the purposes of federal statutory copyright in the U.S.[239] For

238. 531 F.3d 962 (9th Cir. 2008).
239. 17U.S.C.A. § 201(b).

example, in Integral Development Corporation v. Tolat, the court held that a software development company owned the copyright in source code sufficient to support a copyright infringement claim against its former chief technology officer. The court ruled that the company obtained the copyright in the source code when it was written, and that the company did not need to register the source code before the right attached. As the source code was created by various individuals working within the scope of their employment, the law deems the company as the author of the source code and the owner.[240]

284. This legal presumption can be reversed if the parties expressly agree in a written document signed by them that specifies the relative ownership rights of the work. It is important to note that the hired party or employee is often identified as the "author" in some copyright instruments, but this appellation does not itself grant the employee ownership. Moreover, a creator of a work made for hire does not qualify as an owner of the work even if the employee is entitled to copyright royalties. Typically, the work of a web designer, writer, or graphic artist, even if done outside of normal working hours, will be owned by the employer, if that work is related to the creator's employment.

285. At times it is unclear whether a work is created within an employment context or whether the work is created within the independent contractor contest. The law of agency determines whether an individual is an employee or independent contractor. Generally speaking, agency law as it relates to employment and copyright, depends on whether the employer induced the creation of the work, which includes an inquiry into the employer's ability to direct and control the creation of the work.

286. A reviewing court will focus on to the extent to which the employer or hiring party provided the inducement for, participated in, or had the ability to supervise the creation of the work. Courts will also review the "expense" aspect of the transaction, which includes the allocation of resources imparted by the hiring party as they relate to the creation of the work. In such disputes, agency law seeks to award ownership to the party that shoulders the risk associated with the works creation and success.

287. More specifically, courts have also considered a number of factors in determining whether an individual acted as an employee or as an independent contractor. Factors include: the location of the work; the history and duration of the relationship between the parties; the hiring party's right to control the manner and means by which the work is created; which party provides the tools and particularized resources required for the work's creation; the degree of discretion exercised by the creator regarding when and how long to work on the project; the creator's or hired party's role in hiring and paying subordinates; the method of payment; whether the work is part of the regular business of the hiring party; and the tax treatment of the hired party. The consequences for the company of having a particular work determined to have been done by an independent contractor, rather than an employee,

---

240. 675 Fed. Appx. 700 (9th Cir. 2017).

can be severe. The company may find that it does not have any ownership rights in the resulting work, which could be a very significant issue for a company that intends to use the created work for its primary products or services. Accordingly, companies will generally obtain agreements with the creators of copyrightable work in the absence of a very clear employment relationship.

§7. Computer-Generated Works

288. As noted above, within the framework of the copyright law, intellectual property ownership rights depend initially on "authorship."[241] When a computer system or software automatically creates output that is not identical to its own text or coding, some of which is potentially copyrightable, legal issues emerge in determining authorship. Despite its centrality to copyright law in the U.S., authorship in this context has not been formally defined. In many instances, works generated by a computer operate like a typical copyrighted work, even though no individual's actions reflect those of a traditional copyright author. For example, an increasing number of financial and sports news articles on the Internet today are written by computers. Computers draw, paint, and compose music. Over twenty-three years ago, IBM's specialized computer defeated world chess champion Garry Kasparov.

289. The question of who will own what rights in the "output" of such programs largely turns on copyright law, because software is copyrightable. But copyright law is ill-equipped to resolve this legal issue. As is often the case with computer-generated works, the generation and production components are merged. The computer program generates a new, distinguishable work each time it is used. The distinguishing elements to each new work exacerbate the ability to identify a human origin.

290. Although the law is in flux, the current majority rule in the U.S. turns on whether the individual or user is leveraging the computer to generate or modify the user's expression. If a user leverages a computer to help manipulate expression created by the user, the resulting work is copyrightable. Conversely, if a user's interaction with a computer prompts the computer to generate its own expression, the resulting work is not copyrightable, and no legal protection attaches. That said, there is no definitive judicial opinion directly adjudicating the copyrightability of works produced by artificial intelligence. To date, the balance of cases that touch on this issue in other contexts reiterate the need for human creativity.

§8. Orphan Works

291. Because the law does not require registration of copyrighted works as a perquisite to copyright protection, all original works fixed in any tangible medium are

241. Section 201(a) of the Copyright Act provides that statutory copyright "vests initially in the author or authors of the work." 17U.S.C. § 201(a) (1982).

automatically granted copyright protection. An orphan work is a work protected by copyright law whose owner is practically impossible to contact or identify. Without the ability to gain approval of the copyright owner, orphan works often can neither be used in new works nor digitized, except when exceptions like the fair use doctrine apply. The number of orphan works has increased dramatically in the last twenty years with digital media and due to optional registration, rendering the status of many works unknown. Orphan works include, but are not limited to, unclaimed folk music recordings, old poetry and little-known novels, historical photographs and the like.

292. Uncertainty about the owner of an orphan work and the risk of liability for publishing these works without permission often serve to further obscure such works. This has a potentially negative societal effect, because unidentified works cause individuals to abandon projects based on the works. Partly responding to this concern, the U.S. Congress urged the U.S. Copyright Office to investigate and report the effects of orphan works. In its report on Orphan Works ("Report") the U.S. Copyright office sought public comment and analyzed the detriments that content users navigate when attempting to use orphan works.

293. The report identified material obstacles presented by orphan works and recommended that the U.S. Congress address the concern legislatively. Congress considered adopting the Orphan Works Act of 2006,[242] but ultimately failed to enact it into law. The draft legislation attempted to identify a process that a content user may follow to legally proceed with the use of copyrighted material in the absence of an identifiable copyright owner. The draft law also included a process to resolve conflict if the copyright owner was later found.

294. Digital technology has made it easier to create and disseminate copyrightable works, but it has also made it easy to separate a work from its owner. In 2011, the Director of the U.S. Copyright Office, Maria Pallante, estimated that 80% of the images on the Internet are unauthorized, significantly devaluing the intellectual property interests of photographers. Certain media are particularly prone to separation of a work from its owner, including photographs, sound recordings, and film footage. Software, of course can also become an orphan work, and is sometimes referred to as abandonware. Source code escrow has been proposed as a way to stem abandonware, but the practice has yet to gain critical traction.

295. Large-scale digitization projects often falter when confronted with the legal uncertainties involved with using orphan works. The cost of identifying and contacting copyright holders outweighs the cost of digitization and indexing. Some entities, however, proceed anyway, like Google which has scanned and digitized the contents of more than fifteen million books.

242. H.R. 5439, 116th Cong. (2019).

§9. RIGHTS OF THE COPYRIGHT HOLDER

296. Although categorized as "Intellectual Property," a copyright owner does not have a traditional property law interest in the work. Instead, U.S. copyright law protects the owner's exclusive right to publish, reproduce, display, and create "derivative works." A copyright owner also has the right to not publish the work and make it unavailable to the public. The particular rights themselves stem largely from section 106 of the Copyright Act, including the right to:

- produce the copyrighted work in copies or phonorecords;
- prepare derivative works based on the copyrighted work;
- distribute copies or phonorecords of the copyrighted work to the public by sale or other transfer of ownership, or by rental, lease or lending;
- for literary, musical, dramatic, and choreographic works, pantomimes, motion pictures, and other audiovisual works, to perform the copyrighted work publicly;
- in the case of sound recordings, to perform the copyrighted work publicly by means of a digital auto transmission.

The exclusive right to perform the copyrighted work publicly also attaches in the case of sound recordings. This exclusive right to perform often extends to musical, dramatic, and choreographic works, including motion pictures and other audiovisual works. U.S. courts have characterized "performance" to include recitation, a play, a dance, an acting exhibition, or, in the case of a motion picture, displaying the movie's images in an identifiable way. Sculptures, paintings, and other audio-visual works include an owner's right to publicly display the same.

Of course, copyright holders also have the right to transfer all or some of the rights to a work. Transfer may be by sale, gift, bequeath or other such legal methods of transferring property.

I. Lifespan of Copyrighted Work

297. The duration of copyright protection has changed over the years in U.S. copyright law. Even so, it has always been the case that a copyright is inherently limited in time, as required by the U.S. Constitution. The U.S. legislature has authority to extend copyright protection, as long as the extension does not amount to an indefinite copyright. For works created on or after January 1, 1978, copyright protection lasts for the life of the author plus seventy years.[243] The clock begins to run when the work is fixed in a copy or phonorecord for the first time. For different versions of a work, each version typically amounts to a separate work. And for works that are generated over time, the part of the work that has been fixed at any one time, amounts to the work as of that time.

298. For joint works created by two or more authors, copyright protection extends through the life of the last surviving author, plus seventy years after his or

243. 17U.S.C.A. § 302.

her death.[244] Perhaps counterintuitively, for works without an identifiable author, including anonymous works and works made for hire, copyright protection extends for 95 years from the year of its first publication, or 120 years from the year of its creation, whichever expires first. These terms continue through the end of the calendar year in which they expire.

299. A copyright's duration for works created before 1978 is more complicated. Prior to that year, copyrights were protected for twenty-eight years with an option to renew for another twenty-eight years. An amended statute, however, extended the second term to sixty-seven years. As of 2012, any work copyrighted before 1923 has expired. Congress extended copyright protection prospectively and retrospectively by twenty years in 1998 with the passage of the Copyright Term Extension Act, also known as the Sonny Bono Copyright Term Extension Act. The extension made U.S. copyright terms consistent with those in the European Union (EU), which in 1993, required Member States to protect their own copyrights for a term equal to the life of the author plus seventy years. The extension was also politically motivated. The Walt Disney Company had lobbied for copyright extension for its characters like Mickey Mouse and Goofy, which were about to expire.

II. Registration and Notice

300. All works created from 1978 on are protected by U.S. copyright law upon creation. No registration is necessary for copyright protections to attach. Although copyright law protects the owner's rights in the work upon creation, the copyright owner cannot bring a lawsuit for infringement until the work is registered in the U.S. Copyright Office.[245] It is possible to register a work after infringement, but this often delays the lawsuit and in some instances will limit the plaintiff/copyright holder to actual damages. A copyright holder who registers the work before alleged infringement of that work may be awarded statutory damages and attorney fees. This has not always been the case. Before 1978, U.S. copyright law largely required registration before copyright protection attached. In that year, the U.S. relinquished the registration pre-requirement in order to join the Berne Convention for the Protection of Literary and Artistic Works.[246]

301. To register the work, the owner completes an application form and pays a fee to the Copyright Office, along with two copies of a published work or one copy of an unpublished work. The works are stored in the Library of Congress, and the Copyright Office then issues a certificate of registration. The copyright owner may, but is not required to, attach a notice of copyright to the published work. Such notice is not required, but it is often advisable, particularly to rebut a defendant's claim that the defendant was an innocent infringer. The copyright notice may be placed on all

244. 17U.S.C.A. § 305.
245. 17U.S.C.A. § 401(a).
246. Berne Convention for the Protection of Literary and Artistic Works, Sept. 9, 1886, revised at Paris July 24, 1971, 25U.S.T. 1341; 1161 U.N.T.S. 3.

publicly distributed copies from which the work can be visually perceived. Importantly, if a notice of copyright appears on copies of a work it must consist of three elements.

(1) the letter C in a circle, or the word "Copyright," or the abbreviation "Copr.;"
(2) the year of first publication of the work in most instances;
(3) the name of the copyright owner.[247]

302. The law recognizes that the media or nature of some copyrighted works make attachment of notice difficult. Generally speaking, the notice must be affixed to the copies in such manner as to give reasonable notice of the copyright. In one instance, notice of copyright in a computer program was placed on the back of a computer chip. This was determined legally sufficient even though the notice was not visible when the chip was in the circuit board. Importantly, the program could not be copied without removing the chip from the circuit board.

303. Because it is relatively easy to register for a copyright, false registration claims arise with frequency. Section 506(c) of United States Code Title 17 prohibits three distinct acts: (1) placing a false notice of copyright on an article; (2) publicly distributing articles which bear a false copyright notice; and (3) importing for public distribution articles which bear a false copyright notice. In particular, the law states the following:

> (e) False Representation.—
>
> Any person who knowingly makes a false representation of a material fact in the application for copyright registration provided for by section 409, or in any written statement filed in connection with the application, shall be fined not more than $2,500.

304. The prosecution must prove that the Act alleged was committed "with fraudulent intent." Violations are each punishable by a fine of up to USD 2,500. Owing perhaps to this week enforcement tool, some scholars estimate that false claims of copyright over public domain woks is a multimillion-dollar industry. Even so, a few notable cases illustrate the downsides to false copyright registration. In 2013, a documentary film company sued Warner Music/Chappell for falsely claiming copyright to the song "Happy Birthday to You." Warner Music had historically claimed copyright to English language's most popular song, but a federal judge ruled that Warner Music did not hold any valid copyright to the song and never acquired the rights to the "Happy Birthday" lyrics. Warner Music was ordered to pay USD 14 million to end a lawsuit challenging its hold on the popular song. In addition, the settlement stipulated a proposed final judgment and order that would declare the song to be in the public domain. In 2016, photographer Carol M. Highsmith sued Getty Images and Alamy (two stock photography organizations) for

247. 17U.S.C.A. § 401(b)(3).

USD 1.35 billion over their attempts to assert copyright over her images and for charging fees for the use of over 18,000 of her images, which she had released royalty-free.

305. Given the fact that copyright registration and notice is not required, it is not prudent to assume the absence of copyright protection based on lack of a copyright mark or notice. Even with notice, identifying the owner of the copyright can prove challenging, due to transfer of ownership, death, and several other factors. To search for the identity of a copyright holder, most researchers start with the Copyright Office records, which include registration information and now provide online access for more recent works.[248]

III. Publication and Issuance of Copies to the Public

306. Publication occurs when copies or phonorecords are distributed to the public by sale, lease, or other transfer of ownership. Whether a work is published or unpublished it may determine the duration of copyright protections. In particular, the duration of protection for works made for hire may be determined by the date of publication. Moreover, the year of publication may determine the length of the copyright term if the work was created before January 1, 1978, and was published or registered before that date. As noted above, a certificate of registration creates certain legal presumptions particularly in light of subsequent claims of infringement. Most notably, a copyright owner may be entitled to claim statutory damages and attorneys' fees in an infringement lawsuit if the work was registered (and therefore published) before the infringement began or within three months after the first publication of that work. Finally, the deposit requirements for registering a published work differ from the requirements for registering an unpublished work.[249]

307. A public display or performance of a work does not itself constitute publication. Instead, to display or perform a work publicly it must occur at a place open to the public or where a significant number of observers outside those related to or associated with the owner may view or experience the work. Similarly, the transmission of a display or performance to a public place by other processes or devices may constitute publication, regardless of whether the members of public that can access the work, do so in the same location or at the same time.

308. As noted by the Copyright Office, offers to distribute copies of the work to a group of persons for purposes of further distribution, public performance, or public display, constitutes publication. Conversely, granting access to the work to a particular group for an explicit purpose and with the requirement that the work not be further disseminated, does not constitute publication requiring copyright notice.

---

248. *See Public Catalog*, Copyright, www.copyright.gov/records (last visited Jan. 29, 2020).
249. See Copyright Basics, U.S. gov, https://www.copyright.gov/circs/circ01.pdf.

IV. First Sale Doctrine

309. The first sale doctrine provides that a person who buys a copy of a copyrighted work from the copyright owner receives the right to sell, display or otherwise dispose of that particular copy. Such after-sale activities do not violate the copyright owner's rights.[250] The Copyright Act separates expressive conduct, such as an original song that is exclusively controlled by a copyright owner, and the physical object containing that expression, such as a CD, which anyone may own. Although relatively intuitive, the first sale doctrine has generated significant confusion in criminal copyright prosecutions particularly. Notably, the buyer of the work and his/her entitlement to distribute it ends once the buyer has sold that particular copy.[251] For example, a buyer of a movie on DVD may sell it, donate, or otherwise transfer it, but may not digitally duplicate (or burn) copies for further distribution. The first sale doctrine does not protect a defendant who makes unauthorized reproductions of a copyrighted work.

310. Moreover, the defenses created by the first sale doctrine do not extend to those who acquire possession of a copyrighted work from the copyright owner by rental, license, lease, or loan. In other words, those who possess a copy of the copyrighted work but do not have an ownership interest, cannot disseminate or transfer that work under the first sale doctrine.[252] Most computer software, for example, are transferred using licensing agreements. In *Verner v. Autodesk*, the Ninth Circuit Federal Court of Appeals held that the buyer of a copy of software was not entitled to resell it under the first sale doctrine, because the buyer was a licensee, rather than legal owner of the software.[253]

311. Criminal defendants who copy and sell copyrighted works often claim that the works they were selling had been the subject of a legitimate first sale. There is some uncertainty in U.S. courts regarding the burden of proof as to this claim. While many cases maintain that the government prosecutor must prove that the copyrighted work was not the subject of a first sale, other courts have concluded that the issue of a first sale is an affirmative defense that must be proved by the defendant.

312. In *John Wiley & Sons, Inc., v. Kirtsaeng*, a doctoral student from Thailand helped pay for his American education by importing foreign editions of U.S. textbooks sold at discounted prices in Asia. The student than resold the discounted textbooks on eBay at lower prices than those offered by copyright holders in the U.S. When the student was prosecuted in federal U.S. court, the student claimed that the first sale doctrine immunized his reselling because he was the lawful owner of the

250. 17U.S.C. § 109.
251. 17U.S.C. § 109(a) & (c).
252. 17U.S.C. § 109(d).
253. Vernor v. Autodesk, 621 F.3d 1102 (2010).

books. The appellate court held that the student did not lawfully acquire the textbooks and that the Copyright Act prohibits the importation into the U.S. of copies acquired outside the U.S., absent the authorization of the copyright holder.[254]

313. The U.S. Supreme Court however, reversed the appellate court decision. The U.S. Supreme Court held that Kirtsaeng's sale of lawfully made copies purchased overseas was protected by the first sale doctrine. The court reasoned that the first sale doctrine applies to works manufactured outside of the U.S., and the protections and exceptions offered by the Copyright Act to works is not limited by geographical borders. The court then concluded that copyright protections apply to all copies legally made anywhere, not just in the United States. In other words, the first sale doctrine does not apply only to copies manufactured domestically. Wherever a copy of a book is first made and sold, it can be resold in the U.S. without permission from the publisher.[255]

§10. Infringement

314. Generally, copyright law gives the owner of the copyrighted work the exclusive right to reproduce, publish, perform, display, or create "derivative works" from it. Duplicating, distributing, publicly displaying, or performing a derivative version of the protected work without the copyright owner's consent constitutes infringement. Posting on a website another person's original material, for example, without their permission constitutes copying, display, and publication of such work, which could constitute a copyright infringement. Changing, modifying, or editing the work prior to posting it does not necessarily relieve the poster of liability. Under U.S. copyright law, a modified version of an original work would likely be a "derivative work" of the original, which only the copyright owner has the right to make. Downloading an image from the Internet and modifying it does not create a new work; it arguably creates a derivative work, which violates copyright law.

315. Notably, U.S. copyright law does not grant copyright holders absolute control over the use of their work. Only certain types of works and only certain kinds of uses are protected. As detailed more fully below, the "fair use" exception includes several uses of copyrighted material that do not legally infringe on the copyright holder's rights. These non-infringing uses are typically justified as promoting freedom of expression. Generally speaking, fair uses include but are not limited to educational use, criticism, parody, comment, news reporting, scholarship, and research.

316. In the U.S., civil liability for copyright infringement is a strict liability offense. The onus rests with the alleged infringer, because the infringer has the opportunity to inquire as to copyright protection before copying, displaying or otherwise publishing. A copyright holder need not prove that the defendant intended to infringe. The court made this clear in *Pinkham v. Sara Lee Corp*:

---

254. 654 F. 3d 210 (2nd Cir. 2011).
255. 568U.S. 519 (2013).

> Once a plaintiff has proven that he or she owns the copyright on a particular work, and that the defendant has infringed upon those "exclusive rights," the defendant is liable for the infringement and this liability is absolute. The defendant's intent is simply not relevant: The defendant is liable even for "innocent" or "accidental" infringements.[256]

317. Courts have developed secondary liability, even though the same is not stated expressly in the Copyright statue. Persons who "knowingly" cause others to infringe, but have not actually infringed themselves can be liable. Illegal file sharing, for example, demonstrates both direct and indirect infringement. Sharing copyrighted games, music and videos directly violates copyright law. With regard to music, the Recording Industry of America filed lawsuits against more than 30,000 file traders. In MGM *Studios v. Grokster*, the court held Grokster, a West Indies software company, contributorily and vicariously liable for infringing upon MGM Studio copyrights. Grokster's software that facilitated users to engage in illegal file trading was held to be an indirect infringement on the plaintiff's copyrights. The software essentially encouraged and profited from direct copyright infringement.[257]

318. In 2020, the Copyright Alternative in Small-Claims Enforcement Act was enacted, which directed the Copyright Office to establish a small claims court-type process for low-value copyright disputes. In particular, this new three-member tribunal will be available for copyright claims of less than USD 30,000. According to the Copyright Office, this new procedure should be available by the beginning of 2022.[258]

I. Copy Protection and Digital Rights Management

319. Several software products initially included mechanisms to deter copying. Diverse approaches embedded in software restricted the operation of the software to the user alone. Without a uniform approach, however, market forces in conjunction with copyright owners who did not install such restrictions forced most producers and copyright owners to forgo such strategies. Even so, several software products and other technologies have revisited the approach.

320. Relatedly, notification to users that a product is copyright protected is more difficult for digital products. Most analogue works, like a printed text, included copyright details into the text itself. Increasingly, producers of digital works incorporate copyright information into the work as well. As indicated above, digital technologies coupled with the ease of Internet dissemination complicates the rights of copyright owners and the understanding of consumers and users. As a result, embedding copyright data into digital works helps address such confusion. Indeed,

256. 983 F.2d 824, 828 (1992).
257. 545U.S. 417 (1984).
258. Additional details of the copyright small claims process are available here: https://www.copyright.gov/about/small-claims/.

the Digital Millennium Copyright Act restricts users from disabling a technical control that limits access to a work that is protected under the Copyright Act. This includes, but is not limited to, decrypting an encrypted work as well as deactivating, bypassing, or otherwise impairing a technical measure designed to protect a copyright owner's rights.

321. In 2010, Blizzard, the owner of the video game, World of Warcraft, won a multimillion-dollar lawsuit by successfully proving that the defendant enabled users to circumvent the game's authentication software. Disabling the game's authentication software allowed the defendant to use a private server that hosted 427,393 players who played the game on the private server instead of on Blizzard's servers. The court awarded USD 88 million to Blizzard, in part, by multiplying the number of users by the statutory minimum of USD 200.[259]

322. Typically, an illegal circumvention does not include a user's manipulation of software for other reasons, like server overload or obtaining and using a password. In other words, the circumvention must either infringe or facilitate the infringement of a right protected under copyright law. For example, the provision is not violated by decrypting a software to gain access to software fault symptom codes, absent a showing that the decryption allowed or facilitated copyright infringement.

323. Second those entities and persons that design and sell products for the purpose of circumventing digital copyright protections may be liable under U.S. copyright law. Those programs or services that primarily exist only to circumvent protection and are advertised for that purpose are illegal.

324. Examples of infringing acts with regard to disabling technological measures that seek to protect copyright owners include the following:

- software that disables a mechanism that mandates the entry of a security key before the copyright holder's protected software will install;
- software products that enabled decryption and copying of DVDs by manipulating technological protections;
- development of an alternative web address that mimics the copyright owner's online gaming service, which allowed other users to access the copyright owner's software for multiple-user interaction without accessing the copyright owner's server;
- software that removed a registry key used by a website operator to number coupons it issued sequentially so that each coupon would have been one in a numerically limited series.

325. Outside these examples, difficulty remains with regard to software and services that facilitate interoperability of digital devices and services. For example, computer programs that enable wireless telephone devices to execute software

259. Blizzard Entm't, Inc. v. Reeves, 2010U.S. Dist. LEXIS 85560 (C.D. Cal., Aug. 10, 2010).

applications for the sole purpose of enabling interoperability of those applications, might technically circumvent copyright instrumentalities. Interoperability technology might include video games accessible on personal computers, e-books, and screen readers, and increasingly irrelevant hardwire connected devices. In addition, there are a multitude of exceptions to the anti-circumvention rules, as set forth below.

A. *Nonprofits and Education*

326. A nonprofit library, archive, or educational institution does not violate the rule regarding circumvention of technological measures, if such an entity acquires access to a copyrighted work that has been exploited, but does so with the sole intention of determining how or whether to legally use the work. Importantly, a copy of an exploited work by a nonprofit or education institution may not be kept for a period of time longer than necessary to decide whether to buy or otherwise legally use the work. During this time, the exploited work may not be used for any other purpose. This limited exemption does not apply if an identical, non-exploited copy of the work is reasonably available. Repeated violations of the exemption can result in forfeiture of the exemption, as well as civil liability.

B. *Government Process*

327. The U.S. government, under statute, is absolved from liability for circumventing technological measures in some instances. In particular, when the circumvention occurs in the pursuit of a lawfully authorized investigative, protective, information security, or intelligence activity, the circumvention is legal. Under the statute "information security"means activities conducted to identify and address the vulnerabilities of a government computer, computer system, or computer network.[260]

> (e) Law Enforcement, Intelligence, and Other Government Activities:—
>
> This section does not prohibit any lawfully authorized investigative, protective, information security, or intelligence activity of an officer, agent, or employee of the United States, a State, or a political subdivision of a State, or a person acting pursuant to a contract with the United States, a State, or a political subdivision of a State. For purposes of this subsection, the term "information security" means activities carried out in order to identify and address the vulnerabilities of a government computer, computer system, or computer network.[261]

---

260. 17U.S.C.A. § 1201(e).
261. *Id.*

C. Encryption Research

328. It does not violate the prohibition on circumventing copyright protection measures for a person to circumvent a technological measure of a copyrighted work in the course of an act of good faith encryption research. Importantly, the encryption researcher must have lawfully obtained the encrypted copy, and the encryption researcher must have made a good faith effort to obtain permission before the circumvention.

The statute identifies a few factors to determine whether this encryption research exemption applies:

(A) whether the information derived from the encryption research was disseminated, and if so, whether it was disseminated in a manner reasonably calculated to advance the state of knowledge or development of encryption technology, versus whether it was disseminated in a manner that facilitates infringement under this title or a violation of applicable law other than this section, including a violation of privacy or breach of security;

(B) whether the person is engaged in a legitimate course of study, is employed, or is appropriately trained or experienced, in the field of encryption technology; and

(C) whether the person provides the copyright owner of the work to which the technological measure is applied with notice of the findings and documentation of the research, and the time when such notice is provided.[262]

"Encryption research" is defined as "activities necessary to identify and analyze flaws and vulnerabilities of encryption technologies applied to copyrighted works, if those activities are conducted to advance the state of knowledge in the field of encryption technology or to assist in the development of encryption products." "Encryption technology" is defined as "the scrambling and descrambling of information using mathematical formulas or algorithms."[263]

D. Minors

329. Parents and guardians sometimes disable copyright protection measures in order to limit their children's access. U.S. law makes some allowance for this phenomenon if the circumvention "has the sole purpose to prevent the access of minors to the material on the Internet."[264]

---

262. 17U.S.C.A. § 1201(g)(3).
263. 17U.S.C.A. § 1201(g)(1).
264. 17U.S.C.A. § 1201(h).

E. Personally Identifying Information

330. It is not a violation of the prohibition on circumventing copyright protection measures for a person to circumvent a technological measure if that measure also collects or disseminates personally identifying information. The exemption is limited if the work and/or its technological measure provide conspicuous notice that personal information will be gleaned or offers the user an option to prevent or restrict the collection or dissemination of personally identifiable information. Notably the circumvention must be "carried out solely for the purpose of preventing the collection or dissemination of personally identifying information about a natural person who seeks to gain access to the work protected."[265]

II. Internet Service Providers

331. The Digital Millennium Copyright Act which, generally speaking, statutorily limited liability relating to material online, was specifically designed to reduce the liability of ISPs for acts of copyright infringement. This exemption for ISPs shields them from infringement actions brought by their subscribers and from infringement actions based on linking to sites that contain infringing information. To qualify for one of the exemptions under the DMCA, the service provider's activities at issue must involve functions described in one of four specified categories: (1) Transitory Digital Network Communications, (2) System Caching, (3) Information Residing on Systems or Networks At Direction of Users, and (4) Information Location Tools.[266] Those four categories are distinct, and a service provider's ability to qualify for the exemption associated with any one of the categories must be based solely on the criteria in the applicable category. The liability exemption is arguably justified due to the automatic nature of an ISP's servers. Providing universal access through automated means, dissipates allegations of intentional or volitional wrongdoing.[267]

Of course, the exemption from liability is not unlimited. The exemption applies as long as the service provider is not aware of the "facts and circumstances from which infringing activity is apparent," gets no financial benefit from the infringing activity, and does not itself take part in editing the material or selecting its audience. In other words, an ISP or other computer system operator is contributorily liable for copyright infringement if it has actual knowledge about discrete infringing material on its system and could have exercised reasonable means to prevent further infringement, but nevertheless continues to provide access to infringing

265. 17U.S.C.A. § 1201(i)(1)(D).
266. 17U.S.C.A. § 1201(a)(b)(c)(d).
267. Rosen v. Hosting Services, Inc., 771 F. Supp. 2d 1219 (C.D. Cal. 2010).

works.[268] For example, in a 2009 California case, the fact that a video-sharing website hosted an entire category of content—music—that was subject to copyright protection did not establish that the operator had actual knowledge of infringement, as required to prove that it was not entitled to coverage under the safe harbor provision.[269]

In *Arista Records LLC v. Usenet.com, Inc.*, operators of a file distribution service were not protected under this provision because they actively engaged in conduct that facilitated direct infringement of recording companies' copyrights. The plaintiffs in that case were able to prove that the operators were aware that digital music files were among the most popular items on the service and took active measures to create servers dedicated to music files. The operators also purposely increased retention times of particular groups containing those files and engaged in several overt efforts that demonstrated their control over the groups that could access their servers.[270]

A. *Transitory Digital Network Communications*

332. The first discrete category for service providers under the Act deals with transitory storage. In this category, a service provider is not liable for monetary relief, or, subject to an exception on when injunctive relief is allowed, for copyright infringement by reason of the provider's transmitting, routing, or providing connections for material through a system or network controlled or operated by or for the service provider, or by reason of the intermediate and transient storage of that material in the course of transmitting, routing, or providing connections, if:

- the transmission of the material was initiated by or at the direction of a person other than the service provider;
- the transmission, routing, provision of connections, or storage is done through an automatic technical process without selection of the material by the service provider;
- the service provider does not select the recipients of the material, except as an automatic response to the request of another person;
- no copy of the material made by the service provider in the course of such intermediate or transient storage is maintained on the system or network in a manner ordinarily accessible to anyone other than anticipated recipients, or in a manner ordinarily accessible to anticipated recipients for a longer period than is reasonably necessary for the transmission, routing, or provision of connections; and
- the material is transmitted through the system or network without modification of its content.[271]

---

268. 17U.S.C.A. § 512(c)(1).
269. *UMG Recordings, Inc. v. Veoh Networks Inc.*, 665 F. Supp. 2d 1099 (C.D. Cal. 2009).
270. *Arista Records LLC v. Usenet.com, Inc.*, 633 F. Supp. 2d 124 (S.D. N.Y. 2009).
271. 17U.S.C.A. § 512(a).

B. Linking to Infringing Matter

333. A service provider is not liable for copyright infringement by reason of the provider referring or linking users to an online location containing infringing material or infringing activity. The mere linking to an infringing source, or using information location tools, including a directory, index, reference, or hypertext link, will not create liability for the service provider unless the service provider has actual knowledge that the material or activity is infringing. However, upon obtaining such knowledge or awareness, the ISP must act expeditiously to remove, or disable access to, the infringing material. If the service provider derives a financial benefit directly from the infringing material, liability is likely to attach.

III. Contributory and Vicarious Copyright Infringement

334. As noted above, it is often difficult to enforce copyright protections against individual infringers when a widely shared application is used to commit that infringement. There may be a long list of direct infringers who are themselves difficult to identify. The legal alternative focuses contributory or vicarious infringement on a theory of secondary liability. This typically concerns the distributor of the infringing device, itself. Notably, the U.S. Copyright Act does not expressly impose liability for contributory infringement. Instead, contributory infringement is understood as an extension of general tort law and the principle in tort law that in addition to the tortfeasor, anyone who contributed to the tort should also be held liable. Generally speaking, a claimant has the burden of proving that the defendant had knowledge of a direct infringement and the defendant materially contributed to or facilitated that infringement.

As the U.S. Supreme Court stated in *Metro-Goldwyn-Mayer Studios, Inc. v. Grokster*, Ltd., vicarious infringement necessarily requires direct infringement: "One infringes contributorily by intentionally inducing or encouraging direct infringement, and infringes vicariously by profiting from direct infringement while declining to exercise a right to stop or limit it."[272] If a facilitating entity knows of the direct infringement and then induces or significantly contributes to continued direct infringement, the entity can be held contributorily liable.

This legal construct is often complicated, however, by the fair use defense, which allows the use of copyrighted works without the copyright owner's consent in certain situations. Several recent cases have addressed fair use defense as it relates to digitizing certain media, like books, for the purpose of allowing users to search the books using databases. In one recent case, the Second Circuit Court of Appeals ruled that digitization of copyrighted works to facilitate full-text searching of those works and to allow patrons with versions of the works absent the ability to print constituted fair use and was not a copyright infringement.

The defendant, HathiTrust Digital Library, was a spin-off of the Google Books Library Project. A group of California universities had Google digitize the books in each university's library. The collections of these university libraries were digitized

272. 545U.S. 913, 930 (2005).

by Google and then combined by HathiTrust Digital Library.[273] Notably, the digitization by Google has been the subject of a separate lawsuit.

In the underlying case, however, the court found the full-text search function to be fair use because the full-text search did not itself equate to the books being searched as the search function did not permit access to the underlying text. As a result, the plaintiffs could not demonstrate a legally recognized economic harm under the Copyright Act; the database and search function did not impede the market for the work. Moreover, the result of a word search was "different in purpose, character, expression, meaning, and message from the page (and the book) from which it is drawn."[274]

In a related case, a U.S. court exonerated a defendant that was charged with copyright infringement when an online advertising provider had no notice of infringing activity from the copyright holder. The defendant used an infringing free download site, but the court found no evidence of knowing infringement and therefore no liability for contributory infringement. The plaintiff had argued that the defendant "materially contributed to the infringement" because the shared advertising revenue made it easier for the website owner's infringement to be profitable. This argument was rejected by the court.[275]

Another high-profile case involving contributory infringement involved the infringement of copyrights through the "Music Share" software of Napster. Once the Napster software was activated on a computer, the software collected data about the MP3 files stored on that computer and transmitted the data to Napster servers. Napster then used the data to compile an index of music files available for download on the Napster network. Importantly, when a user wanted to download a music file, the software accessed the Napster index to locate a different user who already had that file on their system. Napster then connected the two users directly to facilitate the download of the music file. This process occurred without routing the file itself through Napster's servers. Even though Napster did not itself directly infringe, the Ninth Circuit Court of Appeals found Napster liable for both "contributory infringement" and "vicarious infringement." The court found that Napster had "actual knowledge" of infringing activity, and that by providing its software and services to the infringers, Napster had "materially contributed" to the infringement.[276]

IV. Resale, the Internet and Secondary Infringement

335. The proliferation of the ability to copy, transfer, and download digital files has disrupted the music industry, particularly as it relates to third parties that merely act as a go-between or host to music files downloaded or uploaded by users.

---

273. *Authors Guild, Inc v. Hathi Trust*, 755 F.3d 87 (2d Cir. 2014).
274. *Id.*
275. 826 F. Supp. 2d 398 (DC, Mass. 2011).
276. 239 F.3d 1004 (9th Cir. 2001).

In *Capitol Records, LLC v. ReDigi Inc.*, the defendant, ReDigi Inc., provided an online service that allowed resale of digital musical tracks that were originally purchased by users from other sources, like the iTunes Store.[277] The plaintiff, record label Capitol Records, claimed copyright infringement. The novel question before the court was whether digital music purchases are eligible for resale under the first sale doctrine. Although the trial court initially denied the plaintiff's motion for preliminary injunction, the court eventually granted the plaintiff's motion for summary judgment. In so doing, the court ruled that defendant, as the operator of an online digital music marketplace, was liable for the direct and secondary infringement of the plaintiff's reproduction and distribution rights.

The reproduction right was triggered by the transference of the music file into a new hard drive, constituting a new material object. As a result, the argument that the music file merely "migrated" from the user's computer to the defendant's cloud storage was rejected. The transfer was not merely a transfer or movement of the file, but a duplication thereof. The court concluded that "the fact that a file has moved from one material object—the user's computer—to another—the ReDigi server—means that a reproduction has occurred. Similarly, when a ReDigi user downloads a new purchase from the ReDigi website to her computer, yet another reproduction is created. It is beside the point that the original phonorecord no longer exists. It matters only that a new phonorecord has been created."[278] The court's ruling signals that under the first sale doctrine, digital music files, lawfully made and purchased, may not be resold by users through an online used digital marketplace.

V. News Aggregation

336. The Internet has become a primary news source for most Americans. Increased reliance on the Internet as a source of news has coincided with declining profits in the traditional news media and the failure of a spate of news media organizations across the U.S. News aggregators like Google News and The Huffington Post are characterized by some as simply reselling and profiting from the factual news gathered by traditional news media. In fact, Rupert Murdoch, the American media mogul who founded News Corp., has characterized Google's aggregation and display of newspaper headlines as "theft."

Because a news aggregator features the content of others, it may appear illegitimate or infringing, particularly when the aggregator benefits from the labor of others' news gathering and writing. But the aggregator's site often links or otherwise refers readers to the original source, where that original publisher benefits from the user's presence on the publisher's website. Additionally, new users are often introduced to a publisher through news aggregators.

A few courts have reviewed the online practices of certain blogs and news-oriented websites with regard to the practice of news aggregation. The question arises whether a news organization has recourse when aggregators purportedly

277. 934 F. Supp. 2d 640 (S.D.N.Y. 2013).
278. *Id.*

engage in certain acts of unlawful copying and misappropriation, or for misappropriation of its breaking news. In *Associated Press v. Meltwater U.S. Holdings, Inc.*, for example, an online news aggregator lifted news articles from others and provided selected excerpts of those stories (including many stories published by the Associated Press) to subscribers. The federal district court in New York ruled that the fair use defense did not protect news aggregators from copyright infringement claims.[279]

§11. NONINFRINGEMENT

I. Freedom of Expression

337. As identified above, the U.S. Constitution contains strong protection for the right of free expression. Interestingly, the U.S. Supreme Court has characterized copyright restrictions on copying other's works as "the engine of free expression," because copyright laws promote the creation of works by protecting their economic value as against indiscriminate copying.[280] As a result, there is no conflict between copyright protection and First Amendment freedom of expression. The copyright protections are not content-specific, but instead turn on the idea versus author expression dichotomy. For example, the popular entertainment show Saturday Night Live frequently uses copyrighted works for parody, comment or criticism. A sketch featuring Harry Potter or a sketch parodying Kylo Ren from the Star Wars franchise do not infringe on the copyright holders of those respective works. Such uses promote freedom of expression and constitute a non-infringing use.

II. Fair Use

338. The Copyright Act provides for "fair use" of a work, even without the copyright owner's permission in certain instances.[281] The fair use doctrine originally developed through common law in the U.S. and was justified on the theory that every author, by the act of publishing her work and making it available for public consumption, impliedly consented to "reasonable and customary use" of the work by subsequent writers. It also promotes freedom of expression. According to the U.S. Supreme Court, fair uses often include "criticism, comment, news reporting, teaching (including multiple copies for classroom use), scholarship, or research."[282] Although fair use is simple enough as a generalized concept, it is also frustratingly ambiguous.

339. Fair use is often raised as a defense to claims of copying. This doctrine allows flexibility in deciding infringement cases but has been criticized for the

279. 931 F. Supp. 2d 537 (S.D.N.Y. 2013).
280. *Harper & Row v. Nation Enterprises*, 471U.S. 539, 558 (1985).
281. 17U.S.C. § 107 (2007).
282. *Campbell v. Acuff-Rose Music, Inc.*, 510U.S. 569, 578 (1994).

ambiguity inherent in the doctrine. The several factors used to determine fair use illustrate the nebulous nature of the doctrine. In section 107, Congress provided a list of four factors that could be used to determine whether the doctrine was applicable to a given situation. These factors are:

(1) the purpose and character of the use, including whether such use is of a commercial nature or is for nonprofit educational purposes;
(2) the nature of the copyrighted work;
(3) the amount and substantiality of the portion used in relation to the copyrighted work as a whole; and
(4) the effect of the use upon the potential market for or value of the copyrighted work.[283]

340. No one factor is determinative of outcome. Courts weigh the results of the factors in light of copyright law's more general objectives. Notably, Congress intentionally sought to maintain the flexibility of the doctrine. Congress considered but rejected absolute and explicit definitions of fair use and instead indicated that case law applications would continue to be given deference and allowed to control. As noted above, the factors are balanced in light of the underlying policies motivating copyright law generally. There is no definitive list of "fair uses," leaving courts to address such claims on a case-by-case basis.

341. In evaluating the first factor, the court will identify how the work was used, noting whether the use promoted commercial or nonprofit objectives. If the allegedly unlawful use of a protected work was noncommercial or not used to generate a profit, the use will more likely be considered "fair." Courts also consider the degree of transformation attending the allegedly unlawful use. While transformation is not essential, "the more transformative the new work, the less will be the significance of other factors, like commercialism, that may weigh against a finding of fair use."[284]

342. The second factor, the nature of the copyrighted work, examines the aspects and dimensions of the copyrighted work itself. Courts, for example, are less likely to find that there was infringement under this factor of the fair use doctrine, if the original work was published, rather than unpublished, and if it was a factual work. Owners of works that have been published have already exposed the work to the public, and excising factual works from public use stunts societal progress.

343. The third factor is similarly intuitive, but simultaneously amorphous. The amount and substantiality of the work used in relation to the whole, clearly suggest that a court will be less inclined to extend fair use protection to a use that encompasses all or a substantial amount of the protected work. No formula or percentage provides a quantitative metric. Instead, courts adhere to a general understanding that the smaller the use, the more likely it will receive fair use protection. That said, even

283. 17U.S.C. § 107 (2007).
284. *Campbell v. Acuff-Rose Music, Inc.*, 510U.S. 569, 579 (1994).

a small use will violate copyright law if that use leverages the heart of the work, as illustrated in the Harper & Row case discussed below.

344. The fourth factor is the most important factor when determining fair use protection. Analyzing the effect of the unauthorized use on the potential market or value of the protected work reflects the underlying policy that motivates copyright law. Creators and owners of copyright works are incentivized to create such works, in part, by the remuneration attending the same. An unauthorized use that is commercial and that impairs the market for a work undermines that central policy. This factor extends to derivative rights, as illustrated by J. K. Rowling's successful lawsuit against a defendant who sought to publish an encyclopedia that detailed Harry Potter lexicon. The court enjoined defendant from publishing such an encyclopedia as interfering with Rowling's plans to pursue a similar project.[285]

A. *News and Fair Use*

345. These factors often take on slightly different dimensions depending on context. News and matters of public concern, are often claimed as deserving more protection under the four fair use factors. The court addressed all four factors within the context of the news in *Harper & Row, Publishers, Inc. v. Nation Enterprises.*[286] In that case, a copyright infringement claim was brought against a magazine for publishing exact quotes of President Ford that were pulled from a novel containing President Ford's memoirs just before its publication date.

346. The court held that the unauthorized publication of the quotes did not fall within the fair use exception. In so doing, the court explained the way in which the four factors could be applied to news media and matters of public concern. With regard to the first fair use factor which distinguishes between commercial and noncommercial uses, the court stated that "every commercial use of copyrighted material is presumptively an unfair exploitation of the monopoly privilege that belongs to the owner of the copyright."[287] Applied in this case, the subsequent use was for reporting the news, an example of something which the statute gives as a possible fair use. Even so, the court said that Congress did not mean for this list to be dispositive or controlling of the fair use issue without analysis of the other factors.

347. In so doing, the court relied on an undergirding policy objective of copyright law—"the propriety of the defendant's conduct."[288] In the case at bar, the defendant magazine had used ethically suspicious means to get a copy of the Ford quotes. Noting that the fair use defense was an equitable doctrine, the court took the illicit appropriation into consideration. Finally, the defendant's work—publishing

285. *Warner Bros. Entertainment, Inc. v. RDR Books*, 07 Civ. 9667 (S.D. N.Y. 2008).
286. 471U.S. 539 (1985).
287. *Id.* at 562.
288. *Id.*

Ford's quotes—did not add to or improve upon the appropriated information. It did not increase or benefit the public marketplace of ideas in any significant way.

348. The second fair use factor, the nature of the copyrighted use, was also analyzed by the court in the *Harper & Row* decision. The unpublished book that included Ford's memoirs was characterized by the court as a historical narrative or biography. The court opined that the law generally favors works based on fact over those based on fiction. But even within those categories, the court indicated that "within the field of fact works, there are gradations as to the relative proportion of fact and fancy."[289] In other words, historical fictions often invite fair use exceptions. But here, the court determined that the subsequent writer had appropriated "the subjective descriptions and portraits of public figures whose power lies in the author's individualized expression."[290] The court found that fair use was improper despite the fact that the work was a historical narrative.

349. The third fair use factor addresses the "amount and substantiality of the portion used in relation to the copyrighted work as a whole." The U.S. Copyright office has noted that under this factor, courts look at both the quantity and quality of the copyrighted material that was used. Intuitively, if the use includes a large portion of the copyrighted work, fair use is less likely to protect the user. Conversely, if the use employs only a small amount of copyrighted material, fair use is more likely. Even so, in some contexts courts have found use of an entire work to be fair. And in other contexts, using even a small amount of a copyrighted work was determined not to be fair because the selection was an important part—or the "heart" ––of the work. In the *Harper & Row* decision, the court held that while the appropriated material constituted only a very small proportion of the Ford memoir, the "qualitative nature of the taking" negated a fair use defense as far as that factor was concerned. The quotes from Ford were considered to be the heart of the book, and, as such, the defendant's use could not be appropriately classified as fair.

350. The fourth fair use factor addresses the effect of the use upon the potential market for or value of the copyrighted work. The U.S. Copyright office states that this includes whether, and to what extent, the unauthorized use harms the existing or future market for the copyright owner's original work. Courts consider whether the use is hurting the current market for the original work (for example, by displacing sales of the original) and/or whether the use could cause substantial harm if it were to become widespread. In the *Harper & Row* decision, the court identified this as the most important element of fair use. It found that the subsequent writing by the infringing magazine negatively affected the marketability of the Ford memoirs. The court stated, "to negate fair use one need only show that if the challenged use 'should become widespread, it would adversely affect the potential market for the copyrighted work.' "

289. *Id.* at 563.
290. *Id.*

B. Parodies and Fair Use

351. A parody is fair use of a copyrighted work when it is a humorous form of social commentary or literary criticism in which one work imitates another. It is a work that ridicules another, usually well-known work, by imitating it in a comic way. Although a parody falls under "use of a copyrighted work for the purpose of criticism or comment" as provided under 17 U.S.C § 107, the determination of whether the work qualifies as a parody depends on the current case law. Courts understand that, by its nature, parody requires some taking from the original work being parodied. Unlike other forms of fair use, a fairly extensive use of the original work is permitted in a parody in order to identify or "conjure up" the original.

352. Similarly a parody mocking a copyrighted work can qualify as fair use even if the parody was generated for commercial profit. The courts have also rejected the argument that a parody violates copyright law because it could harm the derivative value of the copyrighted work. To qualify as a fair use parody, the parody must criticize or mock the copyrighted work. The transformed use of Dr. Seuss' work, the Cat in the Hat, to criticize O.J. Simpson's trial, for example was not a parody under fair use, because the parody criticized O.J.'s trial, not Dr. Seuss' work.[291]

353. By way of contrast, use of a famous photograph of a naked pregnant Demi Moore, taken by Annie Leibovitz for Vanity Fair, to make fun of it, did qualify as parody. In that case the parody placed the superimposed head of Leslie Nielsen on the body of a naked pregnant woman, using the same lighting and body positioning as the famous photograph, and was ruled as fair use.[292]

C. GIFs and Fair Use

354. GIF is a graphic image file that facilitates brief animation by combining several images or frames into a single file. These short repeating animations that draw from other—often copyrighted works—have created uncertainty in copyright law. GIFs as we well know are an image format which have become popular through their use in sharing short repeating animations and are primarily seen on the Internet to help convey creative and entertaining responses to contemporary issues that could not be readily expressed using words alone.

355. Crucially, the content of GIFs that are widely available tend to range from snippets of existing copyright material (e.g., a short sequence from a film or similar motion video) or an original animation. In each case the GIF is either itself an original creation subject to copyright, or derived from preexisting copyrighted work. This presents a problem in relation to the legal use of GIFs, as it may be argued that they contain unlicensed copyright protected material. As such, in principle, freely sharing GIFs could infringe on the rights of copyright holders.

291. *Dr. Seuss Enterprises, L.P. v. Penguin Books U.S.A, Inc.*, 109 F.3d 1394, (9th Cir. 1997).
292. *See Leibovitz v. Paramount Pictures Corp.* 137 F.3d 109 (2d Cir. N.Y. 1998).

356. Although there is little case law to support how the courts would decide this particular issue, applying the four fair use factors appear to allow the ongoing practice. Typically, the primary purpose of GIFs is to illustrate a certain feeling, expression, or reaction. The devaluation of the copyrighted work is minor, and the amount and quality of the copyrighted work used in GIFs is usually very small. Courts have not yet resolved the legality of GIFs due to their nascent arrival new to the Internet and social media world.

D. Linking and Fair Use

357. Posting content obtained from other sources is restricted under copyright law in many instances. It is also often restricted by the terms of any agreements with the owners of that material, or contained within a website's terms and conditions. Generally speaking, copyright law does not bar the act of directing one's website visitors to useful information elsewhere on the Internet by providing links to other sites where such information appears. Even so, U.S. courts will scrutinize linking when the evidence suggests that the entity providing the link knows that the link connects to a site that facilitates infringement or publishes infringing material. In *Universal City Studios v. Corley*, the Second Circuit court of appeals considered the legality of a link which transmitted users to a computer program created to circumvent the CSS encryption technology used in DVDs. Several film studios sued, and the court ultimately concluded that "the government interest in preventing unauthorized access to encrypted copyrighted material is unquestionably substantial," and that the links were not protected by free speech principles because regulation of the links was content-neutral.[293]

358. Linking typically enhances the usability and value of a website. However, in some instances links infringe copyrights owned by the linked site. When links actually mimic or duplicate the information contained in the linked page, they are closer to infringement. As a result, links should merely direct the user to the linked site, without duplicating the content therein.

359. In addition, many sites contain terms and conditions of use that prohibit what has been termed, "deep linking," which is the process of linking to an internal page and bypassing a website's homepage. Although there are few cases on the enforceability of such provisions, the terms and conditions listed on any site being linked to may create legal obligations. The legality of "in-line linking" is also somewhat unclear. In-line linking also known as hotlinking, is the use of a linked object, often an image, on one site by a web page belonging to a second site. It creates the illusion that an image is part of both websites. In *Perfect 10 v. Amazon*, the Ninth Circuit found no infringement for an in-line link that itself resembled thumbnail-sized images of the full-sized images accessed through the link. The court found that

293. *Universal City Studios v. Corley*, 273 F.3d 429 (2001).

Google did not directly infringe on the full-sized images because it never stored the full-sized images on its server and because the thumbnail size was sufficiently transformative.[294]

360. Internet users routinely use in-line linking to embed videos to their own works using video-sharing sites, like YouTube. Notably, most prominent video-sharing sites like Vimeo and YouTube require those who upload videos to simultaneously relinquish rights to those videos. In their terms of service, YouTube requires those who post videos to allow others to use the posted content. As long as the original party posting the video also owned the content, it is legal for others to embed that content.

E. Social Networking and Fair Use

361. When a user posts creative work on social media, the user generally continues to own the copyright if the work is otherwise eligible. However, several social media platforms, like YouTube and Twitter include terms of use that apply merely by using those platforms. Those terms purport to give the platform a license to use the creative work posted by the user.

362. Moreover, the terms of use often include language allowing other users of the platform to share the work. The legal enforceability of these terms of use is unclear. Perhaps surprisingly, given the ubiquity of social networking media, there have been few dispositive cases of users suing each other for copyright infringement based on sharing or altering posts or tweets without permission. In conjunction with the terms of use, it is common practice to republish tweets, for example, and to do so in diverse media.

363. Importantly, many social media providers include similar terms of service to those terms found on video-sharing sites like YouTube. When registering for the social networking site, reddit users, for example, agree to grant the company a fully transferrable, sublicensable, royalty-free, worldwide right to use copyright protected material posted by subscribers for any purpose. Presuming courts will enforce such terms of use, companies like Twitter and Facebook not only have a legal right to the use of content that consumers upload to their services, but also to sublicense the use of that content to others as well.

F. Sampling and Fair Use

364. Often a new work takes a portion of a copyrighted work and incorporates it. Sampling involves the assimilation of a portion of a video, a sound recording, or photograph into a new work. Historically artists used portions of other's preexisting

294. *Perfect 10 v. Google, Inc*, 416 F. Supp. 2d 828, 843–45 (C.D. Cal. 2006).

work to create a new work, particularly in music. Technological advancements in auditory software and photographic editing facilitated the ability to capture exact duplicates of preexisting works from which to excerpt portions thereof. File sharing, for example made this process easy and inexpensive, making it easy to distribute one's own work and to find others' work for modification and adaptation.

365. With regard to music, large entertainment organizations banded together and pushed to outlaw sampling as violating copyright law. Until 1991, sampling was a common practice in certain genres of music in the U.S. and copyright protections were presumed inapplicable. Due to judicial interpretation, however, samples fell within the ambit of copyright protection as long as they rose "to a level legally cognizable appropriation."[295]

366. This standard allowed for "de minimis" sampling. In other words, no license was required if one artist sampled, or incorporated, another artist's work, as long as the sampling was small enough. Of course, litigation ensued to further clarify what an appropriate "de minimis" sampling means, with one court attempting to eliminate the de minimis doctrine altogether.[296] Suffice it to say, the wise action is to obtain a license from the copyright holder before sampling.

367. There are two categories of works protected by musical licenses, musical works and sound recordings. A musical work is the composition of music and lyrics, generally owned by the songwriter or a music publisher. A sound recording is the final product produced in a studio by musicians, producers, and sound engineers, which is generally owned by the record company. There is also a performance license, which is a license required before playing a musical work. In most instances, public performance rights are negotiated by the broadcasters, businesses, venues, and radio stations that present the music.

368. With regard to movies, a more flexible approach to sampling pervades U.S. copyright law. In 2010, the Copyright Office determined that disabling management software on DVDs in order to integrate small scenes from a movie into a video for purposes like education, criticism, or parody was not an infringement. *See* prior discussion regarding GIFs and the Internet above.

G. Software Application Programming Interfaces and Fair Use

369. Like other areas of intellectual property protection, copyright law struggles with how to deal with the unique challenges posed by software. As discussed above, software has a primarily functional aspect (dictating the operation of a computer device), but software is, by statute, protected as copyrightable subject matter. This intersection of the functionality doctrine and the explicit statutory protection of software come to the fore when considering Application Programming Interfaces

295. *Bridgeport Music, Inc. v. Dimension Films*, 410 F.3d 792 (6th Cir. 2005).
296. *Id.*

(APIs). APIs have as a primary function enabling interoperability of the software with other software. APIs are often also smaller code segments that do not add significant expressive content to their interoperability functionality. Nevertheless, under well-settled copyright doctrine, as long as there is some expressive content, the software is copyrightable.

370. These issues came to a head recently in a case that cycled through the courts for many years and ultimately ended up at the Supreme Court.[297] In the Oracle case, Google was accused of copying portions of Oracle's Java code base in creating its Android software so that programmers could continue to use the function calls from Java that they had grown accustomed to using. Ultimately, the Supreme Court did not address every issue raised with respect to copyrightability and APIs, but the court did resolve the fair use issue. Specifically, the court held that "where Google reimplemented a user interface, taking only what was needed to allow users to put their accrued talents to work in a new and transformative program, Google's copying of the Sun Java API was a fair use of that material as a matter of law."[298] Accordingly, companies reusing code from an API to ensure compatibility with their new programs would seem to be on strong legal footing, at least from a fair use perspective. The question of whether such use would be copyright infringement in the first place (in the absence of a fair use) remains unresolved, however.

III. Reverse Engineering and Decompilation

371. As noted above, circumventing a technological measure that attempts to protect copyright holders, will often violate the law. However, some statutory allowance exempts users from liability for reverse engineering in certain contexts. Under the Copyright Act, "a person who has lawfully obtained the right to use a copy of a computer program may circumvent a technological measure that effectively controls access to a particular portion of that program for the sole purpose of identifying and analyzing those elements of the program that are necessary to achieve interoperability of an independently created computer program with other programs."[299] This exemption applies only if such means have not previously been made available to the person engaging in the circumvention.

372. Similarly, a person may develop and employ technological means to circumvent a technological measure in order to enable the identification and analysis for the purpose of enabling interoperability of an independently created computer program with other programs. Again, this circumvention is allowed only if those means are necessary to achieve interoperability, and to the extent that doing so does not constitute copyright infringement.[300]

297. *Google LLC v. Oracle Am., Inc.*, 141 S. Ct. 1183, 209 L. Ed. 2d 311 (2021).
298. *Id.* at 1209.
299. 17U.S.C.A. § 1201(f).
300. *Id.*

373. Importantly, the information acquired through the circumvention may be made available to others if the person provides such information or means solely for the purpose of "enabling interoperability of an independently created computer program with other programs, and to the extent that doing so does not constitute copyright infringement" or violate applicable law other than the circumvention provision. For these purposes, the term "interoperability" means the ability of computer programs to exchange information and to use the information that has been exchanged.[301]

IV. Enforcement

374. Enforcement of copyright law may take several forms. Copying or posting a copyrighted work without permission, for example, on a website can lead to statutory damages, set by law at a minimum of USD 750 and a maximum of USD 30,000 per work that is infringed, based on the court's discretion.

> (1) Except as provided by clause (2) of this subsection, the copyright owner may elect, at any time before final judgment is rendered, to recover, instead of actual damages and profits, an award of statutory damages for all infringements involved in the action, with respect to any one work, for which any one infringer is liable individually, or for which any two or more infringers are liable jointly and severally, in a sum of not less than USD 750 or more than USD 30,000 as the court considers just.[302]

375. In the alternative, a court can award the plaintiff "actual damages," sometimes termed compensatory damages, in the amount of any demonstrable loss suffered because of the infringement. Generally speaking copyright owners prefer statutory damages over actual damages because it is less burdensome to prove such damages.

376. Purposeful or "willful" copyright infringement is a federal crime punishable by imprisonment or fines. In addition, if the infringement was "willful," the court has the discretion to increase the amount of statutory damages up to USD 150,000 per infringement, and can require the losing party to pay the prevailing party's costs and attorney's fees.

> (2) In a case where the copyright owner sustains the burden of proving, and the court finds, that infringement was committed willfully, the court in its discretion may increase the award of statutory damages to a sum of not more than $150,000. In a case where the infringer sustains the burden of proving, and the court finds, that such infringer was not aware and had no

301. *Id.*
302. 17U.S. Code §504(b).

> reason to believe that his or her acts constituted an infringement of copyright, the court in its discretion may reduce the award of statutory damages to a sum of not less than $200 ...[303]

377. Moreover, any person who infringes a copyright willfully and for purposes of commercial advantage or private financial gain is guilty of criminal infringement.[304] Criminal liability in such instances does not require that the defendant actually obtain advantage or payment stemming from the illegal conduct. Violation of the prohibition on the lease of a phonorecord does not constitute criminal infringement.

378. Willfully infringing a copyright by purposely making it available on a digital network accessible to the public may also constitute criminal infringement if the person knew that the work was intended for commercial distribution. In U.S. *v. Liu*, the appellate court ruled that the trial court erred by wrongly defining "willfulness." Because the jury could have convicted the defendant without finding that he knew that his actions were unlawful, there was insufficient proof that that defendant knew that he was illegally copying copyrighted material and thus he did not willfully infringe the copyrights.[305]

379. Of course, criminal liability under U.S. copyright law extends beyond mere criminal infringement. A person who knowingly makes a false representation of a material fact in the application for copyright registration, may violate federal copyright law. This liability extends to those who fraudulently post a notice of copyright on works that the person knows to be false. Finally, fraudulently removing a copyright notice may result in criminal liability under U.S. copyright law.

303. *Id.*
304. 17U.S.C.A. § 506(a)(1)(A).
305. 731 F.3d 982 (9th Cir. 2013).

Chapter 5. Legal Protection of Software

380. Software-based inventions do not easily fit the traditional patent law regulations. Even so, software inventions are patentable in the U.S. Recent Supreme Court decisions and subsequent lower court opinions have struggled with the awkward marriage of software innovation and traditional patent law. In so doing, U.S. courts have introduced significant ambiguity to an otherwise straightforward analysis. For software to be patent eligible, the software must meet certain technical requirements. For example, the software may be patentable (1) if it improves computer functionality in some way (i.e., it enables certain computations that were previously unavailable, speeds up processes, or requires fewer resources), or (2) if it solves a computing challenge in an unconventional way. Many academics and technology experts argue that software patents actually impede innovation. They contend that the vast majority of software is neither "novel" nor "nonobvious" to other developers who are equally skilled in the same technical field. As detailed below, all inventions must be "novel" and "nonobvious" in order to be patentable.

381. With regard to copyrighting software, computer programs are considered literary works in the U.S. under the Copyright Act.[306] The traditional policy disputes regarding copyright apply with equal force to the rationale for copyrighting software, although a few distinctive issues attend software copyrights. For example, many software programs can be protected only to the extent that they facilitate the programmer's expression of original ideas, as distinguished from the ideas themselves. This dichotomy attempts to distinguish copyrightable aspects of a program from the purely utilitarian and the public domain. Thus, the copyrightability of particular aspects of a given piece of software depends on fact-specific details of the software itself.

382. One important issue that is unique to the protection of software is with respect to open-source software projects, and the resulting litigation surrounding this issue. Each of these will be addressed in turn.

I. Open Source

383. Open source is a method of creating and distributing software. The open-source approach typically allows for the sharing of source code. Source code is the underlying code of a program or application that interacts directly with the computer or operating system. Having access to the source code of an application makes the inner workings of a computer program directly observable. Without access to the source code, a programmer can sometimes observe the inputs, outputs, and behaviors of an application to gather a general sense of the application's operation.

306. 17U.S.C. § 101.

384. Sometimes it is even possible to recreate the application or create a replica of it using only those observations, but this is rarely as effective as access to the source code—especially if a programmer wants to leverage the work of another programmer who created the original application. Consequently, open source can be a useful tool in collaboration and innovation in software engineering. Rather than keeping the source code hidden from the end users, as traditional software companies typically do, the open-source ideology calls for the source code to be available to everyone. This access enables users who are proficient in programming to add to or modify the software code and then redistribute it.

385. The open-source approach uses licensing and copyrights to accomplish its goals. Instead of using copyrights to control and limit access to software, the open-source approach uses copyrights to require freedom and openness. Essentially, open source uses licenses to impose conditions on the use of a work or software. If a user meets the conditions of the licensing, she has permission to use and modify the software and source code. Generally speaking, these conditions require that the subsequent user makes her modified source code available, does not charge royalties for her software, attributes modifications to the maker, and propagates the same terms for redistributed or modified software. This approach helps to make a variety of important software technologies more available to the public.

386. However, software patents can cause issues with the open-source ideology. As with other general patents, new technology (or software) that infringes upon a valid patent does so even if the technology (or software) was independently created. This can bypass the open-source methods of licensing. If an unrelated third party holds the patent rights for a piece of software, they can block open-source users from running the software. Furthermore, third parties could obtain patents to strategically block or disadvantage open-source products.

387. How does patent protection, which circumvents the openness of the open-source approach, work for software? The source code implements an algorithm or "recipe" which may be protected by patent rights. Software patents are written to cover specific algorithms, in specific contexts, that deliver certain tangible results. Even with this specificity and context, they can obtain very broad coverage. . . . A process claim will describe the algorithm in English-language statements. The claim may employ terms of art for skilled programmers, but the claim will not be a direct recitation of the computer program's source code. . . . Such a patent claim could cover a software instructional composite implementing the algorithm written in either the "C" or "C++" or "Pascal" language. Indeed, it is not strictly necessary for the patent applicant to supply any source code with the application disclosure, so long as the disclosure provided enables a person skilled in the relevant programming art to practice the invention. . . . When this process (the claim) maps to a software instructional composite, both its source and object code are effectively shackled if the patentee enforces the patent.[307]

307. Greg R. Vetter, *The Collaborative Integrity of Open-Source Software*, Utah L. Rev., 563, 593 n.84 (2004).

388. With the recent increase in software patents, the risk of conflict with open-source software grows. In addition to more software patents, the open-source movement continues to grow and expand with new projects and products. While there is wide flexibility in how to implement algorithms in the source code, that flexibility is not boundless. As the number of software patents in a specialized area increases, that opportunity to use different algorithms may decrease. Conversely, as open source continues to grow and spread, it may inhibit patent infringement cases due the available source code that may qualify as patent-invalidating prior art. As such, there may be a race to claim as many software patents as possible while they are still available.

II. Patent Wars

389. One of the results of the surge in open-source software is that larger software companies are battling more frequently with patent infringement suits or open-source licensing enforcements. Software patents often have unpredictable claim interpretation, as well as blurred scope and disputed validity. As these software patents rarely include actual code, they often describe the software in broad and general terms of functionality. Because of that, these patents can be ambiguous and lack strong boundaries, which makes them an ideal target for patent trolls.

390. A patent troll is the popular name given to a patent attorney or company, often called nonpracticing entities, that try to acquire large portfolios of patents. Rather than using these patents to conduct business or produce goods or services, these entities use these patents to intimidate and persuade other companies into licensing agreements to allow the practicing company to continue to use the technology. These patent trolls threaten litigation for patent infringement if the technology company does not cooperate. Unfortunately for these technology companies, retaliation against these patent trolls can be difficult because they hide behind their nonpracticing entities. Due to its rapid growth, the open-source industry provides a tempting target and profitable open-source software vendors have become troll targets.

391. In what may be the first "patent troll" lawsuit against an open-source software vendor, IP Innovation LLC filed suit against Red Hat in 2007 for patent infringement.[308] IP Innovation claimed that Red Hat infringed four claims from three U.S. patents that share a common title of "User interface with multiple workspaces for sharing display system objects." Red Hat asked for help from the open-source software community to find prior art that would invalidate IP innovation's patents and, luckily for Red Hat, the jury found all asserted claims as invalid. However, open-source software vendors are not the only ones at risk of attack from patent trolls. Any businesses that invest in technology may be targeted by patent trolls. These target businesses may receive a series of letters from the patent troll that accuse the business of patent infringement and threaten a lawsuit. These patent

308. *IP Innovation LLC v. Red Hat, Inc.*, No. 2:2007-cv-00447, 2010 WL 2635947 (E.D. Tex. 2010).

trolls often do not follow through with their threat of litigation, but rather use fear to basically shake down the target business for money. However, if a lawsuit is brought, it can be harmful to the target business.

392. In 2012, small businesses reported that fighting a patent assertion battle in court cost, on average, USD 857,000, or 24% of their annual revenue. Settling the matter, while less than the cost of an in-court battle, still sets small businesses back, on average, USD 340,000, or 13% of their annual revenue in 2012. Further, the cost of litigation incentivizes patent trolls to drag out litigation as much as possible to increase the settlement value of the case, thereby forcing defendants into often non-meritorious settlements as the cost of fighting in court escalates.[309]

393. In addition to the economic harm suffered by the target businesses, this litigation or threat of litigation from these patent trolls can also cause an impact to innovation. While defending themselves from litigation, the target business must use company funds that could be used for research and development. Additionally, the target business likely will spend extra money in its legal department out of fear of potential infringement suits. These extra costs can take funding away from other departments and potentially impair its ability to innovate and create new technologies, which in turn can impair the patent system's goal of innovation and creation.

309. Tara Feld, *States Hold the Sword to Force "Patent Trolls" Back Under Their Bridges*, Univ. Ill. L. Rev., 1123, 1129 (2016).

Chapter 6. Protection of Databases

§1. General

394. Under U.S. law, databases may garner copyright protection in limited and distinct instances. The structure or composition of a database may be protected by U.S. copyright law if the arrangement or selection of the database derives from the author's intellectual expression or creation. Alternatively, U.S. copyright law protects the content within databases in certain instances.

§2. Databases as Compilations

395. Most frequently, owners seek copyright protection of databases as compilations. Under the Copyright Act, a compilation is defined as a "collection and assembling of preexisting materials or of data that are selected in such a way that the resulting work as a whole constitutes an original work of authorship."[310] In other words, the selection and arrangement of the materials may, itself garner copyright protection, even though individual items themselves are not protected. Conversely, mechanical or automated collection of preexisting material is not protected. The collection of telephone numbers and addresses for a directory, for example, does not involve an original expression through concerted curation or arrangement and would therefore not receive copyright protection.

396. Examples of protected compilations include, a photo book of the greatest political photographs from 2019, a listing of the best novellas from the Victorian era, a website cataloguing culinary recipes collected from world travel, and a directory of the least expensive automotive services in a geographic location. In each example, protection stems from the expressive creation implicit in the selection of which novellas, photographs, recipes, and automotive services to include and the order in which it is included within the compilation.

397. Notably, the preexisting materials or data may be protected in their own right by copyright, or may be unprotectable facts or ideas:

(b) The copyright in a compilation or derivative work extends only to the material contributed by the author of such work, as distinguished from the preexisting material employed in the work, and does not imply any exclusive right in the preexisting material. The copyright in such work is independent of, and does not affect or enlarge the scope, duration, ownership, or subsistence of, any copyright protection in the preexisting material.[311]

310. 17U.S.C. § 101.
311. 17U.S.C. § 103.

398. As a result, a collection of particular academic articles through links or URLs would be protected if the selection and curation reflects original expression. But each link contains only factual information—that a specific academic article can be found at that URL location. No copyright protection extends to each location or academic article itself. Because the copyright protection for compilations is limited to the compilation itself, the individual items within it can be copied by others. The law protects against duplication or unauthorized use of an entire database. If the locations of the academic articles were divided by topic in the database, the organization of the database would also be protected.

399. Compilation copyrights cannot be used to extend copyright protection to ideas or facts that are otherwise unprotectable. Since the underlying data is not protected, U.S. copyright law does not prevent the extraction of unprotected data from an otherwise protectable database. In a database of links to selected academic articles, copying one such link to a specific article would not infringe upon the holder of the database copyright.

§3. Originality and Creativity

400. The seminal case determining whether copyright protection should be afforded to a database compilation is *Feist Publications, Inc. v. Rural Telephone Service Company, Inc.* In that case, the U.S. Supreme Court held that a compilation work such as a database must demonstrate a minimum level of creativity in order to be protectable under the Copyright Act.

401. Rural, was a local telephone company. It published directories based on data it received from its subscribers. A larger company, Feist, published area-wide telephone directories that covered a larger geographic area. To round out its directory, Feist needed the information Rural had listed in Rural's telephone directory. Feist initially asked to license Rural's directory from Rural, but when Rural refused, Feist simply copied the information it needed from Rural's directory without consent. Feist modified some of the data, but much of it was identical to that found in Rural's directory. Rural sued in copyright, claiming infringement of the compilation of its directory data.

402. The U.S. Supreme Court was asked to determine whether the information contained in Rural's phone directory was copyrightable. The court found that the information in Rural's telephone directory was not entitled to copyright protection, since the telephone directory did not meet the statutory requirement for originality. Under section 102(a) of the Copyright Act, a compilation is copyrightable only if its facts have been "selected, coordinated, or arranged in such a way that the resulting work as a whole constitutes an original work of authorship."

403. According to the Supreme Court, some methods or manners of selecting and arranging data are not sufficiently original to merit copyright protection under the statute. In applying this originality requirement, the Supreme Court held that

Rural's telephone directory was merely a listing of subscribers' names, towns, and telephone numbers and lacked the minimum level of original expression required to garner copyright protection. Arranging names and associated data alphabetically in a telephone directory is customary and ordinary.

404. Importantly, this ruling effectively overturned precedent that awarded copyright protection to compilations based on labor—or "sweat of the brow" ––required to complete the compilation. Labor or industriousness is no longer the text of whether a compilation will be protected under copyright law. Under now defunct labor justification, copyright protection extended to each fact contained within the compilation such that no extraction of facts from a compilation was allowed. The Supreme Court expressly renounced this "sweat of the brow" analysis, and limited copyright protection to the original selection, coordination, and arranging of data, and not to any unprotected facts contained within the compilation.

§4. Database Licensing and Preemption

405. The Court's decision in Feist makes it clear that a minimum level of creativity or original expression must attend the selection and/or arrangement of a compilation to merit copyright protection. An alphabetical listing of relevant data will likely not meet this threshold. The decision also made clear that even if a database is protected by copyright law as an original work, this protection will not prevent an individual from extracting factual data from the database as long as extraction does not use or copy the database entirely.

406. Due to limited copyright protection for databases, many database owners attempt to protect their databases through contracts. By licensing use, the consumer or user is restricted from copying or extracting data from the database for unauthorized purposes. For example, a contract could prohibit the end user from sharing data extracted from the licensor's database with third parties.

407. Under U.S. law, contracts are typically enforced under state law. This results in a lack of uniformity, with a few states finding that contractual database protections are preempted by the federal Copyright Act and therefore not enforceable. The majority of states, however have ruled that contracts represent an individualized agreement among the parties and are not the equivalent of protections afforded under the Copyright Act and are therefore enforceable.

408. In *ProCD, Incorporated v. Matthew Zeidenberg and Silken Mountain Web Services, Inc.*, the Seventh Circuit Court of Appeals considered a database similar to the database at issue in Feist.[312] The data included names, addresses, and phone numbers. As a result, the database was not protected under the Copyright Act, but the owners of the database claimed protection under the shrink-wrap license, which

312. 86 F.3d 1447 (7th Cir. 1996).

purported to restrict the end user's ability to copy and publish the data. The defendant had done just that by extracting a large portion of the database and making it available on the Internet.

409. The Seventh Circuit suggested that the database was not sufficiently original to be protected by copyright, but that the end user violated the contract, because the shrink-wrap license for the CD-ROM prohibited the end user's publication of the material to third parties. In other words, the license was enforceable even though no copyright protection existed.

§5. European Database Directive and WIPO Database Treaty

410. Under the Database Directive adopted by the EU in 1996, copyright protection for databases is substantially greater than in the U.S. Whereas copyright protection in the U.S. only extends to original or creative compilations and whereas discrete data can be extracted from protected databases in the U.S., the EU protects much of that data. In the EU a database can be protected in two ways. First, the databases are protected under copyright law where the selection or composition of the contents constitutes the creator's own intellectual creation. This mirrors U.S. law to a large degree. But second, EU law provides for a sui generis right that prohibits the extraction or reuse of any database in which there has been a substantial investment in either collection, verification, or allocation of the content. Importantly, there is no creativity or originality prerequisite. The sui generis right lasts for fifteen years from the date of the database's creation. The sui generis right granted under the Database Directive applies only to databases created by companies based in countries that are members of the EU. Thus, European companies (and European subsidiaries) will have greater protection for their databases than non-European companies.

Chapter 7. Legal Protection of Computer Chips

§1. General

411. Computer chips do not fit neatly into existing copyright law or into existing patent law. As a result, they have not generally garnered intellectual property protection in the U.S. under traditional copyright or patent principles. Instead, intellectual property protection derives from the Semiconductor Chip Protection Act, a statute that is codified next to the 1976 Copyright Act, but that is actually a part of that act.

412. Semiconductor chips typically are constructed using thousands of miniscule electrical circuits affixed to small semiconductor material, like silicon. When connected, these circuits function as microprocessors or memory devices. Although micro-processing chips are common in computing devices, they are increasingly inserted into an array of day-to-day objects and devices, like cars, garage doors, doorbells, and thermostats. Importantly, the two or three-dimensional layout or topography of an integrated circuit are expensive to design, but easy to copy using photolithography.

413. Because integrated circuit layouts that compose such chips are functional, useful products, copyright law is largely inapplicable. Moreover, patent protection requires that functional inventions exceed the abilities of skilled artisans in order to garner patent protection. While chip design is difficult, obvious variations of known circuit layout are commonplace. With both patent and copyright law inapplicable, U.S. Congress moved to protect semiconductor chips through statute.

§2. Semiconductor Chip Protection Act

414. The Semiconductor Chip Protection Act (SCPA) of 1984 affords some legal protection to chip designs. The Act creates a ten-year term for protection of integrated circuit layouts, provides exclusive rights to proprietors to reproduce these layouts and manufacture chips embodying them, and allows others to reverse engineer the layouts to analyze or evaluate them. The Act defines a semiconductor chip product as the final or intermediate form of any product:

(A) having two or more layers of metallic, insulating, or semiconductor material, deposited or otherwise placed on, or etched away or otherwise removed from, a piece of semiconductor material in accordance with a predetermined pattern; and
(B) intended to perform electronic circuitry functions.[313]

313. 17U.S.C. §§ 901–914.

415. The Act defines a "mask work" as a series of related images, however fixed or encoded:

(A) having or representing the predetermined, three-dimensional pattern of metallic, insulating, or semiconductor material present or removed from the layers of a semiconductor chip product; and
(B) in which series the relation of the images to one another is that each image has the pattern of the surface of one form of the semiconductor chip product.[314]

416. The Act grants protection to a "mask work" that is "fixed in a semiconductor chip product." A "mask work" is an intricate and highly individualized pattern that is used like a pattern or stencil in the semiconductor manufacture process to form the varying layers of a semiconductor chip. Notably, mask works must be registered and filed with the Copyright Office, not the U.S. Patent and Trademark Office. Registration includes depositing four chips embodying the mask work, and drawings or plots of each layer of the mask work. Like copyright law, the Act only protects "original" mask works that are "not commonplace or familiar" within the semiconductor industry. Protection under the Act does not include any "idea, procedure, process, system, method of operation, concept, principle or discovery, embodied in a [mask work]," as such concepts typically fall within patent protection. There is also a "reverse engineering" exception embedded in the SCPA:

(a) Notwithstanding the provisions of section 905, it is not an infringement of the exclusive rights of the owner of a mask work for:
  (1) a person to reproduce the mask work solely for the purpose of teaching, analyzing, or evaluating the concepts or techniques embodied in the mask work or the circuitry, logic flow, or organization of components used in the mask work; or
  (2) a person who performs the analysis or evaluation described in paragraph (1) to incorporate the results of such conduct in an original mask work which is made to be distributed.[315]

417. This reverse engineering exception is similar to the "fair use" doctrine in U.S. copyright law, which permits the unlicensed use of copyright protected works in certain circumstances such as, parody comment, news reporting, teaching, scholarship, and research.

418. The Semiconductor Chip Protection Act has been minimally effective. Since its creation in 1984, only a single published case arose in the court system prior to 1992. In *Brooktree Corp. v. Advanced Micro Devices, Inc.*, the claimant, Brooktree owned several original mask works that were registered with the Copyright Office for Semiconductor Chip Protection Act protection. Brooktree alleged that Advanced Micro Devices misappropriated Brooktree's original mask works in

314. *Id.*
315. *Id.* at § 906.

the manufacturing of its own chips. Although the trial court denied Brooktree's preliminary injunction, at trial the jury awarded Brooktree a USD 26 million in damages. This judgment was affirmed by the Court of Appeals for the Federal Circuit.

419. In order to obtain protection under the Semiconductor Chip Protection Act, chip designers/owners must register the work with the Copyright Office:

(a) The owner of a mask work may apply to the Register of Copyrights for registration of a claim of protection in a mask work. Protection of a mask work under this chapter shall terminate if application for registration of a claim of protection in the mask work is not made as provided in this chapter within two years after the date on which the mask work is first commercially exploited anywhere in the world.
***
(c) The application for registration of a mask work shall be made on a form prescribed by the Register of Copyrights. Such form may require any information regarded by the Register as bearing upon the preparation or identification of the mask work, the existence or duration of protection of the mask work under this chapter, or ownership of the mask work. The application shall be accompanied by the fee set pursuant to subsection (d) and the identifying material specified pursuant to such subsection.
(e) If the Register of Copyrights, after examining an application for registration, determines, in accordance with the provisions of this chapter, that the application relates to a mask work which is entitled to protection under this chapter, then the Register shall register the claim of protection and issue to the applicant a certificate of registration of the claim of protection under the seal of the Copyright Office. The effective date of registration of a claim of protection shall be the date on which an application, deposit of identifying material, and fee, which are determined by the Register of Copyrights or by a court of competent jurisdiction to be acceptable for registration of the claim, have all been received in the Copyright Office.
(f) In any action for infringement under this chapter, the certificate of registration of a mask work shall constitute prima facie evidence (1) of the facts stated in the certificate, and (2) that the applicant issued the certificate has met the requirements of this chapter, and the regulations issued under this chapter, with respect to the registration of claims.
(g) Any applicant for registration under this section who is dissatisfied with the refusal of the Register of Copyrights to issue a certificate of registration under this section may seek judicial review of that refusal by bringing an action for such review in an appropriate United States district court not later than sixty days after the refusal. The provisions of chapter 7 of title 5 shall apply to such judicial review. The failure of the Register of Copyrights to issue a certificate of

registration within four months after an application for registration is filed shall be deemed to be a refusal to issue a certificate of registration for purposes of this subsection and section 910(b)(2), except that, upon a showing of good cause, the district court may shorten such four-month period.[316]

316. *Id.* at § 908.

Chapter 8. Protection of Internet Domain Names

§1. General

420. Legal disputes continue to arise from the intersection of Internet domain names and trademark rights. Functionally, domain names substitute identifiable persons and entities, like coke.com, for IP addresses, which are the series of unique numbers used by Internet hosts to locate one another. The .com or.org portion of the domain name is known as the top-level domain name (TLD) and those designations have historically been limited to a relatively small number of categories. The remainder of the domain name listing (coke and amazon, for example) is assigned and monitored by Internet registrars accredited by the ICANN.

421. Commercial Internet domain name registration began in 1993 when the U.S. Department of Commerce entered into a contract and memorandum of understanding with Network Solutions, Inc. (NSI). The agreement authorized NSI to provide registration services for certain top-level domain names. The agreement was extended modified in 1998. Part of the new agreement established ICANN as a non-profit corporation tasked with managing the U.S. government's domain name needs.

422. After further negotiations, the U.S. Government, ICANN, and NSI entered into a series of agreements in which ICANN was tasked with domain name management functions, and NSI was authorized to provide registration services for the top-level domains.com, .org, and .net. In other words, ICANN managed and coordinated Internet domain policies, and NSI operated the hardware and software supporting Internet domain registration.

423. The 1998 agreement also authorized additional registrars to enter into the domain name registration business, with NSI acting as the central registry administrator. Additional companies, accredited by ICANN, also act as registrars. In the face of heavy international pressure, the U.S. gave up unilateral control of ICANN in 2009 to multinational oversight. A multinational advisory committee now supervises ICANN, with the U.S. serving as one of the nations on the committee. Although ICANN is now independent of unilateral U.S. control, the U.S. government asserts outsized control through the Internet Assigned Numbers Authority, (IANA). IANA, a California entity, is authorized to control IP address space allocation, protocol parameter assignment, and management of the DNS and root server functions of the Internet. Critically, IANA administers functions related to the management of the root zone domain name system.

424. Of course, Internet domain names are part of the Uniform Resource Locator (URL), the rough equivalent of a real world business' mailing address. Because the series of numbers that comprise IP addresses are seldom memorable, domain names serve as a de facto directory, allowing Internet users to more readily interact online. As putative Internet addresses, domain names are critical to individuals and organizations in the digital age. Like a real property name and address, domain names both identify and locate Internet sources.

425. As a result, businesses and individuals frequently integrate their trademark into their Internet domain name. In an increasingly online market, Internet visibility and access is vital. Most large clothing companies in the U.S., for example, routinely affix their web address, which incorporates their name or trademark, to advertisements, receipts, and tags. Businesses of every ilk bolster online presence in similar ways.

426. Domain names can include a wide variety of names or indicators, including trademarks, product names, personal names, and more. No legal system, however, connects the registration of domain names with the registration of trademarks. Although this has changed slightly over the last decade, domain names have typically been assigned without reference to who is actually entitled to that name. It takes little effort and no legal vetting to register a domain name that contains someone else's trademark—a practice known as cybersquatting.

427. In other words, an accredited registrar basically assigns domain names on a first-come, first-served basis. The registrar typically performs neither any service mark or trademark search, nor does it attempt to ascertain the connection, if any, between the applicant and the requested domain name. Because the registrar can assign a name to only one owner, the only search performed by a registrar before granting a request for a domain name is a search to ensure that no other party previously registered the domain name.

428. Notably, the registrar will register a domain name even if it is confusingly similar to another domain name. Exponential growth of Internet users and requested registration has added to the confusion. As of 2016, more than 326.4 million domain names had been registered worldwide and across all TLDs.

§2. Cybersquatting

429. Cybersquatting occurs when an entity registers an Internet domain name associated with a different company's trademark, and then seeks to profit by selling or licensing that domain name to the company that is associated with that trademark. U.S. Congress defined cybersquatting as "registering, trafficking in, or using domain names that are identical or confusingly similar to trademarks with the bad faith intent to profit from the goodwill of the trademarks."[317] Cybersquatters do not always reserve domain names in order to extort a purchase price from the company associated with the name. Often, a domain name is not an exact trademarked name, but some close variation, which presents a related problem of trademark dilution.

430. Regardless, the dramatic rise in the digital marketplace has driven demand for specific, distinctive domain names. In 1998, Compaq Computer Corporation

317. 15U.S.C. § 1125(d).

paid USD 3.3 million for the rights to the domain name AltaVista.com. Even outside the realm of trademarks, cybersquatters have taken advantage of limited supply. A host of examples illustrate this phenomenon. A company in Texas, for example, bought the domain name business.com for USD 150,000. The sovereign nation, Bhutan could not register an appropriate domain name because Bhutan.com and Bhutan.net had already been registered by entities that had no affiliation with that country, but that offered to sell the domain name for several thousand dollars. Mecklermedia Corp. paid approximately USD 100,000 for internet.com. and technology businessman John Gotts paid USD 3 million for the domain name wiki-.com.

431. This environment obviously leads to frequent conflict between commercial competitors trying to establish control over domain names appropriate for their businesses. Trademark management in the domain name context is likely to become increasingly difficult as a result of the proliferation of parties purchasing gTLDs and then, in turn, registering domains within their acquired gTLDs. Major companies including Amazon and Google now actively purchase gTLDs and then manage the registration and use of domain names within their gTLDs.

§3. The Anticybersquatting Consumer Protection Act

432. In an effort to address these issues, the U.S. congress passed the Anticybersquatting Consumer Protection Act (ACPA) in 1999. In conjunction with the Lanham Act, the ACPA attempts to reduce the negative secondary effects that attend cybersquatting by adding provisions that protect the holders of distinctive or famous marks from improper registration of their personal names as Internet domain names:

> Under the newly enacted section 43(d) of the Lanham Act, trademark holders now have a cause of action against anyone who, with a bad faith intent to profit from the goodwill of another's trademark, registers, traffics in, or uses a domain name that is identical to, or confusingly similar to a distinctive mark, or dilutive of a famous mark, without regard to the goods or services of the parties.[318]

433. In order to recover under the ACPA, a claimant must prove three basic elements: (1) The defendant demonstrated a bad faith intent to profit from the mark; (2) the mark is a distinctive or famous mark, including a personal name; and (3) the domain name in question is identical or confusingly similar to the mark. Of these elements, the most difficult element to prove is whether the defendant acted in bad faith. The Anticybersquatting Consumer Protection Act includes several factors to determine bad faith:

(1) If registrant has any trademark or other intellectual property rights in the name.

318. *Ibid.*

(2) If this is the legal or nickname of the registrant.
(3) The registrant's prior use of the domain name in connection with the good faith offering of goods and services. According to the legislative history the defendant will have the burden of introducing evidence of lawful use. Note that while the Uniform Domain Name Dispute Resolution Policy (UDRP) provides a defense if the domain name registrant has made demonstrable preparations to use the domain name in a bona fide offering of goods or services, the legislation only provides a defense if there is prior use—not simply preparation to use.
(4) Lawful noncommercial or fair use of the mark in a website under the domain name. According to the legislative history fair use includes comparative advertising, comment, criticism, or parody—even where done for profit. However, simply establishing a website with a fair use, if the actual intent is to sell, will not allow a cybersquatter to avoid a bad faith determination.
(5) Intent to divert to a site that could harm the trademark owner's goodwill—either for commercial gain or with intent to tarnish by creating likelihood of confusion as to source, sponsorship or affiliation, or endorsement of the site.
(6) Offer to sell the domain name without having used, or having an intent to use, it in the bona fide offering of goods or services, or a prior pattern of such conduct. Language in the legislative history specifically indicates that this section is not supposed to apply to a party who registers a name with the bona fide intent to launch a new product or company but then abandons that plan and sells the name to a trademark holder.
(7) Intentional provision of misleading contact information in the domain name registration application or the history of such conduct.
(8) Warehousing of multiple domain names known to be identical or confusingly similar to distinctive marks or dilutive of famous marks, without regard to the goods or services of the parties. According to the legislative history, cybersquatters have been able to avoid liability by not being the one to initiate or offer to sell. Now, sitting on such marks is sufficient evidence of bad faith and an offer to sell is not required.
(9) The extent to which a mark is distinctive or famous. Under the legislative history, the more distinctive or famous a mark is, the more likely the trademark owner will deserve relief.[319]

434. The first four factors count against a determination of bad faith while the remainder count in favor of a bad faith determination. In *Ford Motor Co. v. Catalanotte*, the Sixth Circuit Court of Appeals found that "registering a famous trademark as a domain name and then offering it for sale to the trademark owner is exactly the wrong Congress intended to remedy when it passed the ACPA."[320] As a result, offers by defendants to sell domain names to entities with identical or similar

319. Id.
320. 342 F3d 543 (6th Cir. 2003).

trademarks serve as strong evidence of bad faith. Additionally, a defendant's submission of misleading contact information when attempting to register a domain name serves as evidence of bad faith, because it suggests that the defendant does not want to be readily identified.

435. The ACPA is not a trademark owner's only legal remedy. ICANN provides for an administrative review of such complaints under ICANN's UDRP. The UDRP facilitates challenges by trademark owners against domain name registrants. One advantage of seeking resolution through UDRP is the expedited resolution of the conflict. Another advantage is that the process is often cheaper and that the outcomes arguably favor trademark-owning plaintiffs because the UDRP arbitrators are also trademark lawyers.

436. Additionally, critics of the Anticybersquatting Consumer Protection Act argue that it is an ineffective law in combatting cybersquatting because trademark rights in the U.S. are tied to use in commerce, and the ACPA turns on bad faith. Unlike domain name registration, ownership of a mark belongs to the first-to-use, not the first-to-file. Thus, trademark policy suggests that one who is not using a particular trademark should not be able to block productive use of that trademark by another party. Conversely, cybersquatters similarly fail to put the domain name in question to use in a meaningful way and simultaneously prevent others from making use of it. As such, many argue that cybersquatting is entirely at odds with the public policy behind established trademark law.

§4. The World Intellectual Property Organization

437. Due to the increasing volume of international trade and the fluidity of the Internet's architecture, international protections for domain name conflicts and trademarks is more and more important. The WIPO partnered with ICANN in 1998 and 1999 to provide an international dispute resolution process. WIPO is an international organization created to promote and protect works of intellectual property. It is one of approximately twenty specialized agencies of the United Nations system of organizations, and it administers two dozen international treaties dealing with intellectual property protection. In addition, the WIPO provides an Internet domain name dispute resolution service.[321]

438. The resolution service provided by the WIPO is also called the UDRP, mentioned above. According to its published policy:

> The UDRP sets out the legal framework for the resolution of disputes between a domain name registrant and a third party (i.e., a party other than the registrar) over the abusive registration and use of an Internet domain name in the

321. *See* WIPO Guide to the Uniform Domain Name Dispute Resolution Policy, WIPO, https://www.wipo.int/amc/en/domains/guide/ (last visited Jan. 29, 2020).

generic top-level domains or gTLDs (e.g.,.biz,.com,.info,.mobi,.name,.net,.org), and those country code top-level domains or ccTLDs that have adopted the UDRP Policy on a voluntary basis.[322]

439. The dispute resolution process is only available in certain instances in which a claimant alleges an "abusive registration of a domain name." The UDRP further identifies such instances using three criteria:

(i) the domain name registered by the domain name registrant is identical or confusingly similar to a trademark or service mark in which the complainant (the person or entity bringing the complaint) has rights; and
(ii) the domain name registrant has no rights or legitimate interests in respect of the domain name in question; and
(iii) the domain name has been registered and is being used in bad faith.[323]

440. The UDRP includes dispute resolution for generic toplevel domains (gTLDs), including.com,.org,.net, as well as the gTLDs selected by ICANN in 2000, which include.aero, for the air transport industry, .biz, for business, .coop, for nonprofit cooperative, .info, for general, .museum, for museums, .name, for individuals, and .pro, for professionals.

441. UDRP officiants analyze three elements in determining whether a domain name has, in fact, infringed upon a trademark. First, the officiants identify whether a domain name is "identical or confusingly similar to a trademark or service mark in which the complainant has rights." Second, the officiants determine whether the defendant has any legitimate interest in or claim to the domain name. This interest may be shown in three ways: (1) if the defendant uses the domain name "in connection with a bona fide offering of goods or services;" (2) if the defendant can show that they "have been commonly known by the domain name;" and (3) if the defendant makes "a legitimate noncommercial or fair use of the domain name without intent for commercial gain to misleadingly divert consumers or to tarnish the mark." Finally, the officiants determine if the domain name was registered in bad faith. If the officiants find that all three elements are met, the plaintiff will be awarded rights in the domain name, and the registrant will lose the ability to use the name.

322. *Id.*
323. *Id.*

Part V. Cybersecurity Law

Chapter 1. Institutional Framework

442. The United States does not have a national law that specifically addresses data security standards for all companies but does have some industry-specific statutes. There have been efforts in the last several years to enact federal legislation for the protection of personal information, but to date nothing has been signed into law. Instead of a federal statutory scheme, U.S. cybersecurity law largely derives from the power of the FTC (an executive agency) through the FTC Act[324].

324. 15 U.S.C. 45

Chapter 2. General Obligations

§1. Obligations under Federal Law

I. Obligations Enforced by the FTC

443. The FTC has been very active in bringing enforcement actions under section 5 of the FTC Act for "unfair or deceptive acts or practices" due to cybersecurity lapses. section 5 of the FTC Act does not specifically address cybersecurity issues, and indeed the Act itself was enacted in 1914, long before any of the technology relevant to cybersecurity was even developed.

444. The FTC Act authorizes the FTC to address two types of business practices; deceptive and unfair. As relevant here, the FTC considers false statements about data security to be covered by the prohibition on deceptive practices. For example, if a company falsely states that they have achieved a certain cybersecurity benchmark or adhere to certain cybersecurity standards, the FTC may bring an enforcement action to stop this deceptive practice.

445. On the contrary, the FTC brings enforcement actions based on inadequate data security measures under the "unfair" prong of the FTC Act. Unfortunately, the FTC has not issued regulations detailing specifically how "unfair" practices will be determined in the cybersecurity context. Instead, the FTC continues to rely on a three-part test developed during the period when cigarette regulations were being considered. Despite the lack of clear regulations, the FTC's authority to pursue actions against companies for insufficient cybersecurity practices has been approved by at least one circuit of appeal.[325] Although technically, this decision only controls in the Third Circuit (a portion of the northeastern U.S.), but as the only federal appeals court decision on the issue, it will carry significant weight until or unless a later appeals court or the Supreme Court takes up the issue.

446. Although the FTC has not issued any regulations detailing what cybersecurity measures are sufficient to avoid an enforcement action, the agency did issue a guide in 2015 titled *Start with Security: A Guide for Business*[326] highlighting ten principles for companies to consider in building and managing cybersecurity programs. The ten principles addressed in the guide (along with selected subtopics) are:

(1) Start with security—do not collect personal information you do not need; hold on to information only as long as you have a legitimate business need; do not use personal information when it is not necessary.
(2) Control access to data sensibly—restrict access to sensitive data; limit administrative access.

---

325. *FTC v. Wyndham Worldwide Corp.*, 799 F.3d 236 (3d Cir. 2015).
326. Available here: https://www.ftc.gov/tips-advice/business-center/guidance/start-security-guide-business.

(3) Require secure passwords and authentication—insist on complex and unique passwords; store passwords securely; guard against brute force attacks; protect against authentication bypass.
(4) Store sensitive personal information securely and protect it during transmission—keep sensitive information secure throughout its lifecycle; use industry-tested and accepted methods; ensure proper configuration.
(5) Segment your network and monitor who is trying to get in and out—segment your network; monitor activity on your network.
(6) Secure remote access to your network—ensure endpoint security; put sensible access limits in place.
(7) Apply sound security practices when developing new products—train your engineers in secure coding; follow platform guidelines for security; verify that privacy and security features work; test for common vulnerabilities.
(8) Make sure your service providers implement reasonable security measures—put it in writing; verify compliance.
(9) Put procedures in place to keep your security current and address vulnerabilities that may arise—update and patch third-party software; heed credible security warnings and move quickly to fix them.
(10) Secure paper, physical media, and devices—securely store sensitive files; protect devices that process personal information; keep safety standards in place when data is *en route*; dispose of sensitive data securely.

447. Although this document is published as a "guide," it incorporates lessons learned from numerous FTC actions against companies in various industries and many of the subtopics refer to specific cases. Accordingly, companies could consider this guidance as indicative of what corporate practices, or lack thereof, could lead to FTC scrutiny and/or investigations. The FTC also provided additional guidance on the ten principles in several blog posts titled *Stick with Security* in 2017.[327] These blog posts did not expand the original guide and instead simply provided additional clarifications and explanation on the original principles. Throughout this time, the FTC also released a series of videos[328] to provide specific cybersecurity advice for particular situations that businesses might face.

II. Obligations under Sarbanes-Oxley

448. The Sarbanes-Oxley Act of 2002 (SOX) was enacted to address a broad range of perceived problems in accounting and other administrative issues within corporations in the U.S. Compliance with SOX is enforced by the Securities and Exchange Commission. Of note with respect to cybersecurity are two provisions: section 302 (codified at 15U.S.C. § 7241) and section 404 (codified at 15U.S.C. § 7262).

327. Available here: https://www.ftc.gov/tips-advice/business-center/guidance/stick-security-business-blog-series
328. Available here: https://www.ftc.gov/news-events/audio-video/business.

449. Section 302 requires corporate management to certify that required reporting information produced by the company is correct. Moreover, this section requires corporate officers to certify that internal controls are in place to ensure that the company produces accurate financial reports.

450. Section 404 requires corporate management to report on their internal controls as part of their otherwise required reporting. These internal control reports must include an assessment of the effectiveness of the internal controls. Moreover, the assessment made by the management must be provided to the company's auditors.

451. Although these sections of SOX are not specific to cybersecurity issues, cyber vulnerabilities and data breaches certainly fall within the ambit of these requirements. In fact, the SEC issued guidance in 2011 and 2018 directed at cybersecurity issues and encouraging regulated companies to disclose cybersecurity risks and events in their required annual reporting. Accordingly, SOX is another way that cybersecurity standards are enforced in the U.S. in the absence of a dedicated statutory scheme for cybersecurity.

§2. Obligations Under State Law

I. State Data Breach Notification Laws

452. The most prevalent form of data security regulation in the U.S. is data breach laws in the various states. All fifty states have enacted some form of data breach law. The laws generally apply to the dissemination of personal information of residents of the enacting state. Thus, companies doing business in multiple states must ensure that they are in compliance with the data breach laws in each of those states. There are some differences in the laws of each state and thus, companies may be subject to notification obligations in one state, but not another. Moreover, not every breach will require notification in every state, or any state. There are many exceptions to the data breach laws in the states that allow a company to avoid disclosing the breach if, for example, the information is not the type of information covered by the statute, the data was encrypted, or the company concludes there is no risk of harm to affected individuals from the breach. In addition to reporting breaches to the impacted individuals, companies may also need to report to other state agencies and/or credit reporting bureaus.

II. State Data Security Laws

453. In addition to breach notification laws, many states also have data security statutes. These statutes generally place obligations on companies in possession of personal information to implement and/or maintain reasonable procedures to protect the information. The extent to which the statutes specify what measures are reasonable varies from state to state.

Chapter 3. Sector-Specific Obligations

§1. Financial Institutions

454. In addition to the requirements stated above in Part III, Chapter 4, regarding online transactions, the Gramm-Leach-Bliley Act (GLBA) also imposes cybersecurity obligations through the so-called Safeguards Rule. The Safeguards Rule does not directly impose obligations on the financial institutions and instead, requires agencies to establish standards for regulated institutions. In particular, the Act requires that "each agency … shall establish appropriate standards for the financial institutions subject to their jurisdiction relating to administrative, technical, and physical safeguards:(1) to insure the security and confidentiality of customer records and information; (2) to protect against any anticipated threats or hazards to the security or integrity of such records; and (3) to protect against unauthorized access to or use of such records or information which could result in substantial harm or inconvenience to any customer." (15 U.S. Code § 6801) Because multiple agencies regulate financial institutions, these institutions need to be aware of the specific regulations adopted by these different agencies. In addition to the federal agency rules, the State of New York has also adopted its own cybersecurity regulations, which is discussed below.

I. Securities and Exchange Commission Regulations

455. The Securities and Exchange Commission implemented the Safeguards Rule at 17 CFR § 248.30. This rule applies to "[e]very broker, dealer, and investment company, and every investment adviser registered with the [SEC]" and requires these institutions to "adopt written policies and procedures that address administrative, technical, and physical safeguards for the protection of customer records and information." The SEC rule requires the adopted policies and procedures to be "reasonably designed to" meet the three requirements specified in the GLBA Safeguards Rule.

II. FTC Regulations

456. The FTC has regulatory authority over a broad range of companies through enforcement of a variety of antitrust and consumer protection laws. In addition to its general authority under section 5 discussed above, the FTC has implemented the Safeguards Rule at 16 CFR § 314.3. In view of the types of institutions that the FTC regulates, the FTC's rule includes considerations of the regulated institutions' capabilities. In particular, the rule states that each regulated institution "shall develop, implement, and maintain a comprehensive information security program that is written in one or more readily accessible parts and contains administrative, technical, and physical safeguards that are appropriate to your size and complexity, the nature and scope of your activities, and the sensitivity of any customer information at issue." Despite this relatively permissive language, the rule does make clear that the safeguards shall include particular elements (set forth at 16 CFR § 314.4) and be "reasonably designed to achieve" the three requirements specified in the GLBA Safeguards Rule. The particular elements that are required under the FTC rule include obligations to:

(a) Designate an employee or employees to coordinate your information security program.
(b) Identify reasonably foreseeable internal and external risks to the security, confidentiality, and integrity of customer information that could result in the unauthorized disclosure, misuse, alteration, destruction or other compromise of such information, and assess the sufficiency of any safeguards in place to control these risks. At a minimum, such a risk assessment should include consideration of risks in each relevant area of your operations, including:
    (1) employee training and management;
    (2) information systems, including network and software design, as well as information processing, storage, transmission and disposal; and
    (3) detecting, preventing and responding to attacks, intrusions, or other systems failures.
(c) Design and implement information safeguards to control the risks you identify through risk assessment, and regularly test or otherwise monitor the effectiveness of the safeguards' key controls, systems, and procedures.
(d) Oversee service providers, by:
    (1) taking reasonable steps to select and retain service providers that are capable of maintaining appropriate safeguards for the customer information at issue; and
    (2) requiring your service providers by contract to implement and maintain such safeguards.
    (e) evaluate and adjust your information security program in light of the results of the testing and monitoring required by paragraph (c) of this section; any material changes to your operations or business arrangements; or any other circumstances that you know or have reason to know may have a material impact on your information security program.

16 CFR § 314.4. In view of the many required elements of the FTC rule, institutions subject to regulation by the FTC have numerous, specific obligations to meet in order to ensure compliance.

III. Collaborative Agency Regulations

457. Other than the FTC and SEC discussed above, multiple agencies that regulate financial institutions have collaborated to generate a set of Interagency Guidelines. It is important to note that each of these agencies has its own regulation, but these separate regulations are very similar. The agencies following this approach include the Office of the Comptroller of the Currency (at 12 CFR § 30), the Federal Reserve Board (at 12 CFR § 208), and the Federal Deposit Insurance Corporation (at 12 CFR § 364). The Interagency Guidelines, as implemented by the various agencies, are quite extensive and detailed. Accordingly, these guidelines, and their implementing regulations, provide significant direction to regulated institutions in developing compliant programs.

IV. New York Department of Financial Services Cybersecurity Regulations

458. In addition to the federal agency regulations discussed above, the State of New York has adopted its own cybersecurity regulations at Title 23, Part 500. (N.Y. Comp. Codes R. & Regs. tit. 23, § 500.0 et seq.) The core requirement of the statute is that "[e]ach Covered Entity shall maintain a cybersecurity program designed to protect the confidentiality, integrity, and availability of the Covered Entity's Information Systems." N.Y. Comp. Codes R. & Regs. tit. 23, § 500.2. The definition of "Covered Entity" is quite expansive and includes "any person operating under or required to operate under a license, registration, charter, certificate, permit, accreditation or similar authorization under the Banking Law, the Insurance Law or the Financial Services Law." N.Y. Comp. Codes R. & Regs. tit. 23, § 500.1. Accordingly, the New York law likely applies to all financial institutions located in New York and many institutions that are not located in New York but do some business there. The statute is quite lengthy and detailed and places many specific obligations on the covered institutions, including the development of compliant programs policies, periodic assessments of their programs, and program monitoring and testing. Accordingly, financial institutions located in, or operating in, New York will need to particularly focus on ensuring their cybersecurity programs comply with this state's requirements.

§2. Payment Processors

459. Companies that process credit card payments are likely also bound to comply with the Payment Card Industry Data Security Standard (PCI DSS). It is important to note that this is not a governmental requirement and instead is a requirement imposed by the card issuers themselves.[329] The standards are maintained and updated by the Payment Card Industry Security Standards Council, an independent body that includes among its members the major credit card brands. The standard has extensive requirements that payment processors must adhere to and includes ongoing compliance reporting requirements. Accordingly, any companies in the U.S. that process credit card payments would need to verify and maintain compliance with the standard.

329. But note that the State of Nevada does have a requirement that merchants conducting business in Nevada comply with the standard. *See* NV Rev Stat § 603A.215 (2019).

§3. Health Providers

460. Health and Human Services (HHS) is an agency within the U.S. government responsible for generating regulations applicable to the health care and related industries. Pursuant to its authority under the Health Insurance Portability and Accountability Act of 1996, HHS has enacted regulations related to information security generally located in 45 CFR Part 160. The regulations apply to "Covered Entities,' which include health plans, health care clearinghouses, and health care providers, but it also applies to "Business Associates," which includes an expansive array of companies that process health data. 45 CFR § 160.103. Although the volume of companies potentially covered by the two definitions may be large, the rules apply specifically to protected health information (another defined term) and thus the scope of the rules (and the companies impacted) is relatively small compared to the overall economy. The core obligations of regulated companies are set forth at 45 CFR 164.306, which states:

> Covered entities and business associates must do the following:
>
> (1) Ensure the confidentiality, integrity, and availability of all electronic protected health information the covered entity or business associate creates, receives, maintains, or transmits.
> (2) Protect against any reasonably anticipated threats or hazards to the security or integrity of such information.
> (3) Protect against any reasonably anticipated uses or disclosures of such information that are not permitted or required under subpart E of this part.
> (4) Ensure compliance with this subpart by its workforce.

461. The regulations then go on to impose specific requirements in each area of administrative, physical, and technical safeguards and additional organizational requirements, including data breach notification obligations.[330]

§4. Energy Transmission and Production

462. Although most of the regulations discussed in this chapter relate to protection of personal information, public utilities are also an important concern for cybersecurity regulators. Accordingly, two U.S. agencies, the Federal Energy Regulatory Commission (FERC) and the Nuclear Regulatory Commission (NRC), have issued guidance and/or regulations directed at protecting the nation's power grid and nuclear power plants from hacking.

463. In 2008, FERC issued Order No. 706, which adopted eight Critical Infrastructure Protection Reliability Standards. The standards were amended and refined over time through the issuance of multiple additional orders. Through this process,

330. 45 CFR § 164.308-16.

many standards have been approved and are now in effect, including multiple standards related to cybersecurity. Some of the standards related to cybersecurity include requirements related to personnel training, change management, vulnerability assessment, and physical and systems security.

464. The NRC adopted a cybersecurity regulations in 2009 that are currently codified at 10 CFR § 73.54. These regulations place specific requirements on licensees operating nuclear power plants with respect to protecting their electronic assets against cyberattacks. Due to the limited scope of the regulated companies, these regulations do not impact most companies doing business in the U.S.

Chapter 4. Liability and Remedies

465. With respect to potential liabilities, and associated remedies, for inadequate or noncompliant cybersecurity measures, the primary sources for such liability are going to be the responsible agencies at the federal level and state enforcement authorities at the individual state level.

466. The FTC has brought numerous actions against companies following data breaches and/or hacking incidents. These actions often result in consent orders or other liability impositions that can place significant ongoing obligations on the companies, including obligations extending many years into the future. Additionally, these cases may result in significant fines for the impacted companies. In cases of extensive data breaches, these fines may be on the order of hundreds of millions of dollars. Companies that have been subject to significant fines in the last several years include[331] Facebook (USD 5 billion), Equifax (approx. USD 575 million), Home Depot (approx. USD 200 million), and Yahoo (approx. USD 85 million).

467. Although the fines may not be as large, the SEC also has enforcement mechanisms to impose liability upon companies due to cybersecurity failures. For example, the SEC brought an administrative action against one company[332] following a data breach that resulted in a settlement requiring the company to come into compliance with the agencies version of the Safeguards Rule and to pay a USD 75,000 fine. The SEC also recently announced fines against several brokerage firms totaling USD 750,000.

468. At the state level, companies can also face significant liability. In one recent case, the State of New York imposed a fine of USD 1.5 million (through a consent order) against a mortgage broker/loan servicer for violations of New York's cybersecurity regulations. The consent order also required the company to take affirmative steps to prevent future cybersecurity problems, including internal training, establishing procedures and controls, and undertaking a comprehensive risk assessment. In another case, Uber settled claims against it by all 50U.S. states for approximately USD 148 million. The settlement also required Uber to improve its cybersecurity practices and make periodic reports to the states going forward.

331. Note that these fines are not exclusively directed at cybersecurity violations and may include privacy violations and other deceptive trade practices.
332. R.T. Jones Capital Equities Management (2015).

Part VI. Cybercrime

Chapter 1. General Legal Development

§1. General

469. Generally speaking, criminal law in the U.S. is primarily statutory, rather than based on the common law or on specific constitutional provisions. This reliance on statutes to identify and prosecute crimes in the U.S. is reflected both in the federal legal scheme as well as in most of the states. Practitioners must be careful to identify both federal statutes and applicable state statutes for any given legal issue. In order to determine applicable criminal statutes, Article III of the U.S. Constitution requires venue of criminal trials to reflect the locus of the alleged crime.[333]

470. Computer-related crimes can be divided into two categories: those crimes that specifically target computer misuse or abuse, and those traditional crimes that are facilitated by computer use. For example, tradition crimes like stalking, misappropriation of trade secrets, and child pornography are increasingly perpetrated through computer systems. Of course, crime enforcement in the Internet age faces several new obstacles. Cybercrime is often borderless in nature. It can be difficult to detect when it is occurring, and unlike traditional criminal acts, the amount of potentially relevant digital evidence is often overwhelming and the resources for distilling the magnitude of data are lacking. Moreover, cybercrimes are increasingly global in nature, complicating efforts to detect and prosecute. Attributing a criminal act is also increasingly difficult. The difficulty of tracing a criminal action to its source is illustrated by the amorphous online collective, Anonymous, which is reputedly responsible for a wide array of computer-related attacks. Such attacks include denial of service attacks, viruses, Trojan Horses, and other malware.

471. A study by the U.S. firm Price-Waterhouse-Cooper in 2014 revealed that 77% of the responding entities reported a security event within the last year. According to the Identity and Theft Resource Center, there were 1,579 data breaches in 2017.[334] In 2018, over one billion records were exposed to data breaches, with large corporations like Google, Apple, Amazon, and Facebook all reporting some form of

333. U.S. Const. Art. III, § 2.
334. *See* 2017 Annual Data Breach Year-End Review, at https://www.idtheftcenter.org/images/breach/2017Breaches/2017AnnualDataBreachYearEndReview.pdf.

data breach. Tellingly, the number of data breaches continues to climb, even as companies attempt to increase security protections, a cost often passed on to the consumer. Cybercrimes cost U.S. companies billions of dollars every year, although a wide area of businesses could have prevented many of these crimes with basic security measures.

472. Initial U.S. legislation responsive to computer-based crime emerged in the 1980s, both on the federal level and among several U.S. states. Before the early 1980s, law enforcement attempted to prosecute computer-related crimes under the statute prohibiting mail and wire fraud.[335] In 1984, U.S. Congress enacted the Comprehensive Crime Control Act to extend the reach of the law beyond wire fraud and mail fraud. Two years later, Congress amended the Comprehensive Crime Control Act to include the Computer Fraud and Abuse Act. The principal statutes through which federal law enforcement prosecutes computer-related crime are the Electronic Communications Privacy Act and the Computer Fraud and Abuse Act.

§2. Computer Fraud and Abuse Act

473. The Computer Fraud and Abuse Act (CFAA) was a necessary extension of preexisting statutes, which themselves covered only those crimes facilitated through the mail or wire systems. The inadequacy of the wire fraud and mail fraud statues was on display in *United States v. LaMacchia.*[336] In the Internet's infancy, a student used a university's computer system to create an electronic bulletin board on the Internet. The student solicited subscribers to upload software and computer games, which the student then planned to illegally copy and distribute. Although a federal prosecutor successfully indicted the student for conspiring to violate the wire fraud statue, the district court ultimately held that the wire fraud statute could not be applied to the prosecution of a criminal copyright case facilitated by a computer-generated bulletin board posted on the Internet. Cases like these illustrated the need for a statutory scheme postured for computer-based crimes.

474. The CFAA is a criminal law designed to outlaw unauthorized access to electronic data. The Act has become the principal tool used by law enforcement to prosecute computer-related crimes, like computer intrusions of varied forms. Congress did this by making it a felony to access classified information in a computer without authorization and making it a misdemeanor to access financial records or credit histories stored in a financial institution or to trespass into a government computer. The Act also makes allowance for state law enforcement by authorizing state Attorneys General to file civil lawsuits seeking damages for those victimized by computer-related crimes. In drafting the legislation, Congress chose to address federal computer-related offenses in a single, new statute rather than add new provisions regarding computers to existing criminal laws. In relevant part, the CFAA has broad application, stating whoever:

335. 18U.S.C. §1341, § 1343.
336. 871 F. Supp. 535, 545 (D. Mass. 1994).

(2) intentionally accesses a computer without authorization or exceeds authorized access, and thereby obtains:
   (A) information contained in a financial record of a financial institution, or of a card issuer as defined in section 1602(n)[1] of title 15, or contained in a file of a consumer reporting agency on a consumer, as such terms are defined in the Fair Credit Reporting Act (15 U.S.C. 1681 et seq.);
   (B) information from any department or agency of the United States; or
   (C) information from any protected computer;
(3) intentionally, without authorization to access any nonpublic computer of a department or agency of the United States, accesses such a computer of that department or agency that is exclusively for the use of the Government of the United States or, in the case of a computer not exclusively for such use, is used by or for the Government of the United States and such conduct affects that use by or for the Government of the United States;
(4) knowingly and with intent to defraud, accesses a protected computer without authorization, or exceeds authorized access, and by means of such conduct furthers the intended fraud and obtains anything of value, unless the object of the fraud and the thing obtained consists only of the use of the computer and the value of such use is not more than $5,000 in any 1-year period;
(5) (A) knowingly causes the transmission of a program, information, code, or command, and as a result of such conduct, intentionally causes damage without authorization, to a protected computer;
   (B) intentionally accesses a protected computer without authorization, and as a result of such conduct, recklessly causes damage; or
   (C) intentionally accesses a protected computer without authorization, and as a result of such conduct, causes damage and loss.
(6) knowingly and with intent to defraud traffics (as defined in section 1029) in any password or similar information through which a computer may be accessed without authorization, if:
   (A) such trafficking affects interstate or foreign commerce; or
   (B) such computer is used by or for the Government of the United States;
(7) with intent to extort from any person any money or other thing of value, transmits in interstate or foreign commerce any communication containing any:
   (A) threat to cause damage to a protected computer;
   (B) threat to obtain information from a protected computer without authorization or in excess of authorization or to impair the confidentiality of information obtained from a protected computer without authorization or by exceeding authorized access; or
   (C) demand or request for money or other thing of value in relation to damage to a protected computer, where such damage was caused to facilitate the extortion;

shall be punished as provided in subsection (c) of this section.

475. While it is relatively clear when a criminal defendant accessed a protected computer "without authorization," it is significantly less clear when the criminal defendant had some authorization to the computer system, but arguably exceeded the scope of that authorization. Courts continue to struggle in drawing that line, as the CFAA does not itself do so. Moreover, the CFAA demonstrates the failure of legal protections to keep pace with technological advancements. For example, the CFAA did not contemplate automated criminal access to a protected computer. Bots and other automated software today routinely extract data from websites and other online systems, which technically fall outside CFAA's purview. As computer crimes continued to grow in sophistication and as prosecutors gained experience with the CFAA, the CFAA required amending, which Congress did in 1988, 1989, 1990, 1994, 1996, 2001, 2002, and 2008. Some amendments, particularly, the Patriot Act have attempted to broaden the definition of a protected computer.

476. Due in large parts to these amendments, the Act now targets the theft of property via computer that is incident to a scheme to defraud. It includes criminal sanctions for those who purposely alter, damage, or destroy information owned by others. The Act encompasses those who distribute malicious code and instigate denial of service attacks. The Act also criminalizes the trafficking in passwords and other confidential access codes. The federal government publishes a manual entitled "Prosecuting Computer Crimes,"' in which the following table summarizes CFAA Penalties:[337]

Offense	Section	Sentence*
Obtaining National Security Information	(a)(1)	10 (20) years
Accessing a Computer and Obtaining Information	(a)(2)	1 or 5 (10)
Trespassing in a Government Computer	(a)(3)	1 (10)
Accessing a Computer to Defraud & Obtain Value	(a)(4)	5 (10)
Intentionally Damaging by Knowing Transmission	(a)(5)(A)	1 or 10 (20)
Recklessly Damaging by Intentional Access	(a)(5)(B)	1 or 5 (20)
Negligently Causing Damage & Loss by Intentional Access	(a)(5)(C)	1 (10)
Trafficking in Passwords	(a)(6)	1 (10)
Extortion Involving Computers	(a)(7)	5 (10)

* The maximum prison sentences for second convictions are noted in parentheses.

477. The CFAA applies, in many cases, across borders in recognition of the borderless flow of information facilitated by computers and the Internet age. In *United States v. Ivanov*, for example, a federal court answered the question of whether a

337. See Prosecuting Computer Crimes, Office of Legal Education Executive Office for United States Attorneys, https://www.justice.gov/sites/default/files/criminal-ccips/legacy/2015/01/14/ccmanual.pdf.

citizen of a foreign country could be prosecuted under the CFAA when the illegal act occurred in the foreign country—Russia.[338] Ivanov was accused of using computer-based systems to extort and he was accused of possessing illegal access devices. The alleged crimes were committed against a U.S. company based in Connecticut. Ivanov was lured to the U.S. and arrested in the U.S., but Ivanov claimed that because the alleged crime occurred in Russia, the CFAA did not apply. The court ruled, however, that effects of the criminal acts occurred in Connecticut, thus allowing the prosecution to proceed. Ivanov plead guilty and was sentenced to forty-eight months in prison.

478. In a headline-grabbing case, prosecutors attempted to use the CFAA to prosecute a homemaker for posing as a teenage boy, and using that ruse to bully a teenage girl, who ultimately committed suicide.[339] Prosecutors charged the homemaker with intentionally accessing a computer without authorization to further the intentional infliction of emotional distress. The prosecutor's principal theory was that the homemaker violated the CFAA by purposely breaching the terms of the social media cite when she created a fictitious account. The court, however, held that violation of a social media's terms of use was not tantamount to an unambiguous statutory violation.

§3. Electronic Communications Privacy Act

479. The Electronic Communications Privacy Act (ECPA), as amended, protects wire, oral, and electronic communications while those communications are being made, are in transit, and when they are stored on computers. The Act applies to email, telephone conversations, and data stored electronically.[340] The ECPA includes several provisions, many civil in nature which are identified in previous chapters. In relevant part, however, the ECPA provides:

> It shall not be unlawful … to intercept or access an electronic communication made through an electronic communication system that is configured so that such electronic communication is readily accessible to the general public.[341]

480. Prosecutors must demonstrate the illegal act was committed intentionally, electronic interception occurred or was attempted, and attempt or use of unlawfully intercepted information. In a 1990 decision, *United States v. Riggs*, computers were fairly common in academic institutions and large companies, but otherwise not common in residential households. In that case, hackers calling themselves

338. 175 F. Supp. 2d 367 (D. Conn. 2001).
339. *United States v. Drew*, 259 F.R.D. 449 (C.D. Cal. 2009).
340. 18U.S.C. §§ 2510–2523.
341. 18U.S.C. § 2511(2)(g)(I).

"Prophet" gained unauthorized access to Bell South's 911 computer files. The hackers published the emergency phone-call data on their newsletter. The hackers communicated by email and even published instructions for breaking into computer systems. One of the hackers pleaded guilty in Georgia and was sentenced to twenty-one months in prison.

481. Shortly after the September 11, 2001 attacks, Congress amended the Act to supplement the ability of federal law enforcement agencies to intercept electronic communications. The "Patriot Act" amended the ECPA to identify crimes which law enforcement may obtain wiretaps to intercept a wide range of electronic communications, including email and monitoring a variety of Internet actions.

§4. Identity Theft

482. In addition to the CFAA, U.S. Congress enacted the Identity Theft Penalty Enhancement Act (ITPEA), which took effect in 2004.[342] The ITPEA establishes penalties for "aggravated" identity theft, which is using the identity of another person to commit felony crimes, including immigration violations, theft of another's Social Security benefits, and acts of domestic terrorism. This Act builds on previous legislative enactments, including the Identity Theft and Assumption Deterrence Act of 1998 in which identity theft was officially listed as a federal crime. The Act strengthened the criminal laws governing identity theft. Specifically, it amended 18U.S.C. § 1028, entitled "Fraud and related activity in connection with identification documents" to make it a federal crime to:

> knowingly transfer or use, without lawful authority, a means of identification of another person with the intent to commit, or to aid or abet, any unlawful activity that constitutes a violation of Federal law, or that constitutes a felony under any applicable State or local law.

483. The Act thus established identity theft a separate crime against the individual whose identity was stolen. It shifted focus from banks and other financial institutions to the individuals effected. It also specified that the FCC would be the federal government's lead agency for monitoring and investigating allegations of identity theft. The Act also increased criminal penalties with a fifteen-year maximum imprisonment sentence and steep financial penalties. Of course, several states have identity theft criminal statutes as well.

§5. Child Pornography

484. While child pornography has been illegal for well before the spread of the personal computer and the Internet, these technological advances have made enforcement difficult and have greatly increased the capacity to create, transmit,

342. 18U.S.C. § 1028(a).

and/or receive child pornography while remaining undetected. U.S. Congress recognized this context stating, "[t]he technological ease, lack of expense, and anonymity in obtaining and distributing child pornography over the Internet has resulted in an explosion in the multijurisdictional distribution of child pornography."[343]

485. Section 2256 of Title 18, United States Code, defines child pornography as any visual depiction of sexually explicit conduct involving a minor (someone under 18). Notably, images within this definition are not protected by the U.S. Constitution's First Amendment regarding free speech. Visual depictions include photographs, videos, digital or computer-generated images indistinguishable from an actual minor, and images created, adapted, or modified, but appear to depict an identifiable, actual minor.

486. States generally have child pornography laws, but federal law will often supersede state provisions. Federal law prohibits the creation, transmission, reception, and possession of an image of child pornography.[344] Specifically, section 2251 makes it illegal to persuade, induce, entice, or coerce a minor to engage in sexually explicit conduct for purposes of producing visual depictions of that conduct. Any individual who attempts or conspires to commit a child pornography offense is also subject to prosecution under federal law. The most common child pornography offenses are the distribution of child pornography in violation of 18U.S.C. § 2252(a)(2) and possessing and accessing child pornography in violation of 18U.S.C. § 2252(a)(4)(B).

487. The critical components relevant to the transmission of child pornography as stated in section 2252(a) and include:

(1) an active intention to give or transfer a specific depiction [of a minor] to another person; and
(2) active participation in the actual delivery. "Sexting is "the practice of sending or posting sexually suggestive text messages and images, including nude or seminude photographs via cellular telephones or over the Internet."

488. Importantly, federal jurisdiction hinges on interstate or foreign commerce. Traditionally, the mail system and common carriers provided the nexus for federal jurisdiction. But today, federal jurisdiction almost always applies when the Internet is used to commit a child pornography violation. Even if the child pornography image itself did not travel across state or international borders, federal law may be implicated if the materials, such as the computer used to download the image or the CD-ROM used to store the image, originated or previously traveled in interstate or

343. Child Pornography Cases, Pub.L. 110–358, § 102, 122 Stat. 4001 (2008).
344. 18 U.S.C. § 2251; 18U.S.C. § 2252.

foreign commerce. Section 2260 of Title 18, United States Code, prohibits any persons outside of the United States to knowingly produce, receive, transport, ship, or distribute child pornography with intent to import or transmit the visual depiction into the United States.

489. Severe statutory penalties attend conviction under child pornography statutes. A first time offender convicted of producing child pornography, for example, faces a statutory minimum of fifteen years in prison. Convicted offenders may face harsher penalties if the offender has prior convictions or if the child pornography offense occurred in aggravated situations defined as the images are violent, sadistic, or masochistic in nature. In such circumstances, a convicted offender may face up to life imprisonment.

490. A case illustrating the difficulty of enforcing child pornography laws as they apply to third parties and digital data is *Backpage.com v. McKenna.*[345] There, the Communications Decency Act was contrasted to a Washington state statute, which sought to criminalize "the offense of advertising commercial sexual abuse of a minor." Backpage.com is a website that operates an online-classified advertising service located at www.backpage.com. The webpage charges a small fee to post ads in the adult category, and the Washington law made it a felony to knowingly publish or to indirectly cause content to be published if it contains a "depiction of a minor" and any "explicit or implicit offer" of sex for "something of value." It is not a defense under the Washington statue that the defendant did not know the age of the person depicted and the defendant may not rely on representation by or the apparent age of the person depicted.

491. The court held that the Washington statute conflicted with section 230 of the federal Communications Decency Act and was thereby preempted. The court noted that online publishers like Backpage.com were not speakers of the information and could not be criminally liable for the advertisements created by third parties, including "ads for commercial sex acts depicting minors." This ruling comports with others in which U.S. courts have given service providers a broad immunity for websites that display third-party content, so long as the service providers are not too involved in the creation of the content.

§6. Other Network Crime Statutes

492. Other network crime statutes address computer-related crimes in a more narrow context. The CAN-SPAM Act creates tools for federal prosecutors to investigate those persons and entities that send large amounts of unsolicited commercial email (a.k.a. "spam").[346] Even though the primary enforcement mechanisms are civil and include penalties, a few criminal offenses are includes in section 1037. The

345. 881 F.Supp. 2d 1262 (W.D. Wash. 2012).
346. Pub. L. No. 108-187, 117 Stat. 2699 (2003).

criminal provisions address instances in which the defendant takes material steps to conceal his identity and/or the origin of the email from recipients, the ISP and/or law enforcement.

493. Whoever, in or affecting interstate or foreign commerce, knowingly:

(1) accesses a protected computer without authorization, and intentionally initiates the transmission of multiple commercial electronic mail messages from or through such computer;
(2) uses a protected computer to relay or retransmit multiple commercial electronic mail messages, with the intent to deceive or mislead recipients, or any Internet access service, as to the origin of such messages:
(3) materially falsifies header information in multiple commercial electronic mail messages and intentionally initiates the transmission of such messages:
(4) registers, using information that materially falsifies the identity of the actual registrant, for five or more electronic mail accounts or online user accounts or two or more domain names, and intentionally initiates the transmission of multiple commercial electronic mail messages from any combination of such accounts or domain names: or
(5) falsely represents oneself to be the registrant or the legitimate successor in interest to the registrant of five or more IP addresses, and intentionally initiates the transmission of multiple commercial electronic mail messages from such addresses, or conspires to do so, shall be punished as provided in subsection (b).[347]

494. In *Omega World Travel, Inc. v. Mummagraphics, Inc.*, the Fourth Circuit held that even though the "from" email addresses were inaccurate and even though the server from which the email originated was inaccurate, the emails included a link through which a recipient could unsubscribe from future messages. The link provided the sender's valid address and telephone number and accurately identified the name and domain name of the sender.[348] Another criminal provision of the CAN-SPAM Act prohibits sending sexually explicit email without labeling it as such. Knowing violations are punishable by imprisonment, but not for more than five years.

495. U.S. law also criminalizes certain access devices in specific circumstances. Prosecutors typically use this provision to investigate "phishing"' cases.[349] In those instances, defendants leverage fraudulent emails to obtain passwords, bank account information, and the like. Phishing scams also include instances where defendants buy, sell, and transfer stolen bank accounts, credit card information and similar data. The term "access device" means:

347. *Id.*
348. 469 F.3d 348 (4th Cir. 2006).
349. 18U.S.C. § 1029.

> any card, plate, code, account number, electronic serial number, mobile identification number, personal identification number, or other telecommunications service, equipment, or instrument identifier, or other means of account access that can be used, alone or in conjunction with another access device, to obtain money, goods, services, or any other thing of value, or that can be used to initiate a transfer of funds (other than a transfer originated solely by paper instrument).[350]

496. Penalties for violations of section 1029 range from a maximum of ten or fifteen years of imprisonment depending on the subsection violated. Second and later offenses are subject to twenty years of imprisonment. In a 2008 case, a defendant used a bar code generator to make false codes which he affixed to items purchased at Walmart. The false codes allowed the defendant to buy items for less than the retail price. The defendant then removed the false codes, returned the items to the store for a full retail credit. The court ruled that the false codes were not "access devices" because they did not facilitate access to a system that monitors an ongoing account relationship between two parties. Instead, the false codes only served as a means of accessing Walmart's internal ledger that tracked payments for inventory purposes.[351]

---

350. 18U.S.C. § 1029(e)(1).
351. *United States v. Lutz*, 2008 WL 4449082 (N.D. Ohio 2008).

Chapter 2. Application of Criminal Procedure Law in the Area of ICT

§1. General

497. Generally speaking, substantive criminal law in the U.S. is primarily statutory, rather than based on the common law or on specific constitutional provisions. This reliance on statutes to identify substantive crimes in the U.S. is reflected both in the federal legal scheme as well as in most of the states. But with regard to criminal procedure, the U.S. Constitution provides the critical foundation. The Fourth Amendment of the U.S. Constitution provides that "[t]he right of the people to be secure in their persons, houses, papers, and effects, against unreasonable searches and seizures, shall not be violated, and no Warrants shall issue, but upon probable cause, supported by Oath or affirmation, and particularly describing the place to be searched, and the persons or things to be seized."[352]

498. This provision in large part protects individual privacy interests from unauthorized government intrusion. Even so, the Fourth Amendment does not guarantee protection from all searches and seizures, but only those effectuated by the government and identified as unreasonable under the law. In most instances, the question of whether the claimant's Fourth Amendment rights have been violated requires that the claimant demonstrates a justifiable expectation of privacy, which was itself arbitrarily violated by the government. The typical example includes law enforcement's warrantless search of an individual's private home. Several examples exist, like search incident to a lawful arrest and probable cause that is supplemented by exigent circumstances.

499. A search under Fourth Amendment occurs when a governmental employee or agent of the government violates an individual's reasonable expectation of privacy. While a reasonable expectation of privacy is clear within an individual's home, the query quickly becomes difficult in other circumstances. The definition of a search also evolves with technology. The question of whether a drug-sniffing dog constitutes a search is different than whether infrared sensors, overhead airplane surveillance, and—increasingly—electronic surveillance will constitute a search.

500. U.S. courts in the past two decades continue to address the Fourth Amendment's applicability to electronic searches and seizures. The penetration of the Internet in the U.S. and the proliferation of personal computers and smartphones continuously raise questions when law enforcement attempts to gather incriminating information through these mediums. Simultaneously, and increasing amount of crime has shifted from traditional on-ground gambits to electronic schemes. Evidence of such schemes emerges more often on computers, digital communications, and hard drives.

---

352. U.S. Const. Amd. 4.

501. Similarly, questions arise as to whether law enforcement may search company-owned computers to seek incriminating information from an employee that uses the company-owned computers. Some jurisdictions protect employees from warrantless searches of their work computers, but the majority of jurisdictions in the U.S. have found that employees do not have a legitimate expectation of privacy in the content stored or communicated in company-owned computers. Indeed, the Supreme Court extended the lack of protection to instances in which text messages are sent and received from an employer-provided pager.

502. With regard to law enforcement interception of telephone conversations, the Fourth Amendment restricts law enforcement in meaningful ways. If the federal government taps a telephone call and monitors content, that act is typically a "search" under the Fourth Amendment. The seminal U.S. Supreme Court case is *Katz v. United States*, where the court extended protection beyond an individual's home into areas in which an individual has a reasonable expectation of privacy.[353] In that case, the Federal Bureau of Investigation placed microphones on the top of a public phone booth that the defendant used to place illegal bets. The court held that monitoring the phone booth without a warrant violated the Fourth Amendment. The Katz test has been used in thousands of cases subsequently, including cases dealing with new technologies that raise new questions regarding expectations of privacy.

503. Criminal procedural protections extend beyond telephone interception. Cell-site data telephone surveillance, text messages, and numbers dialed all convey critical information and in certain contexts require government officials to first obtain a warrant before monitoring these functions. For example, cell-site data includes information about the specific cell towers used to communicate with a particular cell phone while it is in use. In *Smith v. Maryland*, the court considered whether the government-requested installation of a "pen register" at the telephone company office constitutes a search under the Fourth Amendment.[354] A pen register records the numbers dialed from a telephone. The Supreme Court held that the government's use of the pen register did not violate the defendant's reasonable expectation of privacy and was not a Fourth Amendment search. Because the defendant knowingly relayed the numbers to the telephone company, according to the Court, he had no reasonable expectation in the privacy of those numbers.

504. The telephone numbers dialed are not protected under the Smith holding, but the Fourth Amendment likely disallows law enforcement from surveilling cut-through dialed digits without first obtaining a warrant. Cut-through dialed digits are digits entered after the call has connected to its intended destination. Fourth Amendment protection likely applies because the post-connection digits relay content specifically to the recipient rather than to the telephone company. The telephone company is no longer a necessary party to the transaction, and a reasonable expectation of privacy exists.

353. 389U.S. 347 (1967).
354. 442U.S. 735 (1979).

505. Text messages, as a result, are more like cut-through dialed digits than pen registers. Because there is little U.S. Supreme Court precedent addressing text messages and Internet communication, analogies to *Smith* and *Katz* suggest the appropriate legal landscape for law enforcement officials. Lower courts commonly analogize surveillance of computer-based communications to traditional telephone communications for Fourth Amendment purposes. Consequently, most Internet-based communication receives Fourth Amendment protection if the communication is content based, while noncontent Internet communication is unprotected

506. In the Ninth Circuit case of *United States v. Forrester*, the court considered government surveillance of two defendants who were manufacturing ecstasy.[355] The government used several computer surveillance techniques to monitor one of the defendant's email and Internet activity. The government initially installed a pen register device after applying for and getting court approval. The pen register was installed on the defendant's account with his ISP. The pen register enabled the government to assimilate the addresses that the defendant used to send and receive emails. It also revealed IP addresses of the websites that the defendant visited along with the total volume sent to and from the defendant's account.

507. After arrest and indictment, several issues were appealed. The Ninth Circuit's decision is one of the leading opinions that analyzes the Fourth Amendment's application to noncontent Internet communication. According to the Ninth Circuit, the pen register surveillance was not a search because it resembled the pen register case in *Smith v. Maryland.* Although the email information and gathering techniques were more sophisticated than that in *Smith*, the reasoning was the same. Because the email address was "visible" to the third-party carriers that transmit it to its intended location, no reasonable expectation of privacy attends that noncontent information. Just like the address on the front of a physical package sent through the mail can be surveilled without violating the Fourth Amendment, so can email addresses. Just like the government cannot open the contents of a mailed package without a search warrant, the government cannot open the contents of the emails it captures. The court relied on a long line of cases dating back to the 1800s regarding warrantless searches of the contents of sealed mail packages. The outside address is visible to third-party carriers, whereas the sender expects that the contents will be viewed only by the intended recipient.

508. In conformity with this construct, the Sixth Circuit Court of Appeals in *United States v. Warshak*, held that the contents of Internet communications including email were protected by the Fourth Amendment.[356] The defendants in that case operated a company that sold herbal supplements that purportedly enhanced male sexual performance. Many of the advertisements generated by the defendants included patently false information, including the 96% customer satisfaction rating, the false surveys, and the testimony of supposed medical professionals. Defendants

355. 512 F.3d 500 (9th Cir. 2008).
356. 631 F.3d 266 (6th Cir. 2010).

also created deceitful billing practices to trick customers into paying for the supplement automatically and making it difficult for customers to stop the automatic withdrawals.

509. Much of the information about these practices were memorialized in the defendant's emails. As a part of the government's investigation, it seized almost 27,000 emails from the defendant's ISP. The court ruled that the Fourth Amendment protected against government seizure of the contents of the emails without first obtaining a warrant based on probable cause. The court stated that "the Fourth Amendment must keep pace with the inexorable march of technological progress," and that "given the fundamental similarities between email and traditional forms of communication, it would defy common sense to afford emails lesser Fourth Amendment protection."' Even so, under the Stored Communications Act, government agents may request access to emails in order to obtain a court order. And because government agents obtained a subpoena to direct the ISP to turn over the information, the email evidence did not have to be excluded, and the defendant's convictions were affirmed.

510. In general, the court's opinion recognizes that in the last fifteen years email has dominated over traditional forms of communication and has become a necessary means of communication and self-expression. Fourth Amendment protection is warranted to forestall unfettered governmental surveillance of private communications. Of course, the line between content and noncontent is not always clear. The subject line in an email is likely content-based and protected under the Fourth Amendment, but court precedent is unclear on that point. Email addresses, IP addresses, and the data that records volume of transferred data, by contrast are likely noncontent information. Email addresses are not always noncontent data. For example, an email from sender to recipient that attaches a list of other email addresses would likely constitute protected content.

511. Even if an Internet-based communication is protected under the Fourth Amendment as content based, the circumstances of that communication may nullify any protection under the Fourth Amendment. To use an analogue example, a post card in the mail includes content-based information that would ordinarily be protected from government search and seizure under the Fourth Amendment. But because the contents of the communication on the post card are openly visible to everyone, the content would likely not be protected. Some electronic communications are similarly transparent. Governmentally issued email addresses, particularly to employees of the federal government arguably have less privacy protection for the content in the emails generated by government employees. Likewise, the terms of use that accompany registration of an email address provided by ISPs can affect the reasonable expectation of privacy – and thus Fourth Amendment protections – that users may harbor. Terms of service vary widely; some indicate that the ISP protects privacy and others do not.

512. Finally, one of the biggest procedural difficulties in prosecuting crimes in the area of ICT law involves jurisdiction. Applying traditional criminal law concepts to cyberspace generates significant inconsistencies and procedural roadblocks. Traditionally, crimes occur either where the defendant instigates actions which cause the prohibited effect, or where the victim of the offense is located. But cyberspace is everywhere, and a criminal or defamatory message posted on the Internet often achieves global accessibility. To some degree, this exposes criminal defendants to a much wider range of criminal sanctions from varying nations.

513. In one important case, a software developer posted encryption software on the Internet. Government prosecutors had to determine whether the posting of the encryption software constituted an "export'" of the software under the applicable criminal statute. Although courts are mixed, government prosecutors maintain that posting restricted programs on the Internet irretrievably places such programs in the stream of international commerce, and therefore amounts to "exportation" ––despite any evidence that the program actually left the United States.

Selected Bibliography

§1. General Reference Works

Copyrights and Intellectual Property, 18 C.J.S. Copyrights (2019).
Copyright Infringement Litigation, 77 Am. Jur. Trials 449 (2000).
Copying – Computer programs and software, 1 Computer and Information Law Digest § 1:26 (2019).
George B. Delta; Jeffrey H. Matsuura, *Law of the Internet,* Wolters Kluwer Law & Business, 2009.
Lisa T. Oratz, *Social media law*, Law Journal Press, 2013.

§2. Textbooks

A. Hugh Scott, *Computer and Intellectual Property Crime: Federal and State* Law, Bureau of National Affairs, 2001
Lisa J. Sotto, *Privacy and Data Security Law Deskbook*, Wolters Kluwer, 2010.
Jane Kaufman Winn, Benjamin Wright, *Law of Electronic Commerce*, 4th ed. Wolters Kluwer, 2019.
Jeff Koseff, Cybersecurity Law, 2nd ed., John Wiley & Sons, 2020.

§3. Journals

Sony, Cyber Security, and Free Speech: Preserving the First Amendment in the Modern World, 16 U.C. Davis Bus. L.J. 309 (2016).

Selected Bibliography

Index

The numbers here refer to paragraph numbers.

www.ingramcontent.com/pod-product-compliance
Ingram Content Group UK Ltd.
Pitfield, Milton Keynes, MK11 3LW, UK
UKHW020136290926
15471UKWH00003B/526

9 789403 549750